# 15-MINUTE
# SPANISH
## LEARN IN JUST 12 WEEKS

Ana Bremón

**REVISED EDITION**
**DK LONDON**
**Senior Editor** Ankita Awasthi Tröger
**Senior Art Editor** Clare Shedden
**Managing Editor** Carine Tracanelli
**Managing Art Editor** Anna Hall
**US Editor** Heather Wilcox
**US Executive Editor** Lori Hand
**Senior Production Editor** Andy Hilliard
**Senior Production Controller** Poppy David
**Jacket Design Development Manager** Sophia MTT
**Associate Publishing Director** Liz Wheeler
**Art Director** Karen Self
**Publishing Director** Jonathan Metcalf

**DK DELHI**
**Project Editor** Priyanjali Narain
**Project Art Editor** Anjali Sachar
**Senior Art Editor** Pooja Pipil
**Art Editor** Aarushi Dhawan
**Senior Managing Editor** Rohan Sinha
**Managing Art Editor** Sudakshina Basu
**Senior Jackets Coordinator** Priyanka Sharma-Saddi
**DTP Designers** Rakesh Kumar, Mrinmoy Mazumdar
**Hi-Res Coordinators** Neeraj Bhatia, Jagtar Singh
**Production Editor** Vishal Bhatia
**Production Manager** Pankaj Sharma
**Pre-production Manager** Balwant Singh
**Senior Picture Researcher** Sumedha Chopra
**Picture Research Manager** Taiyaba Khatoon
**Creative Head** Malavika Talukder

Language content for Dorling Kindersley by
g-and-w publishing.
Additional translations for 2023 edition by
Andiamo! Language Services Ltd.

This American Edition, 2023
First American Edition, 2005
Published in the United States by DK Publishing
1745 Broadway, 20th Floor, New York, NY 10019

Copyright © 2005, 2012, 2018, 2023
Dorling Kindersley Limited
DK, a Division of Penguin Random House LLC
24 25 26 27  10 9 8 7 6 5 4 3 2
003–329221–Jul/2023

A catalog record for this book
is available from the Library of Congress.
ISBN 978-0-7440-7372-0

DK books are available at special discounts when
purchased in bulk for sales promotions, premiums,
fundraising, or educational use. For details, contact:
DK Publishing Special Markets, 1745 Broadway,
20th Floor, New York, NY 10019
SpecialSales@dk.com

Printed in China

**For the curious**
**www.dk.com**

**MIX**
Paper | Supporting
responsible forestry
**FSC™ C018179**
www.fsc.org

This book was made with Forest
Stewardship Council™ certified
paper – one small step in DK's
commitment to a sustainable future.
**For more information go to**
**www.dk.com/our-green-pledge**

# Contents

# How to use this book

Twelve themed chapters are broken down into five daily 15-minute lessons, allowing you to work through four teaching units and one revision unit each week. The lessons cover a range of practical themes, including leisure, business, food and drink, and travel. A reference section at the end contains a menu guide and English-to-Spanish and Spanish-to-English dictionaries.

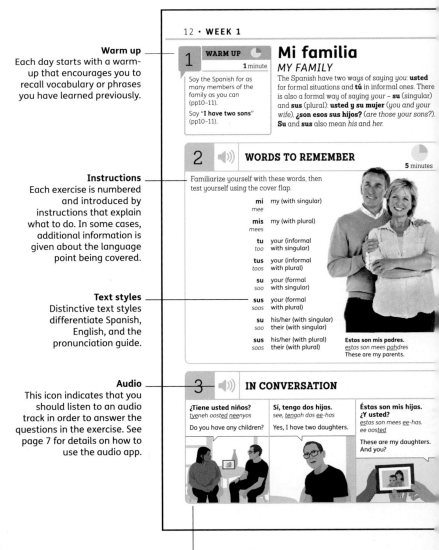

**Warm up**
Each day starts with a warm-up that encourages you to recall vocabulary or phrases you have learned previously.

**Instructions**
Each exercise is numbered and introduced by instructions that explain what to do. In some cases, additional information is given about the language point being covered.

**Text styles**
Distinctive text styles differentiate Spanish, English, and the pronunciation guide.

**Audio**
This icon indicates that you should listen to an audio track in order to answer the questions in the exercise. See page 7 for details on how to use the audio app.

---

12 · WEEK 1

### 1 WARM UP
**1 minute**

Say the Spanish for as many members of the family as you can (pp10–11).

Say "**I have two sons**" (pp10–11).

## Mi familia
*MY FAMILY*

The Spanish have two ways of saying *you*: **usted** for formal situations and **tú** in informal ones. There is also a formal way of saying *your* – **su** (singular) and **sus** (plural): **usted y su mujer** (*you and your wife*), **¿son esos sus hijos?** (*are those your sons?*). **Su** and **sus** also mean *his* and *her*.

### 2 WORDS TO REMEMBER
**5 minutes**

Familiarize yourself with these words, then test yourself using the cover flap.

| | |
|---|---|
| **mi** *mee* | my (with singular) |
| **mis** *mees* | my (with plural) |
| **tu** *too* | your (informal with singular) |
| **tus** *toos* | your (informal with plural) |
| **su** *soo* | your (formal with singular) |
| **sus** *soos* | your (formal with plural) |
| **su** *soo* | his/her (with singular) their (with singular) |
| **sus** *soos* | his/her (with plural) their (with plural) |

**Estos son mis padres.**
*estos son mees pahdres*
These are my parents.

### 3 IN CONVERSATION

**¿Tiene usted niños?**
*tyeneh oosted neenyos*

Do you have any children?

**Sí, tengo dos hijas.**
*see, tengo dos ee-has*

Yes, I have two daughters.

**Éstas son mis hijas. ¿Y usted?**
*estas son mees ee-has. ee oosted*

These are my daughters. And you?

---

**In conversation**
Illustrated dialogues reflecting how vocabulary and phrases are used in everyday situations appear throughout the book.

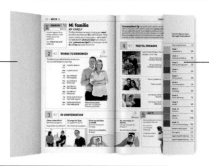

**Learn**
Keep the flaps
open while
you learn.

**Revise**
Use the flaps to
cover the answers
when you are ready
to test yourself.

## INTRODUCTIONS · 13

**Conversational tip** The Spanish ask a question by simply raising the pitch of their voice at the end of a statement: **¿quieres un poco de vino?** (*do you want a little wine?*). You'll notice inverted question marks and exclamation marks at the start of some sentences, as in **¡hola!** (*hello!*). These are added to flag that the following text is a question or exclamation and also to avoid misunderstandings when sentences are very long.

**Cultural/Conversational tip**
These panels provide
additional insights
into life in Spain and
language usage.

4 ((•)) **USEFUL PHRASES**

**3** minutes

Learn these phrases, then test yourself
using the cover flap.

| | |
|---|---|
| Do you have any brothers? (formal) | **¿Tiene usted hermanos?** *tyeneh oosted airmanos* |
| Do you have any brothers? (informal) | **¿Tienes hermanos?** *tyenes airmanos* |

| | |
|---|---|
| This is my husband. | **Este es mi marido.** *esteh es mee mareedoh* |
| That's my wife. | **Esa es mi mujer.** *esah es mee moo-hair* |

| | |
|---|---|
| Is that your sister? (formal) | **¿Es esa su hermana?** *es esah soo airmanah* |
| Is that your sister? (informal) | **¿Es esa tu hermana?** *es esah too airmanah* |

**Exercises**
Familiarizing you with
terms relevant to each
topic, these help you
build your vocabulary,
learn useful phrases,
connect words to
visuals, and practice
what you learn.

**4** minutes

No, pero tengo un
hijastro.
*noh, peroh tengoh oon
ee-hastroh*

No, but I have a stepson.

5 **SAY IT**

**2** minutes

Do you have any brothers
and sisters? (formal)

Do you have
any children?
(informal)

I have two sisters.

This is my wife.

**Time yourself**
This icon and text to the
right of the heading shows
you how long you need to
spend on each exercise.

**Say it**
In these exercises you are asked
to apply what you have learned
using different vocabulary.

»

## Revision

At the end of every week's lessons, a revision unit lets you test yourself on what you have learned so far. A recap of selected elements from previous lessons helps reinforce your knowledge.

**Test yourself**
Use the cover flap to conceal the answers while you study.

## Reference

This section appears at the end of the book and brings together all the words and phrases you have learned over the weeks. While the menu guide focuses on food and drink, the dictionary lists Spanish translations of common words and phrases.

**Dictionaries**
Mini-dictionaries provide ready reference from English to Spanish and Spanish to English for 2,500 words.

**Menu guide**
Use this guide as a reference for food terminology and popular Spanish dishes.

# PRONUNCIATION GUIDE

This book teaches European Spanish, which differs in pronunciation from the various dialects spoken in Latin America. A few Spanish sounds require special explanation:

**c**    a Spanish **c** is pronounced *th* before **i** or **e** but **k** before other vowels: **cinco** *theen*koh (*five*)

**h**    **h** is is always silent: **hola** o-*lah* (*hello*)

**j (g)**    a Spanish **j** (and **g** before **i** or **e**) is pronounced as a strong **h**, as if saying *hat* emphasizing the first letter

**ll**    pronounced *y* as in *yes*

**ñ**    pronounced **ny** like the sound in the middle of *canyon*

**r**    a Spanish **r** is trilled like a Scottish **r**, especially at the beginning of a word and when doubled

**v**    a Spanish **v** is halfway between an English **b** and **v**

**z**    a Spanish **z** is pronounced *th*

Spanish vowels tend to be pronounced shorter than their English equivalents:

**a**    as the English *father*

**e**    as the English *wet*

**i**    as the English *keep*

**o**    as the English *boat*

**u**    as the English *boot*

Below each Spanish word or phrase you will find a pronunciation transcription. Read this, bearing in mind the tips above, and you will achieve a comprehensible result. But remember that the transcription can only ever be an approximation and that there is no real substitute for listening to native speakers.

# HOW TO USE THE AUDIO APP

The free audio app accompanying this book contains audio recordings for all numbered exercises on the teaching pages, except for the Warm Up and Say It exercises (look out for the audio icon). There is no audio for the revision pages.

To start using the audio with this book, download the **DK 15 Minute Language Course** app on your tablet or smartphone from the App Store or Google Play and select your book from the list of available titles. Please note that this app is not a stand-alone course, but is designed to be used together with the book to familiarize you with the language and provide examples for you to repeat aloud.

There are two ways in which you can use the audio. The first is to read through the 15-minute lessons using just the book, then go back and work with the audio and the book together. Or you can combine the book and the audio from the start, pausing the app to read the instructions on the page.

You are encouraged to listen to the audio and repeat the words and sentences out loud until you are confident you understand and can pronounce what has been said. Remember that repetition is vital for language learning. The more often you listen to a conversation or repeat an oral exercise, the more the new language will sink in.

### SUPPORTING AUDIO
This icon indicates that audio recordings are available for you to listen to.

**FREE AUDIO APP**

# Hola
## *HELLO*

In Spain, women often greet people with one or two kisses on the cheek, and men shake other men's hands, although men may also kiss or embrace younger male relatives or close friends. In more formal situations—among strangers or in a business context—a handshake is the norm.

---

**2**  **WORDS TO REMEMBER**

2 minutes

Familiarize yourself with these words by reading them aloud several times, then test yourself by concealing the Spanish on the left with the cover flap.

| | |
|---|---|
| **Buenos días** *bwenos deeyas* | Good morning/day |
| **Buenas tardes (noches)** *bwenas tardes (noches)* | Good afternoon/evening (night) |
| **Encantado/-a** *enkan-tadoh/-ah* | Pleased to meet you (man/woman speaking) |
| **Gracias** *grathyas* | Thank you |
| **Adiós** *addy-os* | Goodbye |

**¡Hola!**
*o-lah*
Hello!

---

**3**  **IN CONVERSATION**: FORMAL

3 minutes

**Buenos días. Me llamo Concha García.**
*bwenos deeyas. meh yamoh konchah garthee-ah*

Good day. My name's Concha García.

**Señor López, encantado.**
*senyor lopeth, enkan-tadoh*

Mr. López, pleased to meet you.

**Encantada.**
*enkan-tadah*

Pleased to meet you.

## 4  PUT INTO PRACTICE

**3** minutes

Read the Spanish on the left and follow the instructions to complete this dialogue. Then, test yourself by concealing the Spanish on the right with the cover flap.

**Buenas tardes señor.**
*bwenas tardes senyor*

Good evening, sir.

Say: Good evening, madam.

**Buenas tardes señora.**
*bwenas tardes senyorah*

**Me llamo Julia.**
*meh yamoh hoolyah*

My name is Julia.

Say: Pleased to meet you.

**Encantado.**
*enkan-tadoh*

---

### Cultural tip

The Spanish greet each other with **señor** (*sir*), **señora** (*madam*), and **señorita** (*miss*, for young women) much more than English-speakers do. With first names, always use **Don** for men or **Doña** for women—for example, **Don Juan, Doña Ana**.

## 5  USEFUL PHRASES

**3** minutes

Learn these phrases by reading them aloud several times, then test yourself by concealing the Spanish on the right with the cover flap.

What's your name? **¿Cómo se llama?**
*komoh seh yamah*

My name is Ana. **Me llamo Ana.**
*meh yamoh annah*

See you soon/tomorrow. **Hasta pronto/mañana.**
*astah prontoh/manyanah*

---

## 6  IN CONVERSATION: INFORMAL

**3** minutes

**Entonces, ¿hasta mañana?**
*entonthes, astah manyanah*

So, see you tomorrow?

**Sí, adiós.**
*see, addy-os*

Yes, goodbye.

**Adiós. Hasta pronto.**
*addy-os. astah prontoh*

Goodbye. See you soon.

# Los parientes
## *RELATIVES*

Say **"hello"** and **"goodbye"** in Spanish (pp8–9).

Now say **"My name is…"** (pp8–9).

Say **"sir"** and **"madam"** (pp8–9).

In Spanish, the male plural can refer to both sexes—for example, **niños** (*boys* and *children*), **padres** (*fathers* and *parents*), **abuelos** (*grandfathers* and *grandparents*), **tíos** (*uncles* and *aunt and uncle*), **hermanos** (*brothers* and *siblings*), and so on. The Spanish equivalents of *mom* and *dad* are **mamá** and **papá**.

| 2 |  | **MATCH AND REPEAT** |
|---|---|---|
| | | **5** minutes |

Look at the people in this scene and match their numbers to the vocabulary list on the left. Then, test yourself by concealing the Spanish on the left, using the cover flap.

❶ **el padre**
 *el pahdreh*

❷ **la madre**
 *lah mahdreh*

❸ **la hermana**
 *lah airmanah*

❹ **el hermano**
 *el airmanoh*

❺ **la hija**
 *lah ee-hah*

❻ **el hijo**
 *el ee-hoh*

❼ **la abuela**
 *lah abwelah*

❽ **el abuelo**
 *el abweloh*

father ❶  mother ❷
sister ❸  brother ❹
daughter ❺  son ❻
grandmother ❼  grandfather ❽

**Conversational tip** In Spanish, things as well as people are masculine (m) or feminine (f). The Spanish for *the* (singular) is **el** or **la**, and *a/an* is **un** or **una**, depending on whether the word is masculine or feminine. For example, *wine* is masculine (**el vino**), but *milk* is feminine (**la leche**). For plurals, **los** is used for masculine and **las** for feminine words, respectively.

## 3  WORDS TO REMEMBER: RELATIVES

**4** minutes

**la mujer**
*lah moo-hair*
wife

**el marido**
*el mareedoh*
husband

**Estoy casado/-a.**
*estoy kasadoh/-ah*
I'm married (m/f).

Familiarize yourself with these words, then test yourself, using the cover flap.

| | |
|---|---|
| father/mother-in-law | **el suegro/la suegra** *el swegroh/lah swegrah* |
| stepfather | **el padrastro** *el padras-troh* |
| stepmother | **la madrastra** *lah madras-trah* |
| children (male/female) | **los niños/las niñas** *los neenyos/las neenyas* |
| uncle/aunt | **el tío/la tía** *el tee-oh/lah tee-ah* |
| cousin | **el primo/la prima** *el preemoh/lah preemah* |
| I have four children. | **Tengo cuatro niños.** *tengoh kwatroh neenyos* |
| I have two stepdaughters and a stepson. | **Tengo dos hijastras y un hijastro.** *tengoh dos ee-hastras ee oon ee-hastroh* |

## 4  WORDS TO REMEMBER: NUMBERS

**3** minutes

Familiarize yourself with these words, then test yourself, using the cover flap.

Be careful when you use the number *one*. When you use **uno** before a word, it changes to **un** or **una**, depending on whether that word is masculine or feminine. For example: **tengo un hijo** (*I have one son*), **tengo una hija** (*I have one daughter*).

| | |
|---|---|
| one | **uno/-a** *oonoh/-ah* |
| two | **dos** *dos* |
| three | **tres** *tres* |
| four | **cuatro** *kwatroh* |
| five | **cinco** *theenkoh* |
| six | **seis** *seh-ees* |
| seven | **siete** *syeteh* |
| eight | **ocho** *ochoh* |
| nine | **nueve** *nwebeh* |
| ten | **diez** *dyeth* |

## 5 SAY IT

**2** minutes

I have five sons.

I have three sisters and a brother.

I have two children.

# Mi familia
## MY FAMILY

Say the Spanish for as many members of the family as you can (pp10–11).

Say "I have two sons" (pp10–11).

The Spanish have two ways of saying *you*: **usted** for formal situations and **tú** in informal ones. There is also a formal way of saying *your*—**su** (singular) and **sus** (plural): **usted y su mujer** (*you and your wife*), **¿son esos sus hijos?** (*are those your sons?*). **Su** and **sus** also mean *his* and *her*.

**2**  **WORDS TO REMEMBER**

**5** minutes

Familiarize yourself with these words, then test yourself, using the cover flap.

| | |
|---|---|
| **mi**<br>*mee* | my (with singular) |
| **mis**<br>*mees* | my (with plural) |
| **tu**<br>*too* | your (informal with singular) |
| **tus**<br>*toos* | your (informal with plural) |
| **su**<br>*soo* | your (formal with singular) |
| **sus**<br>*soos* | your (formal with plural) |
| **su**<br>*soo* | his/her (with singular)<br>their (with singular) |
| **sus**<br>*soos* | his/her (with plural)<br>their (with plural) |

**Estos son mis padres.**
*estos son mees pahdres*
These are my parents.

**3**  **IN CONVERSATION**

**¿Tiene usted niños?**
*tyeneh oosted neenyos*

Do you have any children?

**Sí, tengo dos hijas.**
*see, tengoh dos ee-has*

Yes, I have two daughters.

**Estas son mis hijas.**
**¿Y usted?**
*estas son mees ee-has.*
*ee oosted*

These are my daughters. And you?

**Conversational tip** The Spanish ask a question by simply raising the pitch of their voice at the end of a statement: **¿quieres un poco de vino?** (*do you want a little wine?*). You'll notice inverted question marks and exclamation marks at the start of some sentences, as in **¡hola!** (*hello!*). These are added to flag that the following text is a question or exclamation and also to avoid misunderstandings when sentences are very long.

## 4  USEFUL PHRASES

**3** minutes

Learn these phrases, then test yourself, using the cover flap.

| | |
|---|---|
| Do you have any brothers? (formal) | **¿Tiene usted hermanos?** *tyeneh oosted airmanos* |
| Do you have any brothers? (informal) | **¿Tienes hermanos?** *tyenes airmanos* |

| | |
|---|---|
| This is my husband. | **Este es mi marido.** *esteh es mee mareedoh* |
| That's my wife. | **Esa es mi mujer.** *esah es mee moo-hair* |

| | |
|---|---|
| Is that your sister? (formal) | **¿Es esa su hermana?** *es esah soo airmanah* |
| Is that your sister? (informal) | **¿Es esa tu hermana?** *es esah too airmanah* |

**4** minutes

**No, pero tengo un hijastro.**
*noh, peroh tengoh oon ee-hastroh*

No, but I have a stepson.

## 5 SAY IT

**2** minutes

Do you have any brothers and sisters? (formal)

Do you have any children? (informal)

I have two sisters.

This is my wife.

# Ser y tener
## *TO BE AND TO HAVE*

Say "**See you soon**" (pp8–9).

Say "**I am married**" (pp10–11) and "**I have a wife**" (pp12–13).

Two of the most important verbs are **ser** (*to be*) and **tener** (*to have*). Note that there are different ways of saying *you*, *we*, and *they*, with formal and informal, singular and plural, and masculine and feminine forms. Pronouns (*I*, *you*, etc.) are omitted where the sense is clear.

---

**2**  **SER:** TO BE

**5** minutes

Practise **ser** (*to be*) and the sample sentences, then test yourself, using the cover flap. Note that there is another verb meaning *to be*—**estar**, which is discussed on page 49.

| | |
|---|---|
| **yo soy** *yoh soy* | I am |
| **tú eres** *too eh-res* | you are (informal singular) |
| **usted es** *oosted es* | you are (formal singular) |
| **él/ella es** *el/eh-yah es* | he/she is |
| **nosotros/-as somos** *nosotros/-as somos* | we are (m/f) |
| **vosotros/-as sois** *bosotros/-as soys* | you are (informal plural m/f) |
| **ustedes son** *oostedes son* | you are (formal plural m/f) |
| **ellos/-as son** *eh-yos/-yas son* | they are (m/f) |

**Yo soy inglesa.**
*yoh soy eenglesah*
I'm English.

---

| | |
|---|---|
| **Soy editor. Trabajo mucho y estoy cansado.** *soy edeetor. traba-hoh moochoh ee estoy kansadoh* | I'm an editor. I work a lot, and I'm tired. |
| **¡Es feliz!** *es felith* | She is a happy person. |
| **Somos españoles.** *somos espanyoles* | We're Spanish. |

## 3  TENER: TO HAVE

**5** minutes

Practice **tener** (*to have*) and the sample sentences, then test yourself, using the cover flap.

| | |
|---|---|
| I have | **yo tengo** |
| | *yoh tengoh* |
| you have (informal singular) | **tú tienes** |
| | *too tyenes* |
| you have (formal singular) | **usted tiene** |
| | *oosted tyeneh* |
| he/she has | **él/ella tiene** |
| | *el/eh-yah tyeneh* |
| we have (m/f) | **nosotros/-as tenemos** |
| | *nosotros/-as tenehmos* |
| you have (informal plural m/f) | **vosotros/-as tenéis** |
| | *bosotros/-as teneh-ees* |
| you have (formal plural) | **ustedes tienen** |
| | *oostedes tyenen* |
| they have (m/f) | **ellos/-as tienen** |
| | *eh-yos/-yas tyenen* |

**¿Tiene rosas rojas?**
*tyeneh rosas rohas*
Do you have red roses?

| | |
|---|---|
| He has a meeting. | **Tiene una reunión.** |
| | *tyeneh oonah re-oonyon* |
| Do you have a cell phone? | **¿Tiene usted móvil?** |
| | *tyeneh oosted mobeel?* |
| How many brothers and sisters do you have? | **¿Cuántos hermanos tiene usted?** |
| | *kwantos airmanos tyeneh oosted* |

## 4  NEGATIVES

**4** minutes

To make a sentence negative in Spanish, put **no** in front of the verb: **no somos americanos** (*we're not American*). Read these sentences aloud, then test yourself, using the cover flap.

**la bicicleta**
*lah beetheekletah*
bicycle

**No tengo coche.**
*noh tengoh kocheh*
I don't have a car.

| | |
|---|---|
| I'm not Spanish. | **No soy español.** |
| | *noh soy espanyol* |
| He's not a vegetarian. | **No es vegetariano.** |
| | *noh es be-hetaryanoh* |
| We don't have any children. | **No tenemos niños.** |
| | *noh tenehmos neenyos* |

# Repase y repita
## *REVIEW AND REPEAT*

**Respuestas** *Answers*
(Cover with flap)

### How many?

❶ **tres**
*tres*

❷ **nueve**
*n<u>we</u>beh*

❸ **cuatro**
*k<u>wa</u>troh*

❹ **dos**
*dos*

❺ **ocho**
*<u>o</u>choh*

❻ **diez**
*dy<u>eth</u>*

❼ **cinco**
*<u>theen</u>koh*

❽ **siete**
*s<u>ye</u>teh*

❾ **seis**
*<u>seh</u>-ees*

### Hello

❶ **Buenos días. Me llamo... [your name].**
*<u>bwe</u>nos <u>dee</u>yas. meh <u>ya</u>moh...*

❷ **Encantado/-a.**
*enkan-<u>ta</u>doh/-ah*

❸ **Sí, y tengo dos hijos. ¿Y usted?**
*see, ee <u>ten</u>goh dos <u>ee</u>-hos. ee oo<u>sted</u>*

❹ **Adiós. Hasta mañana.**
*addy-<u>os</u>. <u>as</u>tah man<u>ya</u>nah*

## 1 HOW MANY?

**2** minutes

Say these numbers in Spanish, then test yourself, using the cover flap.

## 2 HELLO

**4** minutes

You meet someone in a formal situation. Join in the conversation, replying in Spanish, following the numbered English prompts.

**Buenos días. Me llamo María.**
❶ Good day. My name is... [your name].

**Este es mi marido, Juan.**
❷ Pleased to meet you.

**¿Está usted casado/-a?**
❸ Yes, and I have two sons. And you?

**Nosotros tenemos tres hijas.**
❹ Goodbye. See you tomorrow.

## 3 BE OR HAVE

**5** minutes

Fill in the blanks with the correct form of **tener** (*to have*) or **ser** (*to be*).

❶ Yo _____ inglesa.
❷ Nosotros _____ cuatro niños.
❸ Yo no _____ feliz.
❹ ¿ _____ coche?
❺ Yo no _____ móvil.
❻ Tú no _____ español.
❼ ¿ _____ usted hijos?
❽ Él _____ mi marido.

### Be or have

❶ **soy**
*soy*

❷ **tenemos**
*tenehmos*

❸ **soy**
*soy*

❹ **tienes**
*tyenes*

❺ **tengo**
*tengoh*

❻ **eres**
*eh-res*

❼ **tiene**
*tyeneh*

❽ **es**
*es*

## 4 RELATIVES

**4** minutes

Name these family members in Spanish.

grandmother ❶     grandfather ❷
❸ father          ❹ mother
sister ❺          brother ❻
daughter ❼        ❽ son

### Relatives

❶ **la abuela**
*lah abwelah*

❷ **el abuelo**
*el abweloh*

❸ **el padre**
*el pahdreh*

❹ **la madre**
*lah mahdreh*

❺ **la hermana**
*lah airmanah*

❻ **el hermano**
*el airmanoh*

❼ **la hija**
*lah ee-hah*

❽ **el hijo**
*el ee-hoh*

## 1 WARM UP  1 minute

Count to ten (pp10–11).

Remind yourself of how to say "**hello**" and "**goodbye**" (pp8–9).

Ask "**Do you have a son?**" (pp14–15).

# En la cafetería
## *IN THE CAFÉ*

In a Spanish **cafetería** (*café*), you can get coffee in the morning accompanied by bread, pastries, or **churros**, sweet, fried dough sticks that are a popular Spanish snack. You can either sit at the counter or have table service. It is usual to tip the server, but a good rounding up will be enough.

## 2  WORDS TO REMEMBER

Familiarize yourself with these words, then test yourself, using the cover flap.

**el pan con jamón**
*el pan kon ha<u>mon</u>*
bread with ham

**el pan con tomate**
*el pan kon to<u>mateh</u>*
bread with tomato

**la tostada con mantequilla y mermelada**
*lah to<u>sta</u>dah kon mante<u>kee</u>-yah ee merme<u>la</u>dah*
toast with butter and jam

**el azúcar**
*el ah-<u>thoo</u>kar*
sugar

**el cortado**
*el kor<u>ta</u>doh*
espresso with a bit of milk

**el café con leche**
*el ka<u>feh</u> kon <u>le</u>cheh*
coffee with milk

**el chocolate caliente**
*el choko<u>la</u>teh ka<u>lee</u>-enteh*
hot chocolate

**la tortilla**
*lah tor<u>tee</u>-yah*
tortilla

## 3  IN CONVERSATION

**Buenos días. Un café con leche, por favor.**
*<u>bwe</u>nos <u>dee</u>yas. oon ka<u>feh</u> kon <u>le</u>cheh, por fa<u>bor</u>*

Hello. I'll have a coffee with milk, please.

**¿Eso es todo?**
*<u>e</u>soh es <u>to</u>doh*

Is that all?

**¿Tiene churros?**
*<u>tye</u>neh <u>choo</u>rros*

Do you have any churros?

**Cultural tip** A standard coffee is small and black. You'll need to ask if you want it any other way. Ask for **té con leche** to get tea with milk or **té con limón** for tea with lemon. If you just ask for **té**, you are likely to get plain black tea.

**5** minutes

**el café solo**
el kafeh soloh
espresso

**los churros**
los choorros
churros

Learn these phrases, then test yourself, using the cover flap.

**¿Me pone un café americano?**
meh poneh oon kafeh amerikanoh

Can I have a black coffee?

**¿Eso es todo?**
esoh es todoh

Is that all?

**Yo voy a tomar churros.**
yoh boy ah tomar choorros

I'm going to have some churros.

**¿Cuánto es?**
kwantoh es

How much is that?

**4** minutes

**Sí, señora.**
see, senyorah

Yes, madam.

**Gracias. ¿Cuánto es?**
grathyas. kwantoh es

Thank you. How much is that?

**Ocho euros, por favor.**
ochoh eh-ooros, por fabor

Eight euros, please.

# En el restaurante
## IN THE RESTAURANT

## 1 WARM UP
**1** minute

Ask "**How much is that?**" (pp18–19).

Say "**I don't have a brother**" (pp14–15).

Ask "**Do you have any churros?**" (pp18–19).

There are a variety of eating places in Spain. A **cafetería** (*café*) is great for breakfast or the **merienda** (*afternoon snack*), with coffee, other drinks, and snacks (pp18–19). A **tasca** or **taberna** (*bar*) offers **tapas** (*small plates*) and Spanish staples alongside alcoholic drinks. Lunch is the main meal of the day and can be eaten in a more formal **restaurante**.

## 2 🔊 MATCH AND REPEAT
**5** minutes

Match the numbered items to the list, then test yourself, using the cover flap.

❶ **el platillo**
   *el plateeyoh*

❷ **la taza**
   *lah tathah*

❸ **la copa**
   *lah kopah*

❹ **el tenedor**
   *el tenedor*

❺ **el cuchillo**
   *el koochee-yoh*

❻ **la cuchara**
   *lah koocharah*

❼ **el plato**
   *el platoh*

❽ **la servilleta**
   *lah serbee-yetah*

cup ❷  glass ❸  saucer ❶  ❹ fork  ❻ spoon  knife ❺  plate ❼  napkin ❽

## 3 🔊 IN CONVERSATION

**Hola. Una mesa para cuatro, por favor.**
*o-lah. oonah mesah parah kwatroh, por fabor*

Hello. A table for four, please.

**¿Tiene una reserva?**
*tyeneh oonah reserbah*

Do you have a reservation?

**Sí, a nombre de Cortés.**
*see, ah nombreh deh kortes*

Yes, in the name of Cortés.

## 4  WORDS TO REMEMBER

**3** minutes

Familiarize yourself with these words, then test yourself, using the cover flap.

| | |
|---|---|
| menu | **la carta** <br> *lah kartah* |
| wine list | **la carta de vinos** <br> *lah kartah deh beenos* |
| starters | **los entrantes** <br> *los entrantes* |
| main course | **el plato principal** <br> *el platoh preer:theepal* |
| desserts | **los postres** <br> *los postres* |
| breakfast | **el desayuno** <br> *el desah-yoonoh* |
| lunch | **el almuerzo** <br> *el almooairthoh* |
| dinner | **la cena** <br> *lah thenah* |

**Estoy almorzando con mi familia.**
*estoy almorthandoh kon mee fameelee-ah*
I am having lunch with my family.

## 5  USEFUL PHRASES

**2** minutes

Learn these phrases, then test yourself, using the cover flap.

| | |
|---|---|
| We have a reservation. | **Tenemos una reserva.** <br> *tenehmos oonah resairbah* |
| What do you have for dessert? | **¿Qué tiene de postre?** <br> *keh tyeneh deh postreh* |
| The bill, please. | **La cuenta, por favor.** <br> *lah kwentah, por fabor* |

**4** minutes

**Muy bien. ¿Qué mesa le gustaría?**
*mwee byen. keh mesah leh goostareeyah*

Very good. Which table would you like?

**Cerca de la ventana, por favor.**
*therkah deh lah bentanah, por fabor*

Near the window, please.

**Síganme, por favor.**
*seegan-meh, por fabor.*

Follow me, please.

## 1 WARM UP
**1** minute

Say "**I'm Spanish**" and "**She has a bicycle**" (pp14–15).

Ask "**Do you have a fork?**" (pp20–21).

Say "**I'd like a coffee with milk**" (pp18–19).

# Los platos
## DISHES

Spain offers a large variety of regional dishes. Plenty of garlic and olive oil are a feature of many typical dishes. Several restaurants now offer a vegetarian or vegan menu, but even if they don't, there are many traditional Spanish dishes available that do not contain meat. Ask your server for advice.

## 2 ◀))) MATCH AND REPEAT
**4** minutes

Match the numbered items to the list, then test yourself, using the cover flap.

❶ **las verduras**
*las berdooras*

❷ **la fruta**
*lah frootah*

❸ **el queso**
*el kesoh*

❹ **los frutos secos**
*los frootos sekos*

❺ **la sopa**
*lah sopah*

❻ **las aves**
*las ahbes*

❼ **la pasta**
*lah pastah*

❽ **el pescado**
*el peskadoh*

❾ **el marisco**
*el mareeskoh*

❿ **la carne**
*lah karneh*

❶ vegetables  fruit ❷

❸ cheese

soup ❺

nuts ❹

❻ poultry

pasta ❼

fish ❽  ❾ seafood  meat ❿

**Cultural tip** At lunch time, you will find that many restaurants offer **el menú del día** (*the day's set menu*). This is usually a three-course meal, with bread for the table and a drink included in the price.

## 3  WORDS TO REMEMBER: COOKING METHODS

 **3** minutes

Familiarize yourself with these words, then test yourself, using the cover flap. Note that the ending often varies, depending on the gender of item described.

| | |
|---|---|
| fried (m/f) | **frito/-a** *freetoh/-ah* |
| grilled | **a la plancha** *ah lah planchah* |
| roasted (m/f) | **asado/-a** *ahsadoh/-ah* |
| boiled (m/f) | **hervido/-a** *erbeedoh/-ah* |
| steamed | **al vapor** *al bapor* |
| rare (m/f) | **poco hecho/-a** *pokoh eh-choh/-ah* |

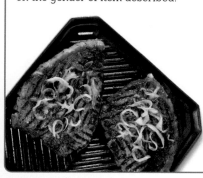

**Quisiera mi filete bien hecho.**
*keesyairah mee feeleteh byen eh-choh*
I'd like my steak well done.

## 4  WORDS TO REMEMBER: DRINKS

 **3** minutes

Familiarize yourself with these words, then test yourself, using the cover flap.

| | |
|---|---|
| water | **el agua** *el ahgwah* |
| still water | **el agua sin gas** *el ahgwah seen gas* |
| wine | **el vino** *el beenoh* |
| beer | **la cerveza** *lah thairbehthah* |
| fruit juice | **el zumo** *el thoomoh* |

**el agua con gas**
*el ahgwah kon gas*
fizzy water

## 5 USEFUL PHRASES

**2** minutes

Learn these phrases, then test yourself, using the cover flap.

| | |
|---|---|
| I am a vegetarian. (m/f) | **Soy vegetariano/-a.** *soy be-hetareeanoh/-ah* |
| I am allergic to nuts. (m/f) | **Soy alérgico/-a a los frutos secos.** *soy ahler-heekoh/-ah ah los frootos sekos* |
| What is "conejo"? | **¿Qué es el "conejo"?** *keh es el kone-hoh* |

## 6 SAY IT

**2** minutes

What is "tortilla"?

I'm allergic to seafood.

I'd like a beer.

# Querer
## *TO WANT*

What are "**breakfast**," "**lunch**," and "**dinner**" in Spanish? (pp20–21).

Say "**I**," "**you**" (informal), "**he**," "**she**," "**we**," "**you**" (plural/formal), "**they**" (masculine), and "**they**" (feminine) (pp14–15).

In this section, you will learn the present tense of a verb that is essential to everyday conversation—**querer** (*to want*)—as well as a useful polite form, **quisiera** (*I'd like*). Remember to use this form when requesting something because **quiero** (*I want*) may sound too strong: **¿qué quiere beber?** (*what do you want to drink?*); **quisiera una cerveza** (*I'd like a beer*).

---

**2**  **QUERER**: TO WANT

**6** minutes

Practice **querer** (*to want*) and the sample sentences, then test yourself, using the cover flap.

| | |
|---|---|
| **yo quiero** <br> *yoh kyairoh* | I want |
| **tú quieres/usted quiere** <br> *too kyaires/oosted kyaireh* | you want (informal/ formal singular) |
| **él/ella quiere** <br> *el/eh-yah kyaireh* | he/she wants |
| **nosotros/-as queremos** <br> *nosotros/-as kerehmos* | we want (m/f) |
| **vosotros/-as queréis/ ustedes quieren** <br> *bosotros/-as kereh-ees/ oostedes kyairen* | you want (informal/ formal plural m/f) |
| **ellos/-as quieren** <br> *eh-yos/-as-yas kyairen* | they want (m/f) |

| | |
|---|---|
| **¿Quieres vino?** <br> *kyaires beenoh?* | Do you want some wine? |
| **Quiere un coche nuevo.** <br> *kyaireh oon kocheh nweboh* | She wants a new car. |

**Quiero caramelos.**
*kyairoh karamelos*
I want some sweets.

---

**Conversational tip** Although it may sound rude to you, the Spanish don't say *please* (**por favor**) or *thank you* (**gracias**) very often, and they hardly ever say *excuse me* (**perdón**) or *I'm sorry* (**lo siento**), but they use the tone of their voices and choice of words to imply politeness, such as **quisiera** (*I'd like*) instead of **quiero** (*I want*).

## 3  POLITE REQUESTS

**4** minutes

There is a form of **quiero** (*I want*) used for polite requests: **quisiera** (*I'd like*). Practice the sample sentences, then test yourself, using the cover flap.

| I'd like a beer. | **Quisiera una cerveza.** |
| | *keesyairah oonah therbehthah* |

| I'd like a table for tonight. | **Quisiera una mesa para esta noche.** |
| | *keesyairah oonah mesah parah estah nocheh* |

| I'd like to see the menu, please. | **Quisiera ver la carta, por favor.** |
| | *keesyairah ber lah kartah, por fabor* |

## 4  PUT INTO PRACTICE

**4** minutes

Complete this dialogue, then test yourself, using the cover flap.

**Buenas tardes señor. ¿Tiene una reserva?**
*bwenas tardes senyor. tyeneh oonah reserbah*

Good evening, sir. Do you have a reservation?

Say: No, but I would like a table for three.

**No, pero quisiera una mesa para tres.**
*noh, peroh keesyairah oonah mesah parah tres*

**Muy bien. ¿Qué mesa le gustaría?**
*mwee byen. keh mesah leh goostareeyah*

Very good. Which table would you like?

Say: Near the window, please.

**Cerca de la ventana, por favor.**
*therkah deh lah bentanah, por fabor*

# Repase y repita
## REVIEW AND REPEAT

### At the table

❶ **los frutos secos**
*los frootos sekos*

❷ **el azúcar**
*el ah-thookar*

❸ **el marisco**
*el mareeskoh*

❹ **la carne**
*lah karneh*

❺ **la copa**
*lah kopah*

## 1 AT THE TABLE

Name these items in Spanish.

❶ nuts

sugar ❷

❸ seafood

meat ❹

glass ❺

### This is my…

❶ **Esta es mi mujer.**
*estah es mee moo-hair*

❷ **Aquí están sus hijas.**
*ahkee estan soos ee-has*

❸ **Mis hijos están cansados.**
*mis eehos estan kansahdos*

❹ **Mi mesa está en la terraza**
*mee mesah estah en lah terrathah*

## 2 THIS IS MY…

4 minutes

Say these sentences in Spanish.
Use **mi(-s)**, **tu(-us)**, or **su(-s)**.

❶ This is my wife.

❷ Here are her daughters.

❸ My children are tired.

❹ My table is on the terrace.

### I'd like…

❶ **Quisiera la tortilla**
*keesyairah lah tortee-yah*

❷ **Quisiera el chocolate caliente**
*keesyairah el chokolateh kalee-enteh*

❸ **Quisiera churros.**
*keesyairah choorros*

## 3 I'D LIKE…

3 minutes

Say that you'd like these items in Spanish.

❶ tortilla    ❷ hot chocolate    ❸ churros

**4** minutes

⑥ pasta

⑦ cheese

knife ⑧

⑨ napkin

⑩ beer

## At the table

⑥ **la pasta**
*lah pastah*

⑦ **el queso**
*el kesoh*

⑧ **el cuchillo**
*el koochee-yoh*

⑨ **la servilleta**
*lah serbee-yetah*

⑩ **la cerveza**
*lah thairbeh;thah*

---

## 4   RESTAURANT

**4** minutes

You arrive at a restaurant. Join in the conversation, replying in Spanish, following the numbered English prompts.

**Buenas tardes señora, señor.**
① Good evening, I would like a table for six.

**¿Tiene una reserva?**
② Yes, in the name of López.

**Síganme, por favor.**
③ I'd like the menu, please.

**¿Quiere la carta de vinos?**
④ No. Fizzy water, please.

**Muy bien.**
⑤ I don't have a glass.

## Restaurant

① **Buenas tardes, quisiera una mesa para seis.**
*bwenas tardes. keesyairah oonah mesah parah seh-ees*

② **Sí, a nombre de López.**
*see, ah nombren deh lopeth*

③ **Quisiera la carta, por favor.**
*keesyairah lah kortah, por fabor*

④ **No. Agua con gas, por favor.**
*noh. ahgwah kon gas, por fabor*

⑤ **No tengo copa.**
*noh tengoh kopah*

# 1 WARM UP
**1** minute

Say "**He is**" and "**They are**" (pp14–15).

Say "**He is not**" and "**They are not**" (pp14–15).

What is Spanish for "**the children**" (pp10–11)?

# Los días y los meses
## *DAYS AND MONTHS*

In Spanish, the days of the week (**los días de la semana**) and months of the year (**los meses del año**) do not have capital letters. The months have similar names to the English terms. You use **en** with months: **en abril** (*in April*), but **el** or **los** with days: **el/los lunes** (*on Monday/Mondays*).

# 2  WORDS TO REMEMBER:
## DAYS
**5** minutes

Familiarize yourself with these words, then test yourself, using the cover flap.

| | |
|---|---|
| **lunes** *loones* | Monday |
| **martes** *martes* | Tuesday |
| **miércoles** *myairkoles* | Wednesday |
| **jueves** *hwebes* | Thursday |
| **viernes** *byernes* | Friday |
| **sábado** *sabadoh* | Saturday |
| **domingo** *domeengoh* | Sunday |
| **hoy** *oy* | today |
| **mañana** *manyanah* | tomorrow |
| **ayer** *ah-yair* | yesterday |

**Nos reunimos mañana.**
*mos reh-ooneemos manyanah*
We meet tomorrow.

**Tengo una reserva para hoy.**
*tengoh oonah reserbah parah oy*
I have a reservation for today.

# 3  USEFUL PHRASES: DAYS
**2** minutes

Learn these phrases, then test yourself, using the cover flap.

**La reunión no es el martes.**
*lah reh-oonyon noh es el martes*
The meeting isn't on Tuesday.

**Trabajo los domingos.**
*traba-hoh los domeengos*
I work on Sundays.

## 4  WORDS TO REMEMBER: MONTHS

 **5** minutes

Familiarize yourself with these words, then test yourself, using the cover flap.

**Nuestro aniversario de boda es en julio.**
*nwestroh aneebairsaree-oh deh bohdah es en hoolee-oh*
Our wedding anniversary is in July.

**Navidad es en diciembre.**
*nabeedad es en deethyembreh*
Christmas is in December.

| January | **enero** |
| | *ehneroh* |
| February | **febrero** |
| | *febreroh* |
| March | **marzo** |
| | *marthoh* |
| April | **abril** |
| | *abreel* |
| May | **mayo** |
| | *mah-yoh* |
| June | **junio** |
| | *hoonee-oh* |
| July | **julio** |
| | *hoolee-oh* |
| August | **agosto** |
| | *agostoh* |
| September | **septiembre** |
| | *septyembreh* |
| October | **octubre** |
| | *oktoobreh* |
| November | **noviembre** |
| | *nobyembreh* |
| December | **diciembre** |
| | *deethyembreh* |
| month | **el mes** |
| | *el mes* |
| year | **el año** |
| | *el anyoh* |

## 5  USEFUL PHRASES: MONTHS

 **2** minutes

Learn these phrases, then test yourself, using the cover flap.

My children are on vacation in August.
**Mis hijos están de vacaciones en agosto.**
*mees ee-hos estan deh bakathyones en agostoh*

My birthday is in June.
**Mi cumpleaños es en junio.**
*mee kompleh-anyos es en hoonee-oh*

# La hora y los números
## *TIME AND NUMBERS*

**1** **WARM UP**
**1** minute

Count in Spanish from 1 to 10 (pp10–11).

Say "**I have a reservation**" (pp20–21).

Say "**The meeting is on Wednesday**" (pp28–29).

The hour is preceded by **la**, as in **la una** (*one o'clock*), and **las** for the other numbers: **las dos, las tres,** and so on. In English, the minutes come first: ten to five; in Spanish, the hour comes first: **las cinco menos diez** (*five minus ten*).

**2**  **WORDS TO REMEMBER**: TIME

**4** minutes

Familiarize yourself with these words, then test yourself, using the cover flap.

| | |
|---|---|
| **la una**<br>*lah oonah* | one o'clock |
| **la una y cinco**<br>*lah oonah ee theenkoh* | five past one |
| **la una y cuarto**<br>*lah oonah ee kwartoh* | quarter past one |
| **la una y veinte**<br>*lah oonah ee beynteh* | twenty past one |
| **la una y media**<br>*lah oonah ee medee-ah* | half past one |
| **las dos menos cuarto**<br>*las dos menos kwartoh* | quarter to two |
| **las dos menos diez**<br>*las dos menos dyeth* | ten to two |

**3**  **USEFUL PHRASES**

**2** minutes

Learn these phrases, then test yourself, using the cover flap.

| | |
|---|---|
| **¿Qué hora es?**<br>*keh orah es* | What time is it? |
| **¿A qué hora quiere el desayuno?**<br>*ah keh orah kyaireh el desah-yoonoh* | What time do you want breakfast? |
| **La reunión es a mediodía.**<br>*lah reh-oonyon es ah mehdyodee-ah* | The meeting is at midday. |

# 4 WORDS TO REMEMBER:
HIGHER NUMBERS

**6** minutes

In Spanish, when you say 21, you use **veinti** and add **uno** (*one*): **veintiuno**. Successive numbers are created in the same way—for example, **veintidós** (22), **veintitrés** (23), and so on. After 30, link the numbers with **y** (*and*): **treinta y uno** (31), **cuarenta y cinco** (45), **sesenta y seis** (66).

Note the special forms used for 500, 700, and 900: **quinientos**, **setecientos**, and **novecientos**.

Familiarize yourself with these words, then test yourself, using the cover flap.

**He pagado ochenta y cinco euros mediante pago sin contacto.**
*eh pag<u>a</u>doh <u>o</u>ch<u>en</u>tah ee th<u>een</u>koh eh-<u>oo</u>ros m<u>edee</u>anteh p<u>a</u>goh seen kon<u>tak</u>toh*
I've paid eighty-five euros by contactless payment.

| | | |
|---|---|---|
| eleven | **once** | *<u>on</u>theh* |
| twelve | **doce** | *<u>do</u>theh* |
| thirteen | **trece** | *<u>tre</u>theh* |
| fourteen | **catorce** | *kat<u>or</u>theh* |
| fifteen | **quince** | *<u>keen</u>theh* |
| sixteen | **dieciséis** | *deeehthee<u>se</u>hees* |
| seventeen | **diecisiete** | *deeehthee<u>sye</u>yteh* |
| eighteen | **dieciocho** | *deeehthy<u>o</u>choh* |
| nineteen | **diecinueve** | *deeehthy<u>nwe</u>beh* |
| twenty | **veinte** | *<u>beyn</u>teh* |
| thirty | **treinta** | *<u>treyn</u>tah* |
| forty | **cuarenta** | *kwa<u>ren</u>tah* |
| fifty | **cincuenta** | *theen<u>kwen</u>tah* |
| sixty | **sesenta** | *se<u>sen</u>tah* |
| seventy | **setenta** | *se<u>ten</u>tah* |
| eighty | **ochenta** | *o<u>chen</u>tah* |
| ninety | **noventa** | *no<u>ben</u>tah* |
| hundred | **cien** | *thee-en* |
| three hundred | **trescientos** | *tresthee<u>en</u>tos* |
| thousand | **mil** | *meel* |
| ten thousand | **diez mil** | *d<u>yeth</u> meel* |
| two hundred thousand | **doscientos mil** | *dosthee<u>en</u>tos meel* |
| one million | **un millón** | *oon mee<u>yon</u>* |

# 5 SAY IT

**2** minutes

twenty-five

sixty-eight

eighty-four

ninety-one

five to ten

half past eleven

What time is lunch?

Say the days of the week in Spanish (pp28–29).

Say "**It's three o'clock**" (pp30–31).

What's the Spanish for "**today**," "**tomorrow**," and "**yesterday**" (pp28–29)?

# Las citas
## *APPOINTMENTS*

Business in Spain is generally conducted more formally than in Britain or the United States; always address business contacts as **usted**, **ustedes** (formal *you*). The Spanish tend to leave the office for the lunch hour, often having a sit-down meal in a restaurant or, less commonly, at home.

## 2  USEFUL PHRASES

**5** minutes

Learn these phrases, then test yourself, using the cover flap.

| | |
|---|---|
| **¿Nos reunimos mañana?**<br>*nos reh-ooneemos manyanah* | Shall we meet tomorrow? |
| **¿Con quién?**<br>*kon kee-en* | With whom? |
| **¿Cuándo está libre?**<br>*kwandoh estah leebreh* | When are you free? |
| **Lo siento, estoy ocupado(-a).**<br>*loh syentoh, estoy okoopadoh(-ah)* | I'm sorry, I'm busy. |
| **¿Qué tal el jueves?**<br>*keh tal el hwebes* | How about Thursday? |
| **A mí me va bien.**<br>*ah mee meh bah byen* | That's good for me. |

**el apretón de manos**
*el apreton deh manos*
handshake

**Bienvenido.**
*byenveneedoh*
Welcome.

## 3  IN CONVERSATION

**Buenos días. Tengo una cita.**
*bwenos deeyas. tengoh oonah theetah*

Good morning. I have an appointment.

**¿Con quién es la cita?**
*kon kee-en es lah theetah*

With whom is the appointment?

**Con el señor Montoya.**
*kon el senyor montoyah*

With Mr. Montoya.

# 4  PUT INTO PRACTICE

**5** minutes

Complete this dialogue, then test yourself, using the cover flap.

**¿Nos reunimos el jueves?**
*nos reh-ooneemos el hwebes*

Shall we meet on Thursday?

Say: Sorry, I'm busy.

**Lo siento, estoy ocupado.**
*loh syentoh, estoy okoopadoh*

**¿Cuándo está libre?**
*kwandoh estah leebreh*

When are you free?

Say: Tuesday afternoon.

**El martes por la tarde.**
*el martes por lah tardeh*

**A mí me va bien.**
*ah mee meh bah byen*

That's good for me.

Ask: At what time?

**¿A qué hora?**
*ah keh orah*

**A las cuatro, si a usted le va bien.**
*ah las kwatroh, see ah oosted le bah byen*

At four o'clock, if that's good for you.

Say: Yes, it's good for me.

**Sí, me va bien.**
*see, meh bah byen*

---

**4** minutes

**Muy bien. ¿A qué hora?**
*mwee byen. ah keh orah?*

Very good. What time?

**A las tres, pero llego un poco tarde.**
*ah las tres, peroh yegoh oon pokoh tardeh*

At three o'clock, but I'm a little late.

**No se preocupe. Tome asiento, por favor.**
*noh seh pre-ohkoopeh. tomeh asyaintoh, por fabor*

Don't worry. Take a seat, please.

# Por teléfono
## ON THE TELEPHONE

**1** **WARM UP** 🕐
**1** minute

Say "**I'm sorry**" (pp32–33).

What is the Spanish for "**I'd like an appointment**" (pp32–33)?

How do you say "**when?**" in Spanish (pp32–33)?

The emergency number for police, ambulance, or fire services across the European Union is 112. You can dial it free of charge from cell phones or landlines anywhere in the EU. To make direct international calls from Spain, dial the access code 00 followed by the country code, area code (omit the initial 0), and then the phone number. The country code for Spain is 34.

**2** 🔊 **MATCH AND REPEAT**

Match the numbered items to the list, then test yourself, using the cover flap.

**1** **los auriculares**
los aooreekoo*la*res

**2** **los cascos**
los *kas*kos

**3** **el teléfono**
el te*le*fonoh

**4** **el móvil**
el *mo*beel

**5** **el cargador**
el karga*dor*

**6** **la tarjeta SIM**
lah tar*he*tah seem

**7** **el contestador automático**
el kontesta*dor* aooto*ma*teekoh

**1** earphones  **2** headphones

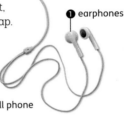

**4** cell phone

**5** charger

**6** SIM card

**Quisiera comprar una tarjeta SIM.**
kee*syai*rah komprar *oo*nah tar*he*tah seem
I'd like to buy a SIM card.

**3** 🔊 **IN CONVERSATION**

**Dígame, Susana Castillo al habla.**
*dee*gameh, soo*sa*nah kas*tee*yoh al *a*blah

Hello. Susana Castillo speaking.

**Buenos días. Quisiera hablar con Julián López, por favor.**
*bwe*nos *dee*yas. kee*syair*-ah *a*blar kon hoolee*an* *lo*peth, por fa*bor*

Hello. I'd like to speak to Julián López, please.

**¿De parte de quién?**
deh *par*teh deh kee-*en*?

May I know who's calling?

## 5 SAY IT
*2 minutes*

I'd like to speak to Mr. Girona.

Can I leave a message for Antonio?

Can she call me back on Wednesday, please?

*4 minutes*

❸ telephone

answering machine ❼

## 4 🔊 USEFUL PHRASES
*4 minutes*

Learn these phrases, then test yourself, using the cover flap.

I'd like the number for Juan.

**Quisiera el número de Juan.**
*keesyairah el noomeroh deh hooan*

I'd like to speak to María Alfaro.

**Quisiera hablar con María Alfaro.**
*keesyairah ablar kon mareeah alfaroh*

Can I leave a message?

**¿Puedo dejar un mensaje?**
*pwedoh dehar oon mensaheh*

Sorry, I have the wrong number.

**Perdone, me he equivocado de número.**
*perdoneh, meh eh ekeebokadoh deh noomeroh*

*4 minutes*

**José Ortega, de Imprentas Lacuesta.**
*hoseh ortegah, deh eemprentas lakwestah*

José Ortega of Lacuesta Printers.

**Lo siento. La línea está comunicando.**
*loh syaintoh. lah leeneah estah komooneekandoh*

I'm sorry. The line is busy.

**¿Le puede decir que me llame, por favor?**
*leh pwedeh detheer keh meh yameh, por fabor*

Can you ask him to call me, please?

# Repase y repita
## *REVIEW AND REPEAT*

### Telephones

❶ **el móvil**
*el mobeel*

❷ **el teléfono**
*el telefonoh*

❸ **el contestador automático**
*el kontestador aootomateekoh*

❹ **los cascos**
*los kaskos*

❺ **la tarjeta SIM**
*lah tarhetah seem*

## 1 TELEPHONES

Name these items in Spanish.

❶ cell phone
❷ telephone
❸ answering machine
headphones ❹

### When?

❶ I have a meeting on Monday, May 20.

❷ My birthday is in September.

❸ Today is Sunday.

❹ I don't work in August.

## 2 WHEN?

**2** minutes

What do these sentences mean?

❶ Tengo una cita el lunes, veinte de mayo.
❷ Mi cumpleaños es en septiembre.
❸ Hoy es domingo.
❹ No trabajo en agosto.

### Time

❶ **la una**
*lah oonah*

❷ **la una y cinco**
*lah oonah ee theenkoh*

❸ **la una y cuarto**
*lah oonah ee kwartoh*

❹ **la una y veinte**
*lah oonah ee beynteh*

❺ **la una y media**
*lah oonah ee medee-ah*

❻ **las dos menos diez**
*las dos menos dyeth*

## 3 TIME

**3** minutes

Say these times in Spanish.

❶  ❷  ❸
❹  ❺  ❻

**3** minutes

## 4 ADDITION

**4** minutes

Say the answers to these problems in Spanish.

❶ 10 + 6 = ?
❷ 14 + 25 = ?
❸ 66 − 13 = ?
❹ 40 + 34 = ?
❺ 90 + 9 = ?

❺ SIM card

### Addition

❶ **dieciséis**
*deeehtheesehees*

❷ **treinta y nueve**
*treyntah ee nwebeh*

❸ **cincuenta y tres**
*theenkwentah ee tres*

❹ **setenta y cuatro**
*setentah ee kwatroh*

❺ **noventa y nueve**
*nobentah ee nwebeh*

## 5 I WANT...

**3** minutes

Fill in the blanks with the correct form of **querer** (*to want*).

❶ ¿ _____ usted un café?
❷ Ella _____ ir de vacaciones.
❸ Nosotros _____ una mesa para tres.
❹ Tú _____ una cerveza.
❺ Ellos _____ una mesa para dos.
❻ Yo _____ caramelos.

### I want...

❶ **Quiere**
*kyaireh*

❷ **quiere**
*kyaireh*

❸ **queremos**
*kerehmos*

❹ **quieres**
*kyaires*

❺ **quieren**
*kyairen*

❻ **quiero**
*kyairoh*

Count to 100 by tens
(pp10–11, pp30–31).

Ask **"At what time?"**
(pp30–31).

Say **"It's half-past one"**
(pp30–31).

# En la taquilla
## *AT THE TICKET OFFICE*

In Spain, before getting on the train, you must
validate (**validar**) your ticket by stamping it.
Special machines are installed in every railway
station for this purpose. Fines are handed out
to those who forget to validate their tickets.
Prices of long-distance trains vary, depending
on what day you travel.

## 2  WORDS TO REMEMBER

**3** minutes

Familiarize yourself with these words,
then test yourself, using the cover flap.

**el andén**
*el an*den
platform

**el tren**
*el tren*
train

**la estación** (train) station
*lah estath*yon

**la terminal** (bus) station
*lah termee*nal

**el billete** ticket
*el bee*yeteh

**de ida** single
*deh* eedah

**de ida y vuelta** return
*deh* eedah *ee* bweltah

**de primera** first class
*deh preem*erah

**de segunda** second class
*deh se*goondah

**el descuento** discount
*el des*kwentoh

**La estación no está llena de gente.**
*lah estath*yon *noh es*tah yenah *deh* henteh
The station is not crowded.

## 3  IN CONVERSATION

**Dos billetes para Bilbao, por favor.**
*dos bee*yetes parah beeba-oh*, por fa*bor

Two tickets for Bilbao,
please.

**¿De ida y vuelta?**
*deh* eedah *ee* bweltah

Return?

**Sí. ¿Necesito reservar asiento?**
*see. nethe*seetoh *rreseer*bar asyaintoh

Yes. Do I need to
reserve seats?

# 4   USEFUL PHRASES

**5** minutes

Learn these phrases, then test yourself, using the cover flap.

**Mi tren va con retraso.**
*mee tren bah kon rretrasoh*
My train is late.

| | |
|---|---|
| How much is a ticket to Madrid? | **¿Cuánto cuesta un billete para Madrid?** <br> *kwantoh kwehstah oon beeyeteh parah madreed* |
| Can I pay by credit card? | **¿Puedo pagar con tarjeta de crédito?** <br> *pwedoh pagar kon tarhetah deh kredeetoh* |
| Do I have to change trains? | **¿Tengo que cambiar de tren?** <br> *tengoh keh kambee-ar deh tren* |
| Which platform does the train leave from? | **¿De qué andén sale el tren?** <br> *deh keh anden saleh el tren* |
| Are there any discounts? | **¿Hay algún descuento?** <br> *ah-ee algoon deskwentoh* |
| What time does the train for Gijón leave? | **¿A qué hora sale el tren para Gijón?** <br> *ah keh orah saleh el tren parah geehon* |

**Cultural tip** Most large railway stations have ticket offices and automatic ticket machines that accept credit and debit cards, cash, and payments via mobile and digital wallets.

# 5  SAY IT

**2** minutes

Which platform does the train for Madrid leave from?

Three return tickets to Murcia, please.

---

**4** minutes

**No hace falta. Trescientos euros, por favor.**
*noh ahtheh faltah. trestheeentos eh-ooros, por fabor*

That's not necessary. Three hundred euros please.

**¿Aceptan tarjetas de crédito?**
*ahtheptan tarhetas deh kredeetoh*

Do you accept credit cards?

**Sí. El tren sale del andén cinco.**
*see. el tren saleh del anden theenkoh*

Certainly. The train leaves from platform five.

## 1 WARM UP
**1** minute

How do you say "**train**" in Spanish (pp38–39)?

What does "**¿De qué andén sale el tren?**" mean (pp38–39)?

Ask "**When are you free?**" (pp32–33).

# Ir y coger
*TO GO AND TO TAKE*

The verbs **ir** (*to go*) and **coger** (*to take*) allow you to create many useful sentences. Note that **coger** can also mean *to catch*: **coger una pelota** (*to catch a ball*), **coger un resfriado** (*to catch a cold*); *to grab*: **coger a alguien** (*to grab someone*); and *to hold*: **coger a un bebé** (*to hold a baby*).

## 2 IR: TO GO

**6** minutes

The present tense in Spanish includes the sense of continuous action. For example, the same form of **ir** is used for both *I go* and *I am going*: **voy a Madrid** (*I am going to Madrid/I go to Madrid*). The same is true of other verbs—for example, **cojo el metro** (*I am taking the metro/I take the metro*). Practice **ir** (*to go*) and the sample sentences, then test yourself, using the cover flap.

| | |
|---|---|
| **yo voy** *yoh boy* | I go |
| **tú vas/usted va** *too bas/oosted bah* | you go (informal/formal singular) |
| **él/ella va** *el/eh-yah bah* | he/she goes |
| **nosotros(-as) vamos** *nosotros(-as) bamos* | we go (m/f) |
| **vosotros(-as) vais/ ustedes van** *bosotros(-as) baees/ oostedes ban* | you go (informal/formal plural m/f) |
| **ellos/ellas van** *eh-yos/eh-yas ban* | they go (m/f) |
| **¿A dónde vas?** *ah dondeh bas* | Where are you going? |
| **Voy a Madrid.** *boy ah madreed* | I am going to Madrid. |

**Voy a la Plaza de España.**
*boy ah lah plathah deh espanyah*
I am going to the Plaza de España.

**Conversational tip** You may have noticed that **de** (*of*) combines with **el** to produce **del**, as in **Museo del Prado** (literally *museum of the Prado*) or **el menú del día** (*menu of the day*). In the same way, **a** (*to*) combines with **el** to produce **al**: **voy al museo** (*I'm going to the museum*). With feminine and plural words, **de** remains separate from **la**, **los**, and **las**.

# 3  COGER: TO TAKE

**6** minutes

Practice **coger** (*to take*) and the sample sentences, then test yourself, using the cover flap.

| | |
|---|---|
| **yo cojo**<br>*yoh kohoh* | I take |
| **tú coges/usted coge**<br>*too kohes/oosted koheh* | you take (informal/<br>formal singular) |
| **él/ella coge**<br>*el/eh-yah koheh* | he/she takes |
| **nosotros(-as)**<br>**cogemos**<br>*nosotros(-as) kohehmos* | we take (m/f) |
| **vosotros(-as) cogéis/**<br>**ustedes cogen**<br>*bosotros(-as) koheh-ees/*<br>*oostedes kohen* | you take (informal/<br>formal plural m/f) |
| **ellos/ellas cogen**<br>*eh-yos/eh-yas kohen* | they take (m/f) |

**Yo cojo el metro todos los días.**
*yoh kohoh el metroh todos los deeyas*
I take the metro every day.

| | |
|---|---|
| **No quiero coger un taxi.**<br>*noh kyairoh koher oon taksee* | I don't want to take a taxi. |

| | |
|---|---|
| **Coja la primera a la izquierda.**<br>*kohah lah preemerah ah lah eethkyairdah* | Take the first on the left. |

# 4  PUT INTO PRACTICE

**2** minutes

Complete this dialogue, then test yourself, using the cover flap.

**¿A dónde va?**
*ah dondeh bah*

Where are you going?

Say: I'm going to the Puerta del Sol.

**Voy a la Puerta del Sol.**
*boy ah lah pwertah del sol*

**¿Quiere coger el autobús?**
*kyaireh koher el aootoboos*

Do you want to take the bus?

Say: No, I want to go by metro.

**No, quiero ir en metro.**
*noh, kyairoh eer en metroh*

# Taxi, autobús, y metro
## *TAXI, BUS, AND METRO*

## 1 — WARM UP
**1** minute

Say "**I'd like to go to the station**" (pp40–41).

Ask "**Where are you going?**" (pp40–41).

Say "**fruit**" and "**cheese**" (pp22–23).

For the metro and some buses you will have to validate your tickets in a machine. There's a standard fare per ride. You can buy single tickets using cash or card, and in some cities you can also buy a book of ten tickets valid on buses and the metro. Some buses may also accept contactless payments.

## 2 🔊 WORDS TO REMEMBER
**4** minutes

| | |
|---|---|
| **el autobús** *el aootoboos* | bus |
| **la estación de autobús** *lah estathyon deh aootoboos* | bus station |
| **la taquilla** *lah takeeyah* | ticket office |
| **la parada de autobús** *lah paradah deh aootoboos* | bus stop |
| **la tarifa** *lah tareefah* | fare |
| **el taxi** *el taksee* | taxi |
| **la parada de taxis** *lah paradah deh taksees* | taxi rank |
| **la estación de metro** *lah estathyon deh metroh* | metro station |

Familiarize yourself with these words, then test yourself, using the cover flap.

**¿Para aquí el 17?**
*parah ahkee el deeaytheeseehteh*
Does the number 17 bus stop here?

## 3 🔊 IN CONVERSATION: TAXI
**2** minutes

**A la Plaza de España, por favor.**
*ah lah plathah deh espanyah, por fabor*

Plaza de España, please.

**Sí, de acuerdo, señor.**
*see, deh akwairdoh, senyor*

Yes, certainly, sir.

**¿Me puede dejar aquí, por favor?**
*meh pwedeh dehar ahkee, por fabor*

Can you drop me here, please?

## 4  USEFUL PHRASES

**4** minutes

Learn these phrases, then test yourself, using the cover flap.

| I'd like a taxi to go to the Prado. | **Quisiera un taxi para ir al Prado.**<br>_keesyairah oon taksee parah eer al pradoh_ |
|---|---|
| Please wait for me. | **Espéreme, por favor.**<br>_esperemeh, por fabor_ |

| How long is the journey? | **¿Cuánto dura el viaje?**<br>_kwantoh doorah el beeaheh_ |
|---|---|

| How do you get to the museum? | **¿Cómo se va al museo?**<br>_komoh seh bah al moosehoh_ |
|---|---|
| When is the next bus? | **¿Cuándo sale el próximo autobús?**<br>_kwandoh saleh el prokseemoh aootoboos_ |

**Cultural tip** Metro lines (**línea de metro**) in Madrid are known by their number. The name of the last station on the line is used to indicate the direction of the train. Follow the signs to the relevant end station—for example, Las Rosas on Line 2. Several other Spanish cities also have metro systems; these can be navigated in a similar way to Madrid's.

## 6 SAY IT

**2** minutes

Do you go near the railway station?

Do you go near the Prado?

When is the next bus to Barcelona?

## 5  IN CONVERSATION: BUS

**2** minutes

**¿Pasa cerca del museo?**
_pasah therkah del moosehoh_

Do you go near the museum?

**Sí. Son dos euros veinte.**
_see. son dos eh-ooros beynteh_

Yes. That's two euros, twenty.

**Avíseme cuando lleguemos.**
_abeesemeh kwandoh yeghemos_

Tell me when we arrive.

# En la carretera
## *ON THE ROAD*

Say "**I have...**" (pp14–15).

Say "**my father**," "**my sister**," and "**my parents**" (pp10–11 and pp12–13).

Say "**I'm going to Madrid**" (pp40–41).

Spanish **autopistas** (*highways*) are fast, but some can be quite expensive, as they have **el peaje** (*toll stations*) along the way. These toll stations have multiple lanes, some of which are for passholders or trucks only. Make sure that you enter a green lane that allows payment by cash or credit card.

---

**2**  **MATCH AND REPEAT**

**❶ el maletero**
  *el maleht**airoh***

**❷ el parabrisas**
  *el para**breesas***

**❸ el cargador**
  *el karga**dor***

**❹ el punto/la estación de carga**
  *el **poon**toh/lah esta**thyon** deh **kargah***

**❺ la puerta**
  *lah **pwer**tah*

**❻ el neumático**
  *el ne-oo**ma**teekoh*

**❼ los faros**
  *los **faros***

**❽ el cable de carga**
  *el **kab**leh deh **kargah***

Match the numbered items to the list, then test yourself, using the cover flap.

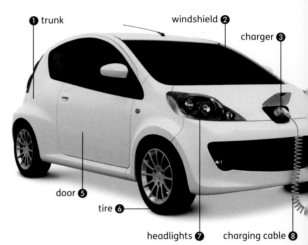

❶ trunk
windshield ❷
charger ❸
door ❺
tire ❻
headlights ❼
charging cable ❽

---

**Cultural tip** At self-service stations, the pump shows the fuel being added and the money owed. At unmanned gas stations, a card payment may need to be authorized before the pump starts working. Electric cars can be charged at public charging stations, paid for by card or app, and could take up to half a day to fully charge.

---

**3**  **ROAD SIGNS**

**Sentido único**
*sen**teedoh** oonee**koh***
One way

**Rotonda**
*rro**tondah***
Roundabout

**Calzada con prioridad**
*kal**thadah** kon preeo**reeduh***
Priority road

## 4  USEFUL PHRASES

**4** minutes

Learn these phrases, then test yourself, using the cover flap.

My turn signal doesn't work.
**El intermitente no funciona.**
*el intairmee<u>tain</u>teh noh foon<u>thyo</u>nah*

Fill it up, please.
**Lleno, por favor.**
*<u>yen</u>noh, por fa<u>bor</u>*

**4** minutes

④ charging point/station

## 5 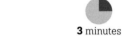 WORDS TO REMEMBER

**3** minutes

Familiarize yourself with these words, then test yourself, using the cover flap.

| | |
|---|---|
| car | **el coche** *el <u>ko</u>cheh* |
| gas | **la gasolina** *lah gaso<u>lee</u>nah* |
| diesel | **el gasoil** *el gas<u>oil</u>* |
| oil | **el aceite** *el ah-the<u>hee</u>teh* |
| engine | **el motor** *el mo<u>tor</u>* |
| transmission | **la caja de cambios** *lah <u>ka</u>hah deh <u>kam</u>byos* |
| flat tire | **la rueda pinchada** *lah <u>rweh</u>dah peen<u>cha</u>dah* |
| exhaust | **el tubo de escape** *el <u>too</u>boh deh es<u>ka</u>peh* |
| driver's license | **el carné de conducir** *el kar<u>neh</u> deh kondoo<u>theer</u>* |

## 6 SAY IT

**1** minute

There's something wrong with my engine.

I have a flat tire.

**2** minutes

**Entrada prohibida**
*en<u>tra</u>dah proee<u>bee</u>dah*
**No entry**

**Ceda el paso**
*<u>the</u>dah el <u>pa</u>soh*
**Yield**

**Estacionamiento prohibido**
*estathyona<u>mee</u>-en<u>toh</u> proee<u>bee</u>doh*
**No parking**

# Repase y repita
## REVIEW AND REPEAT

**Respuestas** *Answers*
(Cover with flap)

## Transport

❶ **el taxi**
   el <u>tak</u>see

❷ **el coche**
   el <u>ko</u>cheh

❸ **el autobús**
   el aooto<u>boos</u>

❹ **el tren**
   el tren

❺ **la bicicleta**
   lah beethee<u>kle</u>tah

❻ **el metro**
   el <u>me</u>troh

### 1 | TRANSPORT

Name these forms of transport in Spanish.

❷ car

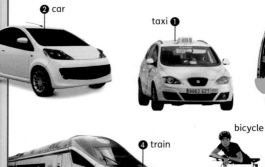

taxi ❶

bicycle ❺

 ❹ train

## Go and take

❶ **ir**
   eer

❷ **cojo**
   <u>ko</u>hoh

❸ **va**
   bah

❹ **vamos**
   <u>ba</u>mos

❺ **cogen**
   <u>ko</u>hen

❻ **voy**
   boy

### 2 | GO AND TAKE

**4 minutes**

Fill in the blanks with the correct form of **ir** (*to go*) or **coger** (*to take*).

❶ **Quiero _____ a la estación.** (ir)

❷ **Yo _____ el metro.** (coger)

❸ **¿A dónde _____ usted?** (ir)

❹ **Nosotros _____ al Museo del Prado.** (ir)

❺ **Ellos _____ un taxi.** (coger)

❻ **Yo _____ a Madrid.** (ir)

**3 minutes**

❸ bus

❻ metro

---

## 3 USTED OR TÚ?

**4 minutes**

Use the correct form of *you*.

❶ You are in a café. Ask, "Do you have churros?"

❷ You are with a friend. Ask, "Do you want a beer?"

❸ A visitor approaches you at your company's reception desk. Ask, "Do you have an appointment?"

❹ You are on the bus. Ask, "Do you go near the station?"

❺ Ask your friend where she's going tomorrow.

---

## 4 TICKETS

**4 minutes**

You are buying tickets at a railway station. Join in the conversation, replying in Spanish, following the numbered English prompts.

**¿Qué desea?**
❶ I'd like two tickets to Sevilla.
**¿De ida o de ida y vuelta?**
❷ Return, please.
**Muy bien. Trescientos euros, por favor.**
❸ What time does the train leave?
**A las tres y diez.**
❹ What platform does the train leave from?
**Andén número siete.**
❺ Thank you very much. Goodbye.

---

**Respuestas** *Answers*
(Cover with flap)

### Usted or tú?

❶ **¿Tiene churros?**
*tyeneh choorros*

❷ **¿Quieres una cerveza?**
*kyaires oonah thairbehthah*

❸ **¿Tiene una cita?**
*tyeneh oonah theetah*

❹ **¿Pasa cerca de la estación?**
*pasah therkah deh lah estathyon*

❺ **¿A dónde vas mañana?**
*ah dondeh bas manyanah*

### Tickets

❶ **Quisiera dos billetes para Sevilla.**
*keesyairah dos beeyetes parah sebeeyah*

❷ **De ida y vuelta, por favor.**
*deh eedah ee bweltah, por fabor*

❸ **¿A qué hora sale el tren?**
*ah keh orah saleh el tren*

❹ **¿De qué andén sale el tren?**
*deh keh anden saleh el tren*

❺ **Muchas gracias. Adiós.**
*moochas grathyas. addy-os*

# En la ciudad
## *ABOUT TOWN*

In Spanish, the word **museo** (*museum*) also means "art gallery" when it's a public building in which works of art are exhibited; **galería de arte** usually refers to a place where works of art are exhibited and sold. Be careful, too, not to confuse **librería** (*bookshop* or *bookshelf*) and **biblioteca** (*library*).

---

## 1 WARM UP
**1** minute

Ask "**How do you get to the museum?**" (pp42–43).

Say "**I want to take the metro**" and "**I don't want to take a taxi**" (pp40–41).

---

## 2 🔊 WORDS TO REMEMBER
**4** minutes

Familiarize yourself with these words, then test yourself, using the cover flap.

| | |
|---|---|
| **la gasolinera** *lah gasoleenerah* | gas station |
| **la oficina de información turística** *lah ohfeetheenah deh eenformathyon tooreesteekah* | tourist office |
| **la piscina municipal** *lah pistheenah mooneetheepal* | public swimming pool |

---

## 3 🔊 MATCH AND REPEAT
**4** minutes

Match the numbered locations to the list, then test yourself, using the cover flap.

❶ **el ayuntamiento**
   *el ahyoonta-myaintoh*

❷ **el museo**
   *el moosehoh*

❸ **el puente**
   *el pwenteh*

❹ **la galería de arte**
   *lah galereeah deh arteh*

❺ **el centro**
   *el thentroh*

❻ **la plaza**
   *lah plathah*

❼ **la iglesia**
   *lah eegleseeah*

❽ **el aparcamiento**
   *el aparka-myaintoh*

❶ town hall

❷ museum

❸ bridge

❹ art gallery

❺ town center

❻ square

# 4  USEFUL PHRASES

**4** minutes

Learn these phrases, then test yourself, using the cover flap.

| | |
|---|---|
| Is there an art gallery in town? | **¿Hay algún museo de arte en la ciudad?** *ah-ee algoon moosehoh deh arteh en lah thyoodad* |
| Is it far from here? | **¿Está lejos de aquí?** *estah lehos deh ahkee* |
| There is a swimming pool near the bridge. | **Hay una piscina cerca del puente.** *ah-ee oonah peestheenah therkah del pwenteh* |

**La catedral está en el centro.**
*lah katedral estah en el thentroh*
The cathedral is in the city center.

❼ church

# 5  PUT INTO PRACTICE

**2** minutes

Complete this dialogue, then test yourself, using the cover flap.

| | |
|---|---|
| **¿Le puedo ayudar?** *leh pwedoh ahyoodar* | **¿Hay alguna biblioteca en la ciudad?** *ah-ee algoonah beebleeotekah en lah thyoodad* |
| Can I help you? | |
| Ask: Is there a library in town? | |
| **No, pero hay un museo.** *noh, peroh ah-ee oon moosehoh* | **¿Cómo se va al museo?** *komoh seh bah al moosehoh* |
| No, but there's a museum. | |
| Ask: How do I get to the museum? | |
| **Está por allí.** *estah por ahyee* | **Muchas gracias.** *moochas grathyas* |
| It's over there. | |
| Say: Thank you very much. | |

❽ parking lot

**Conversational tip** In Spanish, there are two ways of saying *am, is,* or *are.* You have already learned the verb **ser** (p14): **soy inglés/-lesa** (*I am English*); **es vegetariano** (*he is vegetarian*). When talking about where something is, you need to the verb: **estar.** The most important forms of this verb are **estoy** (*I am*), **está** (*he/she/it is*), and **están** (*they are*): **¿dónde está la iglesia?** (*where is the church?*); **el café no está lejos** (*the café isn't far*).

# Las direcciones
## *DIRECTIONS*

To help you find your way, you'll often find a **plano de la ciudad** (*town map*) situated in the town, usually near the town hall or tourist office. In the older parts of Spanish towns, there are often narrow streets in which you will usually find a one-way system in operation. Parking is usually restricted.

**1** | **WARM UP**

**1** minute

How do you say "**Near the station**"? (pp42–43).

Say "**Take the first on the left**" (pp40–41).

Ask "**Where are you going?**" (pp40–41).

## **2** 🔊 **WORDS TO REMEMBER**

Familiarize yourself with these words, then test yourself, using the cover flap.

| | |
|---|---|
| **el semáforo** *el semaforoh* | traffic lights |
| **la calle principal** *lah kayeh preentheepal* | main road |
| **la calle** *lah kayeh* | street/road |
| **la esquina** *lah eskeenah* | corner |
| **el plano** *el planoh* | map |
| **los mapas en línea** *los mahpas en leeneeah* | online maps |

**el bloque de oficinas**
*el blokeh deh ohfeetheenas*
office block

**la fuente**
*lah fwenteh*
fountain

**¿Dónde estamos?**
*dondeh estamos*
Where are we?

**la zona peatonal**
*lah thonah pe-ahtonal*
pedestrian zone

## **3** 🔊 **IN CONVERSATION**

**¿Hay un restaurante cerca?**
*ah-ee oon restaooranteh therkah*

Is there a restaurant nearby?

**Sí, cerca de la estación.**
*see, therkah deh lah estathyon*

Yes, near the station.

**¿Cómo se va a la estación?**
*komoh seh bah ah lah estathyon*

How do I get to the station?

## 5 SAY IT
*2 minutes*

Turn right at the end of the street.

Turn left across from the museum.

It's ten minutes by bus.

---

*4 minutes*

**el centro comercial**
*el thentroh kohmerthyal*
shopping center

---

## 4  USEFUL PHRASES
*4 minutes*

Learn these phrases, then test yourself, using the cover flap.

| | |
|---|---|
| turn left/right | **gire a la izquierda/ derecha** *heereh ah lah eethkyairdah/derechah* |
| first right | **la primera a la derecha** *lah preemerah ah lah derechah* |
| second left | **la segunda a la izquierda** *lah segoondah ah lah eethkyairdah* |
| straight ahead | **todo recto** *todoh rrektoh* |
| at the end of the street | **al final de la calle** *al feenal deh lah kayeh* |
| across from | **enfrente de** *enfrenteh deh* |
| How do I get to the swimming pool? | **¿Cómo se va a la piscina?** *komoh seh bah ah lah peestheenah* |

**Me he perdido.**
*meh eh perdeedoh*
I'm lost.

---

*4 minutes*

**Gire a la izquierda en el semáforo.**
*heereh ah lah eethkyairdah en el semaforoh*

Turn left at the traffic lights.

**¿Está lejos?**
*estah lehos*

Is it far?

**No, cinco minutos andando.**
*noh, theenkoh meenootos andandoh*

No, it's five minutes on foot.

# El turismo
## *SIGHTSEEING*

**WARM UP**

**1** minute

Say "**Is there a museum in town?**" (pp48–49).

How do you say "**At six o'clock**" (pp30–31)?

Ask "**What time is it?**" (pp30–31).

Most national museums and art galleries close one day a week and on public holidays. Although shops are normally closed on Sundays, many will remain open all weekend in tourist areas. It is not unusual, particularly in rural areas, for shops and public buildings to close for an afternoon **siesta** (*nap*) from around 1:30 to 4:30pm.

---

**2**  **WORDS TO REMEMBER**

**4** minutes

Familiarize yourself with these words, then test yourself, using the cover flap.

| | |
|---|---|
| **la guía** | guide, guidebook, |
| *lah gheeah* | travel guide |
| **la entrada** | entrance ticket |
| *lah entradah* | |
| **el horario de apertura** | opening times |
| *el oraryoh deh apertoorah* | |
| **el día festivo** | public holiday |
| *el deeyah festeevoh* | |
| **la entrada libre** | free entrance |
| *lah entradah leebreh* | |

**la visita con guía**
*lah beeseetah kon gheeah*
guided tour

---

**Cultural tip** The majority of public buildings and private offices close for public holiday, and many are also closed in August. If a public holiday falls on a Thursday or a Tuesday, the Spanish will often **hacer puente** (*make a bridge*)— in other words, take Friday or Monday off as well to make a long weekend.

---

**3**  **IN CONVERSATION**

**¿Abren esta tarde?**
*ahbren estah tardeh*

Are you open this afternoon?

**Sí, pero cerramos a las cuatro.**
*see, peroh therramos ah las kwatroh*

Yes, but we close at four o'clock.

**¿Tienen acceso para sillas de ruedas?**
*tyenen akthesoh parah seeyas deh rwedas*

Do you have wheelchair access?

## 4  USEFUL PHRASES

**3** minutes

Learn these phrases, then test yourself, using the cover flap.

What time do you open/close?

**¿A qué hora abre/ cierra?**
*ah keh orah ahbreh/ thyairrah*

Where are the toilets?

**¿Dónde están los servicios?**
*dondeh estan los serbeethyos*

Is there wheelchair access?

**¿Hay acceso para sillas de ruedas?**
*ah-ee akthesoh parah seeyas deh rwedas*

## 5  PUT INTO PRACTICE

**4** minutes

Complete this dialogue, then test yourself, using the cover flap.

**Lo siento, el museo está cerrado.**
*loh syentoh, el moosehoh estah therradoh*

Sorry. The museum is closed.

Ask: Do you open on Tuesdays?

**¿Abren los martes?**
*ahbren los martes*

**Sí, pero cerramos temprano.**
*see, peroh therramos tempranoh*

Yes, but we close early.

Ask: At what time?

**¿A qué hora?**
*ah keh orah*

**3** minutes

**Sí, el ascensor está allí.**
*see, el asthensor estah ah-yee*

Yes, there's an elevator over there.

**Gracias, quisiera cuatro entradas.**
*grathyas, keesyairah kwatroh entradas*

Thank you, I'd like four entrance tickets.

**Aquí tiene, y la guía es gratis.**
*ahkee tyeneh, ee lah gheeah es gratees*

Here you are, and the guidebook is free.

# 1 WARM UP

**1** minute

Say in Spanish "**She is my stepmother**" (pp14–15).

What's the Spanish for "**ticket**" (pp38–39)?

Say "**I am going to New York**" (pp40–41).

# En el aeropuerto
*AT THE AIRPORT*

Although the airport environment is largely international, it is sometimes useful to be able to ask your way around the terminal in Spanish. It's a good idea to make sure you have a few one-euro coins when you arrive at the airport—you may need to pay for a luggage cart.

# 2 WORDS TO REMEMBER

**4** minutes

| | |
|---|---|
| **la facturación** <br> *lah faktoorath<u>yon</u>* | check-in |
| **las salidas** <br> *las sal<u>ee</u>das* | departures |
| **las llegadas** <br> *las yeh<u>ga</u>das* | arrivals |
| **la aduana** <br> *lah a<u>dwa</u>nah* | customs |
| **el control de pasaportes** <br> *el kon<u>trol</u> deh pasa<u>por</u>tes* | passport control |
| **la terminal** <br> *lah termee<u>nal</u>* | terminal |
| **la puerta de embarque** <br> *lah <u>pwer</u>tah deh em<u>bar</u>keh* | boarding gate |
| **el número de vuelo** <br> *el <u>noo</u>meroh deh <u>bwe</u>loh* | flight number |

Familiarize yourself with these words, then test yourself, using the cover flap.

**El vuelo 23 sale de la terminal 2.**
*el <u>bwe</u>loh beyntee<u>tres</u> <u>sa</u>leh deh lah termee<u>nal</u> dos*
Flight 23 leaves from Terminal 2.

# 3 USEFUL PHRASES

**3** minutes

Learn these phrases, then test yourself, using the cover flap.

| | |
|---|---|
| **¿Sale a su hora el vuelo para Sevilla?** <br> *<u>sa</u>leh ah soo orah el <u>bwe</u>loh <u>pa</u>rah se<u>vee</u>yah* | Is the flight for Seville on time? |
| **El vuelo a Londres va con retraso.** <br> *el <u>bwe</u>loh ah <u>lon</u>dres bah kon re<u>tra</u>soh* | The flight to London is delayed. |
| **No encuentro mi equipaje.** <br> *noh en<u>kwen</u>troh mee ehkee<u>pa</u>heh* | I can't find my luggage. |

# 4 PUT INTO PRACTICE

**3** minutes

Complete this dialogue, then test yourself, using the cover flap.

**Hola, ¿le puedo ayudar?**
*o-lah, leh pwedoh ahyoodar*

Hello, can I help you?

Ask: Is the flight to Madrid on time?

**¿Sale a su hora el vuelo para Madrid?**
*saleh ah soo orah el bweloh parah madreed*

**Sí, señor.**
*see senyor*

Yes, sir.

Ask: Which gate does it leave from?

**¿Cuál es la puerta de embarque?**
*kwal es lah pwertah deh embarkeh*

# 5 MATCH AND REPEAT

**4** minutes

check-in desk ❶

boarding pass ❷

ticket ❸

passport ❹

❺ suitcase ❻ carry-on ❼ cart

Match the numbered items to the list, then test yourself, using the cover flap.

❶ **el mostrador de facturación**
*el mostrador deh faktoorathyon*

❷ **la tarjeta de embarque**
*lah tarhetah deh embarkeh*

❸ **el billete**
*el beeyehteh*

❹ **el pasaporte**
*el pasaporteh*

❺ **la maleta**
*lah malehtah*

❻ **el equipaje de mano**
*el ehkeepaheh deh manoh*

❼ **el carrito**
*el karreetoh*

# Repase y repita
*REVIEW AND REPEAT*

## Places

❶ **el museo**
*el moosehoh*

❷ **el ayuntamiento**
*el ahyoonta-myaintoh*

❸ **el puente**
*el pwenteh*

❹ **la galería de arte**
*lah galereeah deh arteh*

❺ **la catedral**
*lah katedral*

❻ **el aparcamiento**
*el ahparka-myaintoh*

❼ **la plaza**
*lah plathah*

## 1 PLACES

**4 minutes**

Name these locations in Spanish.

❶ museum

❷ town hall

❸ bridge

❹ art gallery

❺ cathedral

❻ parking lot    ❼ square

## Car parts

❶ **el parabrisas**
*el parabreesas*

❷ **el cargador**
*el kargador*

❸ **el punto/la estación de carga**
*el poontoh/lah estathyon deh kargah*

❹ **la puerta**
*lah pwertah*

❺ **el neumático**
*el ne-oomateekoh*

❻ **el cable de carga**
*el kableh deh karga*

## 2 CAR PARTS

Name these car parts in Spanish.

windshield ❶

charger ❷

door ❹    tire ❺    charging cable ❻

**Respuestas** *Answers*
(Cover with flap)

## 3 QUESTIONS

4 minutes

Ask the questions in Spanish that match these answers.

**1** El próximo tren es dentro de quince minutos.
el *prokseemoh* tren es *dentroh* deh *keen*theh mee*noo*tos

**2** El autobús sale a las ocho.
el aooto*boos* saleh ah las *ochoh*

**3** El café es dos euros cincuenta.
el ka*feh* es dos eh-*oo*ros theen*kwen*tah

**4** El tren sale del andén cinco.
el tren saleh del an*den* *theen*koh

**5** Nosotros vamos a León.
no*sotros* *bamos* ah leh-*on*

**6** No, no quiero vino.
noh, noh *kyair*oh *bee*noh

### Questions

**1** ¿Cuándo es el próximo tren?
*kwan*doh es el *prok*seemoh tren

**2** ¿A qué hora sale el autobús?
ah keh *orah* *saleh* el aooto*boos*

**3** ¿Cuánto es el café?
*kwan*toh es el ka*feh*

**4** ¿De qué andén sale el tren?
deh keh an*den* *saleh* el tren

**5** ¿A dónde vais?
ah *don*deh baees

**6** ¿Quieres vino?
*kyai*res *bee*noh

---

3 minutes

**3** charging point/station

## 4 VERBS

4 minutes

Fill in the blanks with the correct form of the missing verbs.

**1** Yo _____ inglés. (ser)

**2** Nosotros _____ el metro. (coger)

**3** Ella _____ a Marbella. (ir)

**4** Él _____ casado. (estar)

**5** ¿Tú _____ un té? (querer)

**6** ¿Cuántos niños _____ usted? (tener)

### Verbs

**1** soy
soy

**2** cogemos
ko*heh*mos

**3** va
bah

**4** está
es*tah*

**5** quieres
*kyai*res

**6** tiene
*tye*neh

# Reservar una habitación
## *BOOKING A ROOM*

There are different types of accommodations in Spain: **los hoteles**, categorized from one to five stars; **las pensiones**, small family-run hotels; **los hostales**, cheap and basic; and **los paradores**, state-owned hotels in historic properties or places of great beauty. Airbnb, offering accommodations in private rooms and homes, is also a popular option.

## 1 WARM UP
*1 minute*

Ask in Spanish "**Do you accept credit cards?**" (pp38–39).

Ask "**How much is that?**" (pp18–19).

Ask "**Do you have children?**" (pp10–11).

## 2 ◄))) USEFUL PHRASES
*3 minutes*

Learn these phrases, then test yourself, using the cover flap.

**¿El desayuno está incluido?**
*el dese<u>hoo</u>noh es<u>tah</u> inkloo<u>ee</u>doh*

Is breakfast included?

**¿Aceptan animales de compañía?**
*a<u>thep</u>tan anee<u>ma</u>les deh kompan<u>yee</u>ah*

Do you accept pets?

**¿Tienen servicio de habitaciones?**
*tyenen ser<u>bee</u>thyoh deh abeeta<u>thyon</u>es*

Do you have room service?

**¿A qué hora tengo que dejar la habitación?**
*ah keh orah <u>ten</u>goh keh dehar lah abeeta<u>thyon</u>*

What time do I have to vacate the room?

## 3 ◄))) IN CONVERSATION

**¿Tiene habitaciones libres?**
*<u>tye</u>neh abeeta<u>thyon</u>es <u>lee</u>bres*

Do you have any rooms available?

**Sí, una habitación doble.**
*see, <u>oo</u>nah abeeta<u>thyon</u> <u>dob</u>leh*

Yes, a double room.

**¿Tiene una cuna?**
*<u>tye</u>neh <u>oo</u>nah <u>koo</u>nah*

Do you have a cot?

## 4  WORDS TO REMEMBER

**4** minutes

**¿Tiene la habitación vistas al jardín?**
*tyeneh lah abeetathyon beestas al hardeen*
Does the room have a view over the garden?

Familiarize yourself with these words, then test yourself, using the cover flap.

| | |
|---|---|
| room | **la habitación** *lah abeetathyon* |
| single room | **la habitación individual** *lah abeetathyon indeebeedwal* |
| double room | **la habitación doble** *lah abeetathyon dobleh* |
| bathroom | **el cuarto de baño** *el kwartoh deh banyoh* |
| shower | **la ducha** *lah doochah* |
| balcony | **el balcón** *el balkon* |
| key | **la llave** *lah yabeh* |
| air-conditioning | **el aire acondicionado** *el ah-eereh akondeethyonadoh* |
| breakfast | **el desayuno** *el desehoonoh* |

## 5 SAY IT

**2** minutes

Do you have a single room, please?

For six nights.

Is breakfast included?

---

**Cultural tip** Many places of accommodation, including small and large hotels and **paradores**, offer breakfast, but you will generally be charged extra for it. If your accommodations don't provide breakfast, you'll usually find it easy to discover a bar or a café nearby where you can go for **café con leche** in the mornings.

---

**5** minutes

**Sí, claro. ¿Cuántas noches?**
*see, klaroh. kwantas noches*

Yes, of course. How many nights?

**Para tres noches.**
*parah tres noches*

For three nights.

**Muy bien. Aquí tiene la llave.**
*mwee byen. ahkee tyeneh lah yabeh*

Very good. Here's the key.

## 1 WARM UP

**1** minute

Ask "**Is there…?**" and reply "**There isn't…**" (pp48–49).

What does "**¿Le puedo ayudar?**" mean (pp54–55)?

Say "**They don't have any children**" (pp14–15).

# En el hotel
### *IN THE HOTEL*

Although the larger hotels almost always have bathrooms en suite, there are still some **pensiones** and **hostales** with shared facilities. This can also be the case in some economy hotels, where families can stay the night in low-cost, reasonably priced rooms.

## 2 ◀))) MATCH AND REPEAT

**6** minutes

Match the numbered items to the list, then test yourself, using the cover flap.

**❶ las cortinas**
   *las korteenas*

**❷ el cojín**
   *el koheen*

**❸ el sofá**
   *el sofah*

**❹ la lámpara**
   *lah lamparah*

**❺ la almohada**
   *lah almoh-ahdah*

**❻ el minibar**
   *el meeneebar*

**❼ la cama**
   *lah kamah*

**❽ la manta**
   *lah mantah*

**❾ la colcha**
   *lah kolchah*

**❿ la mesilla de noche**
   *lah meseeyah deh nocheh*

❷ cushion ❶ curtains ❸ sofa ❹ lamp ❺ pillow

❽ blanket ❾ bedspread

❻ minibar ❼ bed bedside table ❿

**Cultural tip** When you arrive in your room, you may sometimes see a long sausage-shaped pillow (**almohada larga**) on the bed—nowadays a largely decorative item. This used to be the usual pillow for a double bed—**cama de matrimonio** (literally *marriage bed*). However, you can usually find soft rectangular pillows (**almohadas blandas cuadradas**) in the cupboard. Do not hesitate to ask if you can't find any. If you don't want to share your bed or pillow, you'll have to ask for **una habitación doble con dos camas** (*a double room with two beds*) to get a twin room.

# 3  USEFUL PHRASES

**5** minutes

Learn these phrases, then test yourself, using the cover flap.

The room is too cold/hot. **Hace demasiado frío/ calor en la habitación.**
*ahtheh dehmasyahdoh freeoh/kalor en lah abeetathyon*

There are no towels. **No hay toallas.**
*noh ah-ee toh-ahyas*

I need some soap. **Necesito jabón.**
*netheseetoh habon*

The shower doesn't work. **La ducha no funciona.**
*lah doochah noh foonthyonah*

The elevator is broken. **El ascensor está roto.**
*el asthensor estah rrotoh*

# 4  PUT INTO PRACTICE

**3** minutes

Complete this dialogue, then test yourself, using the cover flap.

**¿Le atienden?**
*leh atyainden*

Can I help you?

Say: I need some pillows.

**Necesito almohadas.**
*netheseetoh almoh-ahdas*

**El servicio de limpieza traerá algunas.**
*el serbeetheeoh deh limpee- ethah traherah algoonas*

Housekeeping will bring some.

Say: And the television doesn't work.

**Y la televisión no funciona.**
*ee lah telebeesyon noh foonthyonah*

## 1 WARM UP

**1** minute

Ask **"Can I?"** (pp34–35).

What is Spanish for **"the shower"** (pp60–61)?

Say **"I need some towels"** (pp60–61).

# En el camping
*AT THE CAMPSITE*

Camping is very popular in Spain, and the country has numerous well-organized campsites rated by a star system. These include public and private campsites, including luxurious glamping sites. The local tourist office will be able to offer a list of campsites in the area. Book ahead for the summer months.

## 2  USEFUL PHRASES

Learn these phrases, then test yourself, using the cover flap.

**¿Puedo alquilar una bicicleta?** Can I rent a bicycle?
*pwedoh alkeelar oonah beetheekletah*

**¿Es el agua potable?** Is this drinking water?
*es el ahgwah potableh*

**¿Se permiten hogueras?** Are campfires allowed?
*seh permeeten ohgheras*

**La música alta está prohibida.** Loud music is forbidden.
*lah moosikah altah estah proeebeedah*

**El camping es tranquilo.** The campsite is quiet.
*el kampeen es trankeeloh*

**¿Dónde está el grifo?** Where is the tap?
*dondeh estah el greefoh*

**el doble techo** *el dobleh tehchoh* fly sheet
**el punto de luz** *el poontoh deh looth* electrical hook-up
**la cuerda** *lah kwerdah* guy rope
**la clavija** *lah klabeehah* tent peg

## 3  IN CONVERSATION

**Necesito una plaza para tres noches.**
*netheseetoh oonah plathah parah tres noches*

I need a site for three nights.

**Hay una cerca de la piscina.**
*ah-ee oonah therkah deh lah peestheenah*

There's one near the swimming pool.

**¿Cuánto cuesta para una caravana?**
*kwantoh kwestah parah oonah karabanah*

How much is it for a caravan?

## 5 SAY IT

*2 minutes*

I need a site for four nights.

Can I rent a tent?

Where's the electrical hook-up?

---

## 4  WORDS TO REMEMBER

*4 minutes*

Familiarize yourself with these words, then test yourself, using the cover flap.

| | | |
|---|---|---|
| campsite | **el camping** | *el kampeen* |
| site | **la plaza** | *lah plathah* |
| tent | **la tienda** | *lah tyendah* |
| ground sheet | **el suelo aislante** | *el sweloh ah-eeslanteh* |
| sleeping bag | **el saco de dormir** | *el sakoh deh dormeer* |
| air mattress | **la colchoneta** | *lah kolchonetah* |
| caravan | **la caravana** | *lah karabanah* |
| camper van | **la autocaravana** | *lah ah-ootokarabanah* |
| camping gas | **el camping gas** | *el kampeen gas* |
| campfire | **la hoguera** | *lah ohgherah* |
| drinking water | **el agua potable** | *el ahgwah potableh* |
| trash | **la basura** | *lah basoorah* |
| showers | **las duchas** | *las doochas* |

---

*3 minutes*

**la oficina del camping**
*lah ofeetheenah del kampeen*
campsite office

**la papelera**
*lah papehlerah*
litter bin

**los aseos**
*los asehos*
toilets

---

*5 minutes*

**Cuatrocientos euros. Una noche por adelantado.**
*kwatrohtheentos eh-ooros. oonah nocheh por adelantadoh*

Four hundred euros. One night in advance.

**¿Puedo alquilar una barbacoa?**
*pwedoh alkeelar oonah barbakoh-ah*

Can I rent a grill?

**Sí, pero tiene que dejar una fianza.**
*see, peroh tyeneh keh dehar oonah feeanthah*

Yes, but you must pay a deposit.

# Las descripciones
## *DESCRIPTIONS*

**1** WARM UP

**1** minute

Say "**hot**" and "**cold**" (pp60–61).

What is the Spanish for "**room**" (pp58–59), "**bed**," and "**pillow**" (pp60–61)?

Adjectives are words used to describe people, things, and places. In Spanish, you generally put the adjective after the thing it describes in the same gender and number: **una bebida fría** (*a cold drink*, feminine singular); **un café frío** (*a cold coffee*, masculine singular); **dos bebidas frías** (*two cold drinks*, feminine plural).

**2**  | **WORDS TO REMEMBER**

**7** minutes

Adjectives can change slightly, depending on whether the thing described is masculine (**el**) or feminine (**la**). Generally, a final **o** changes to **a** in the feminine, but if the adjective ends with **e** (such as **grande**), it doesn't change for the feminine. To form the plural, just add an **s**. Familiarize yourself with these words, then test yourself, using the cover flap.

| | |
|---|---|
| **grande** *grandeh* | big |
| **pequeño/pequeña** *pekenyoh/pekenyah* | small |
| **caliente** *kalyainteh* | hot |
| **frío/fría** *freeoh/freeah* | cold |
| **bueno/buena** *bwenoh/bwenah* | good |
| **malo/mala** *maloh/malah* | bad |
| **lento/lenta** *lentoh/lentah* | slow |
| **rápido/rápida** *rrapeedoh/rrapeedah* | fast |
| **ruidoso/ruidosa** *rrweedosoh/rrweedosah* | noisy |
| **tranquilo/tranquila** *trankeeloh/trankeelah* | quiet |
| **duro/dura** *dooroh/doorah* | hard |
| **blando/blanda** *blandoh/blandah* | soft |
| **bonito/bonita** *boneetoh/boneetah* | beautiful |
| **feo/fea** *feh-oh/feh-ah* | ugly |

**la montaña alta**
*lah montanyah altah*
high mountain

**la colina baja**
*lah koleenah bahah*
low hill

**la casa pequeña**
*lah kasah pekenyah*
small house

**la iglesia antigua**
*lah eeglesyah anteewah*
old church

**El pueblo es muy bonito.**
*el pwebloh es mwee boneetoh*
The village is very beautiful.

# 3  USEFUL PHRASES

**4** minutes

You can emphasize a description by using **muy** (very), **demasiado** (too), or **más** (more) before the adjective. Learn these phrases, then test yourself, using the cover flap.

This coffee is very hot.

**Este café está muy caliente.**
*esteh kafeh estah mwee kalyainteh*

My room is very noisy.

**Mi habitación es muy ruidosa.**
*mee abeetathyon es mwee rrweedosah*

My car is too small.

**Mi coche es demasiado pequeño.**
*mee koche es demasyahdoh pekenyoh*

I need a softer bed.

**Necesito una cama más blanda.**
*netheseetoh oonah kamah mas blandah*

# 4  PUT INTO PRACTICE

**3** minutes

Complete this dialogue, then test yourself, using the cover flap.

**Esta es la habitación.**
*estah es lah abeetathyon*

This is the bedroom.

Say: The view is very beautiful.

**La vista es muy bonita.**
*lah beestah es mwee boneetah*

**El cuarto de baño está por ahí.**
*el kwartoh deh banyoh estah por ah-ee*

The bathroom is over there.

Say: It is too small.

**Es demasiado pequeño.**
*es demasyahdoh pekenyoh*

**No tenemos otras habitaciones.**
*noh tenehmos otras abeetathyones*

We don't have any other rooms.

Say: It doesn't matter. We'll take the room.

**No importa. Nos quedamos con la habitación.**
*noh importah. nos kedamos kon lah abeetathyon*

**Respuestas** *Answers*
(Cover with flap)

# Repase y repita
*REVIEW AND REPEAT*

## Descriptions

❶ **caliente**
*kalyainteh*

❷ **pequeña**
*pekenyah*

❸ **frío**
*free-oh*

❹ **grande**
*grandeh*

❺ **tranquila**
*trankeelah*

## 1 DESCRIPTIONS

**3** minutes

Fill in the blanks with the correct Spanish masculine or feminine form of the adjective given in brackets.

❶ **El agua está demasiado _____.** (hot)

❷ **La cama es muy _____.** (small)

❸ **El café está _____.** (cold)

❹ **Este cuarto de baño es más _____.** (big)

❺ **Quisiera una habitación más _____.** (quiet)

## Campsite

❶ **la tienda**
*lah tyaindah*

❷ **la autocaravana**
*lah ah-ootokarabanah*

❸ **la papelera**
*lah papehlerah*

❹ **la cuerda**
*lah kwerdah*

❺ **el punto de luz**
*el poontoh deh looth*

❻ **los aseos**
*los asehos*

## 2 CAMPSITE

Name these campsite items in Spanish.

❶ tent    camper van ❷    trash bin ❸

❹ guy rope    ❺ electrical hook-up

## 3 AT THE HOTEL

**4** minutes

You are booking a room in a hotel. Join in the conversation, replying in Spanish, following the numbered English prompts.

**¿Qué desean?**
❶ Do you have any rooms free?

**Sí, una habitación doble.**
❷ Do you accept pets?

**Sí. ¿Cuántas noches?**
❸ Three nights.

**Son doscientos cuarenta euros.**
❹ Is breakfast included?

**Sí. Aquí tiene la llave.**
❺ Thank you very much.

### At the hotel

❶ **¿Tiene habitaciones libres?**
*tyeneh abeetathyones leebres*

❷ **¿Aceptan animales de compañía?**
*atheptan aneemales deh kompanyeeah*

❸ **Tres noches.**
*tres noches*

❹ **¿El desayuno está incluido?**
*el desehoonoh estah inklooeedoh*

❺ **Muchas gracias.**
*moochas grathyas*

**3** minutes

❻ toilets

## 4 NEGATIVES

**5** minutes

Make these sentences negative by using the correct form of the verb in brackets.

❶ **Yo _____ hijos.** (tener)

❷ **Ellos _____ a Madrid mañana.** (ir)

❸ **Él _____ un café.** (querer)

❹ **Yo _____ el metro.** (coger)

❺ **La vista _____ muy bonita.** (ser)

### Negatives

❶ **no tengo**
*noh tengoh*

❷ **no van**
*noh ban*

❸ **no quiere**
*noh kyaireh*

❹ **no cojo**
*noh kohoh*

❺ **no es**
*noh es*

# De compras
## *SHOPPING*

Small, traditional, specialized shops (**tiendas**) are still common in Spanish town centres, although you will see some chains as well. You can also find big supermarkets and shopping centers on the outskirts of major towns. Markets selling fresh local produce can be found everywhere. You can find out the market day at the tourist office.

**2**  **MATCH AND REPEAT**

Match the numbered items to the list, then test yourself, using the cover flap.

❶ **la panadería**
*lah panadaireeah*

❷ **la pastelería**
*lah pastehlaireeah*

❸ **el estanco**
*el estankoh*

❹ **la carnicería**
*lah karnee-thaireeah*

❺ **la charcutería**
*lah charkoo-taireeah*

❻ **la librería**
*lah leebraireeah*

❼ **la pescadería**
*lah peskadaireeah*

❽ **la tienda de alimentación**
*lah teeh-endah deh aleementathyon*

❾ **el banco**
*el bankoh*

❶ **baker**

❷ **cake shop**

❹ **butcher**

❺ **delicatessen**

❼ **fishmonger**

❽ **grocery**

**Cultural tip** A **droguería** (*drugstore*) sells soap and toothpaste, while a **farmacia** (*pharmacy*) has medicines and health products. The **estanco** (*tobacconist*) is the place for newspapers, magazines, postcards, and stamps, but also has sweets, mobile phone top-ups, and souvenirs. **Papelerías** cater to all your stationery needs. Most Spanish shops offer a free gift-wrapping service; just ask **"¿me lo envuelve para regalo?"** (*may I have it gift-wrapped?*).

**¿Dónde está la floristería?**
*dondeh estah lah
floreestaireeah*
Where is the florist?

❸ **tobacconist**

❻ **bookshop**

❾ **bank**

---

5 **SAY IT**
**2** minutes

Where is the bank?

Do you sell cheese?

Where do I pay?

---

3  **USEFUL PHRASES**
**3** minutes

Learn these phrases, then test yourself, using the cover flap.

| | |
|---|---|
| Where is the hairdresser? | **¿Dónde está la peluquería?** *dondeh estah lah pelookaireeah* |
| Where do I pay? | **¿Dónde se paga?** *dondeh seh pagah* |
| I'm just looking, thank you. | **Solo estoy mirando, gracias.** *soloh estoy meerandoh grathyas* |
| Do you sell SIM cards? | **¿Tiene tarjetas SIM?** *tyeneh tarhetas seem* |
| May I have two of these? | **¿Me pone dos de estos?** *meh poneh dos deh estos* |
| Can I place an order? | **¿Puedo hacer un pedido?** *pwedoh ahther oon pedeedoh* |

---

4  **WORDS TO REMEMBER**
**4** minutes

Familiarize yourself with these words, then test yourself, using the cover flap.

| | |
|---|---|
| hardware shop | **la ferretería** *lah ferretaireeah* |
| antiques shop | **el anticuario** *el anteekwareeoh* |
| hairdresser | **la peluquería** *lah pelookaireeah* |
| jeweler | **la joyería** *lah hoyereeah* |
| post office | **la oficina de correos** *lah ofeetheenah deh korrehos* |
| shoe shop | **la zapatería** *lah thapataireeah* |
| dry cleaner | **la tintorería** *lah teentoraireeah* |
| grocery | **la frutería** *lah frootereeah* |

### 1 WARM UP

**1** minute

What is Spanish for "**40**," "**56**," "**77**," "**82**," and "**94**" (pp30–31)?

Say "**I'd like a big room**" (pp64–65).

Ask "**Do you have a small car?**" (pp64–65).

# En el mercado
## *AT THE MARKET*

Spain uses the metric system of weights and measures. You need to ask for produce in kilograms and grams. Some larger or more expensive items, such as melons, pineapples, or artichokes, may be sold as **la pieza** (*single items*); other items, such as lettuce, may be sold in lots of two or three.

---

### 2  MATCH AND REPEAT

Match the numbered items to the list, then test yourself, using the cover flap.

❶ **los tomates**
*los to<u>ma</u>tes*

❷ **los pimientos**
*los pee<u>myai</u>ntos*

❸ **los champiñones**
*los champee<u>nyo</u>nes*

❹ **las uvas**
*las <u>oo</u>bas*

❺ **los pepinos**
*los pe<u>pee</u>nost*

❻ **las alcachofas**
*las alka<u>cho</u>fas*

❼ **los guisantes**
*los ghee<u>san</u>tes*

❽ **las judías**
*las hoo<u>dee</u>as*

tomatoes ❶ bell peppers ❷

❺ cucumbers ❻ artichokes ❼ peas

---

### 3  IN CONVERSATION

**Quisiera tomates.**
*kees<u>ya</u>irah to<u>ma</u>tes*

I'd like some tomatoes.

**¿De los grandes o de los pequeños?**
*deh los <u>gran</u>des oh deh los pe<u>ke</u>nyos*

The large ones or the small ones?

**Dos kilos de los pequeños, por favor.**
*dos <u>kee</u>los deh los pe<u>ke</u>nyos, por fa<u>bor</u>*

Two kilos of the small ones, please.

## 5 SAY IT
**2** minutes

Three kilos of bell peppers, please.

The mushrooms are too expensive.

How much are the grapes?

## 4  USEFUL PHRASES
**5** minutes

Learn these phrases, then test yourself, using the cover flap.

**Esa salchicha es demasiado cara.**
*ehsah salcheechah es demasyahdoh karah*

That sausage is too expensive.

**¿A cuánto está esa?**
*ah kwantoh estah ehsah*

How much is that one?

**Eso es todo.**
*ehsoh es todoh*

That'll be all.

**Cultural tip** Spain uses the common European currency, the euro. This is divided into 100 cents, which the Spanish call **céntimos**. Spanish-speaking countries in Central and South America all have their own currencies. Argentina, Chile, Uruguay, Colombia, and México all call their currency the **peso**, which is divided into 100 **centavos**.

**4** minutes

mushrooms  **3** **4** grapes

**8** beans

**3** minutes

**¿Algo más, señora?**
*algoh mas, senyorah*

Anything else, madam?

**Eso es todo, gracias. ¿Cuánto es?**
*ehsoh es todoh, grathyas. kwantoh es*

That'll be all, thank you. How much?

**Seis euros cincuenta.**
*seh-ees eh-ooros theenkwentah*

Six euros, fifty.

# En el supermercado
*AT THE SUPERMARKET*

Prices in supermarkets are usually lower than in smaller shops. They offer all kinds of products, with the larger **hipermercados** (*hypermarkets*) extending to clothes, household goods, garden furniture, DIY products, wine, full grocery lines, fresh produce, electronic items, and books. They may also stock regional products.

## 1 WARM UP
**1** minute

What are these items you could buy in a supermarket? (pp22–23).

**la carne**
**el pescado**
**el queso**
**el zumo**
**el vino**
**el agua**

## 2 🔊 MATCH AND REPEAT
**5** minutes

Match the numbered items to the list, then test yourself, using the cover flap.

❶ **los productos de limpieza**
*los prodooktos deh limpee-ehthah*

❷ **los productos de belleza**
*los prodooktos deh beyethah*

❸ **la fruta**
*lah frootah*

❹ **las bebidas**
*las bebeedas*

❺ **los platos preparados**
*los platos preparados*

❻ **la verdura**
*lah berdoorah*

❼ **los congelados**
*los konhelados*

❽ **los productos lácteos**
*los prodooktos lakteh-os*

household products ❶

beauty products ❷

fruit ❸

drinks ❹

ready meals ❺

vegetables ❻

frozen foods ❼

dairy products ❽

**Cultural tip** For fruit and vegetables sold by the kilo, you will usually find a self-service weighing machine next to or near the produce. Alternatively, there may occasionally be a separate counter to weigh and price the produce.

# 3  USEFUL PHRASES

**3** minutes

Learn these phrases, then test yourself, using the cover flap.

| May I have a bag, please? | **¿Me da una bolsa, por favor?** |
| | *meh dah oonah bolsah, por fabor* |

| Where are the drinks? | **¿Dónde están las bebidas?** |
| | *dondeh estan las bebeedas* |

| Where is the checkout, please? | **¿Dónde está la caja, por favor?** |
| | *dondeh estah lah kahah, por fabor* |

| Please type in your PIN. | **Por favor, introduzca su PIN.** |
| | *por fabor, introdoothkah soo peen* |

# 4  WORDS TO REMEMBER

**4** minutes

Familiarize yourself with these words, then test yourself, using the cover flap.

| milk | **la leche** |
| | *lah lecheh* |
| bread | **el pan** |
| | *el pan* |
| butter | **la mantequilla** |
| | *lah mantekeeyah* |
| ham | **el jamón** |
| | *el hamon* |
| salt | **la sal** |
| | *lah sal* |
| pepper | **la pimienta** |
| | *lah peemyaintah* |
| laundry detergent | **el detergente en polvo** |
| | *el deterhenteh en polboh* |
| dishwashing liquid | **el líquido lavavajillas** |
| | *el leekeedoh lababaheeyas* |
| toilet paper | **el papel higiénico** |
| | *el papel eehyaineekoh* |
| hand sanitizer | **el desinfectante de manos** |
| | *el deseenfektanteh deh manos* |

## 5 SAY IT

**2** minutes

Where are the dairy products?

May I have some cheese, please?

Where are the frozen foods?

1 **WARM UP**

1 minute

Say "**I'd like...**" (pp24–25).

Ask "**Do you have...?**" (pp14–15).

Say "**38**," "**42**," and "**46**" (pp10–11 and pp30–31).

Say "**big**," "**small**," "**bigger**," and "**smaller**" (pp64–65).

# La ropa y los zapatos
## CLOTHES AND SHOES

Like in most of Europe, clothes and shoes in Spain are measured in metric sizes. Even allowing for conversion of sizes, Spanish clothes tend to be cut smaller than American ones, and measurements may vary according to brand, cut, and style. Note that clothes size is **la talla**, but shoe size is **el número**.

2 ◀)) **MATCH AND REPEAT**

Match the numbered items to the list, then test yourself, using the cover flap.

❶ **la camisa**
   lah kameesah

❷ **la corbata**
   lah korbatah

❸ **la chaqueta**
   lah chaketah

❹ **la manga**
   lah mangah

❺ **el bolsillo**
   el bolseeyoh

❻ **el pantalón**
   el pantalon

❼ **la falda**
   lah faldah

❽ **las medias**
   las medyas

❾ **los zapatos**
   los thapatos

shirt ❶
tie ❷
jacket ❸
sleeve ❹
pocket ❺
trousers ❻
skirt ❼
tights ❽
shoes ❾

**Cultural tip** Dress sizes usually range from 32 (US 0) through to 50 (US 16) and shoe sizes from 35 (US 5) to 46 (US 13). For men's shirts, a size 32 is a 13-inch collar, 35 is a 14-inch collar, 38 is a 15-inch collar, 41 is a 16-inch collar, 44 is a 17-inch collar, and 47 is an 18-inch collar.

## 3  USEFUL PHRASES

**5** minutes

Learn these phrases, then test yourself, using the cover flap.

| Do you have a larger size? | **¿Tiene una talla más grande?** |
| | *tyeneh oonah tayah mas grandeh* |

| It's not what I want. | **No es lo que quiero.** |
| | *noh es loh keh kyairoh* |

| I'll take the pink one. | **Me quedo con el rosa.** |
| | *meh kedoh kon el rrosah* |

**3** minutes

## 4  WORDS TO REMEMBER

**4** minutes

Colors are adjectives (pp64–65) and in most cases have a masculine and a feminine form. The feminine is usually formed by substituting an **a** for the final **o**. Familiarize yourself with these words, then test yourself, using the cover flap.

| red | **rojo/roja** |
| | *rrohoh/rrohah* |
| white | **blanco/blanca** |
| | *blankoh/blankah* |
| blue | **azul** |
| | *athool* |
| yellow | **amarillo/amarilla** |
| | *amareeyoh/amareeyah* |
| green | **verde** |
| | *berdeh* |
| black | **negro/negra** |
| | *negroh/negrah* |

## 5 SAY IT

**2** minutes

What shoe size?

Do you have this jacket in black?

I'd like a 38.

Do you have a smaller size?

# Repase y repita
## *REVIEW AND REPEAT*

## Market

❶ **las alcachofas**
*las alkachofas*

❷ **los pepinos**
*los pepeenost*

❸ **los tomates**
*los tomates*

❹ **los guisantes**
*los gheesantes*

❺ **los pimientos**
*los peemyaintos*

❻ **las judías**
*las hoodeeas*

### 1 MARKET

**3** minutes

Name these vegetables in Spanish.

❶ artichokes  ❸ tomatoes  ❺ bell peppers
❷ cucumbers  ❹ peas  ❻ beans

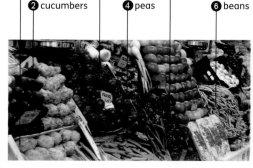

## Description

❶ These shoes are too expensive.
❷ My room is very small.
❸ I need a softer bed.

### 2 DESCRIPTION

**2** minutes

What do these sentences mean?

❶ Estos zapatos son demasiados caros.
❷ Mi habitación es muy pequeña.
❸ Necesito una cama más blanda.

## Shops

❶ **la panadería**
*lah panadaireeah*

❷ **la tienda de alimentación**
*lah teeh-endah deh aleementathyon*

❸ **la librería**
*lah leebraireeah*

❹ **la pescadería**
*lah peskadaireeah*

❺ **la pastelería**
*lah pastaylaireeah*

❻ **la carnicería**
*lah karneethaireeah*

### 3 SHOPS

**3** minutes

Name these shops in Spanish.

❶ baker  ❷ grocery  ❸ bookshop

❹ fishmonger  ❺ cake shop  ❻ butcher

## 4 SUPERMARKET

**3** minutes

Name these products in Spanish.

❶ household products

❷ beauty products

❸ drinks

❹ dairy products

❺ frozen foods

### Supermarket

❶ **los productos de limpieza**
*los prodooktos deh limpee-ehthah*

❷ **los productos de belleza**
*los prodooktos deh beyethah*

❸ **las bebidas**
*las bebeedas*

❹ **los productos lácteos**
*los prodooktos lakteh-os*

❺ **los congelados**
*los konhelados*

## 5 MUSEUM

**4** minutes

You are buying entrance tickets at a museum. Join in the conversation, replying in Spanish, following the numbered English prompts.

**Buenos días. ¿Qué desean?**
❶ I'd like five tickets.

**Son setenta y cinco euros.**
❷ That's very expensive!

**No hacemos descuentos a los niños.**
❸ How much is an audio guide?

**Cinco euros.**
❹ Five tickets and five audio guides, please.

**Cien euros, por favor.**
❺ Here you are. Where are the toilets?

**A la derecha.**
❻ Thank you very much.

### Museum

❶ **Quisiera cinco entradas.**
*keesyairah theenkoh entradas*

❷ **¡Es muy caro!**
*es mwee karoh*

❸ **¿Cuánto cuesta una audioguía?**
*kwantoh kwestah oonah awdeeoh-gheeah*

❹ **Cinco entradas y cinco audioguías, por favor.**
*theenkoh entradas ee theenkoh awdeeoh-ghee-as por fabor*

❺ **Aquí tiene. ¿Dónde están los servicios?**
*ahkee tyeneh. dondeh estan los serbeethyos*

❻ **Muchas gracias.**
*moochas grathyas*

# Los trabajos
## *JOBS*

**1** | **WARM UP**
**1** minute

Ask "**Which platform?**" (pp38–39).

What is the Spanish for these family members: "**sister**", "**brother**", "**son**", "**daughter**", "**mother**", and "**father**"? (pp10–11).

Some occupations have a different form when the person is female—for example, **enfermero** (*male nurse*) and **enfermera** (*female nurse*). Others remain the same for men and women. When you state your occupation, you don't need to use **un/una** (*a*), as in: **soy editor/-a** (*I'm an editor*).

**2**  | **WORDS TO REMEMBER**: JOBS

**7** minutes

Familiarize yourself with these words, then test yourself, using the cover flap. The feminine form is also shown.

| | |
|---|---|
| **el/la médico/-a** <br> *el/lah medeekoh/-ah* | doctor |
| **el/la dentista** <br> *el/lah denteestah* | dentist |
| **el/la enfermero/-a** <br> *el/lah enfermairoh/-ah* | nurse |
| **el/la profesor/-a** <br> *el/lah profaysor/-ah* | teacher |
| **el/la contable** <br> *el/lah kontableh* | accountant |
| **el/la abogado/-a** <br> *el/lah abogadoh/-ah* | lawyer |
| **el/la diseñador/-a** <br> *el/lah deesenyador/-ah* | designer |
| **el/la consultor/-a** <br> *el/lah konsooltor/-ah* | consultant |
| **el/la secretario/-a** <br> *el/lah sekraytareeoh/-ah* | secretary |
| **el/la comerciante** <br> *el/lah komerthyanteh* | shopkeeper |
| **el/la electricista** <br> *el/lah elektreetheestah* | electrician |
| **el/la fontanero/-a** <br> *el/lah fontanairoh/-ah* | plumber |
| **el/la cocinero/-a** <br> *el/lah kotheenairoh/-ah* | cook/chef |
| **el/la ingeniero/-a** <br> *el/lah inheneeairoh/-ah* | engineer |
| **el/la autónomo/-a** <br> *el/lah aootohnomoh/-ah* | self-employed |

**Soy fontanero.**
*soy fontanairoh*
I'm a plumber.

**Es estudiante.**
*es estoodyanteh*
She is a student.

## 3  PUT INTO PRACTICE

**4** minutes

Complete this dialogue, then test yourself, using the cover flap.

**¿Cuál es su profesión?**
*kwal es soo profesyon*
What do you do?
Say: I am a consultant.

**Soy consultor.**
*soy konsooltor*

**¿Para qué empresa trabaja?**
*parah keh empresah trabahah*
What company do you work for?
Say: I'm self-employed.

**Soy autónomo.**
*soy aootohnomoh*

**¡Qué interesante!**
*keh intairaysanteh*
How interesting!
Say: And what is your profession?

**¿Y cuál es su profesión?**
*ee kwal es soo profesyon*

**Soy dentista.**
*soy denteestah*
I'm a dentist.
Say: My sister is a dentist too.

**Mi hermana es dentista también.**
*mee airrmanah es denteestah tambyen*

## 4  WORDS TO REMEMBER: WORKPLACE

**3** minutes

Familiarize yourself with these words, then test yourself, using the cover flap.

**La oficina central está en Madrid.**
*lah ofeetheenah thentral estah en madreed*
The head office is in Madrid.

| | |
|---|---|
| head office | **la oficina central** *lah ofeetheenah thentral* |
| branch | **la sucursal** *lah sookoorsal* |
| department | **el departamento** *el departamaintoh* |
| reception | **la recepción** *lah rrethepthyon* |
| manager | **el/la jefe/-a** *el/lah hefeh/-ah* |
| employee | **el/la empleado/-a** *el/lah employ-ahdoh/-ah* |
| trainee | **el/la aprendiz** *el/lah ahprendeeth* |

# La oficina
## *THE OFFICE*

## 1 WARM UP

**1** minute

Practice different ways of introducing yourself in different situations. Mention your name, your occupation, and any other information you'd like to give (pp8–9, pp14–15, and pp78–79).

An office environment or business situation has its own vocabulary in any language, but there are many items for which the terminology is virtually universal. Note that Spanish computer keyboards have a different layout than the standard English QWERTY convention—they also include **ñ**, vowels with accents, **¡**, and **¿**.

## 2 🔊 WORDS TO REMEMBER

**5** minutes

Familiarize yourself with these words, then test yourself, using the cover flap.

| | |
|---|---|
| **la reunión** *lah reh-oonyon* | meeting |
| **la fotocopiadora** *lah fotokopyadorah* | photocopier |
| **el ordenador** *el ordehnador* | computer |
| **el monitor** *el moneetor* | monitor |
| **el ratón** *el rraton* | mouse |
| **el internet** *el eenternet* | Internet |
| **el correo electrónico** *el korrehoh elektroneekoh* | email |
| **la contraseña** *lah kontrasenyah* | password |
| **la contraseña del wifi** *lah kontrasenyah del weefee* | Wi-Fi password |
| **la conferencia** *lah konfairentheeah* | conference |
| **el orden del día** *el orden del deeah* | agenda |
| **la agenda** *lah ah-hendah* | planner |
| **la tarjeta de visita** *lah tarhetah deh beeseetah* | business card |
| **la mensajería de voz** *lah mensahereeah deh both* | voicemail |

## 3 🔊 MATCH

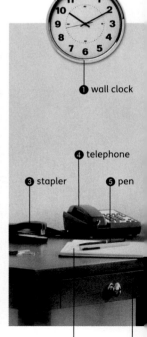

① wall clock

④ telephone

③ stapler    ⑤ pen

notepad ⑩    drawer ⑪

## 4 ◀)) USEFUL PHRASES

**2** minutes

Learn these phrases, then test yourself, using the cover flap.

| I want to send an email. | **Quiero mandar un correo electrónico.** |
| | *kyairoh mandar oon korrehoh elektroneekoh* |

## 5 SAY IT

**2** minutes

I'd like to arrange a conference.

Do you have a business card?

I have a laptop.

| I need to make some photocopies. | **Necesito hacer unas fotocopias.** |
| | *netheseetoh ahther oonas fotokopyas* |

| I'd like to arrange an appointment. | **Quisiera organizar una cita.** |
| | *keesyairah organeethar oonah theetah* |

## ...ND REPEAT

**5** minutes

Match the numbered items to the list, then test yourself, using the cover flap.

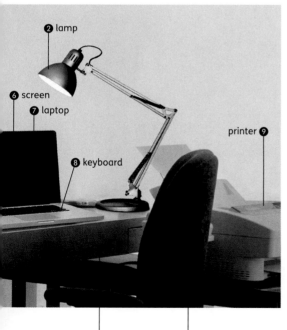

**❶ el reloj de pared**
*el rrelokh deh pareh*

**❷ la lámpara**
*lah lamparah*

**❸ la grapadora**
*lah grapadohrah*

**❹ el teléfono**
*el telefonoh*

**❺ el bolígrafo**
*el boleegrafoh*

**❻ la pantalla**
*lah pantahyah*

**❼ el portátil**
*el portateel*

**❽ el teclado**
*el tekladoh*

**❾ la impresora**
*lah impresorah*

**❿ el bloc**
*el blok*

**⓫ el cajón**
*el kahon*

**⓬ la mesa de escritorio**
*lah mesah deh eskreetoryoh*

**⓭ la silla giratoria**
*lah seeyah heeratoreeah*

# El mundo académico

*ACADEMIC WORLD*

In Spain, as is now becoming standard across the EU, the first degree is **un grado** (*bachelor's*), followed by **un máster** (*master's*) and then by **un doctorado** (*PhD*). Students are selected for the **grado** by an average of secondary school grades and an exam.

## 1 WARM UP

**1** minute

Say "**How interesting!**" (pp78–79), "**library**" (pp48–49), and "**appointment**" (pp32–33).

Ask "**What is your profession?**"; answer "**I'm a designer**" (pp78–79).

## 2  USEFUL PHRASES

**3** minutes

Learn these phrases, then test yourself, using the cover flap.

**¿Cuál es su especialidad?**
*kwal es soo espetheeahleedad*

What is your field?

**Hago investigación en bioquímica.**
*ahgoh inbesteegathyon en beeohkeemeekah*

I am doing research in biochemistry.

**Soy graduado en derecho.**
*soy grahdooahdoh en derechoh*

I have a degree in law.

**Voy a dar una conferencia sobre arquitectura.**
*boy ah dar oonah confairayntheeah sobreh arkeetektoorah*

I'm going to give a lecture on architecture.

## 3  IN CONVERSATION

**Hola, soy la profesora Fernández.**
*o-lah, soy lah profaysorah fernandeth*

Hello, I'm Professor Fernandez.

**¿De qué universidad es usted?**
*deh eh ooneeberseedad es oosted*

Which university are you from?

**De la Universidad de Murcia.**
*deh lah ooneeberseedad deh moortheeah*

From the University of Murcia.

## 4   WORDS TO REMEMBER

**4** minutes

Familiarize yourself with these words, then test yourself, using the cover flap.

**Tenemos un stand en la feria.**
*tenemos oon estand en la fereeah*
We have a stand at the trade fair.

| conference/lecture | **la conferencia** *lah konfairaintheeah* |
|---|---|
| trade fair | **la feria** *lah fereeah* |
| seminar | **el seminario** *el semeenaryoh* |
| lecture hall | **el anfiteatro** *el anfeetay-ahtroh* |
| conference room | **la sala de conferencias** *lah sahlah deh konferaintheeas* |
| exhibition | **la exposición** *lah eksposeethyon* |
| library | **la biblioteca** *lah bibleeotekah* |
| university lecturer | **el/la profesor/-a de universidad** *el/lah profaysor/-ah deh ooneeberseedad* |
| professor | **el/la catedrático/-a** *el/lah katedrateekoh/-ah* |
| medicine | **medicina** *medeetheenah* |
| science | **ciencias** *thyaintheeas* |
| literature | **literatura** *leetairatoorah* |
| engineering | **ingeniería** *inhenyaireeah* |

## 5 SAY IT

**2** minutes

I'm doing research in medicine.

I have a degree in literature.

She's the professor.

---

**5** minutes

**¿Cuál es su especialidad?**
*kwal es soo espethyaleedad*

What's your field?

**Hago investigación en ingeniería.**
*ahgoh inbesteegathyon en inhenyaireeah*

I'm doing research in engineering.

**¡Qué interesante! Yo también.**
*keh intairaysanteh. yoh tambeeayn*

How interesting! Me too.

# 1 WARM UP

**1** minute

Say "**I'm a trainee**" (pp78–79).

Say "**I want to send an email**" (pp80–81).

Say "**I'd like to arrange an appointment**" (pp80–81).

# Los negocios
*IN BUSINESS*

While on business trips to Spain, you will make a good impression and receive a more friendly reception if you make the effort to begin meetings with a short introduction in Spanish, even if your vocabulary is limited. After that, everyone will probably be happy to continue the meeting in English.

# 2  WORDS TO REMEMBER

Familiarize yourself with these words, then test yourself, using the cover flap.

|  |  |
|---|---|
| **el programa** *el programah* | schedule |
| **la entrega** *lah entrehgah* | delivery |
| **el pago** *el pahgoh* | payment |
| **el presupuesto** *el prehsoopwestoh* | budget/estimate/quotation |
| **el precio** *el prehthyoh* | price |
| **el documento** *el dokoomentoh* | document |
| **la factura** *lah faktoorah* | invoice |
| **la propuesta** *lah propwestah* | business proposal |
| **los beneficios** *los behnehfeethyos* | profits |
| **las ventas** *las bentas* | sales |
| **los números** *los noomeros* | figures |

**¿Firmamos el contrato?**
*feermamos el kontratoh*
Shall we sign the contract?

**el ejecutivo**
*el eh-hekooteeboh*
executive

**el contrato**
*el kontratoh*
contract

**Cultural tip** In general, commercial dealings are formal, but a lunch with wine is still part of doing business in Spain. As a client, you can expect to be taken out to a restaurant, and as a supplier, you should consider entertaining your customers.

## 3  USEFUL PHRASES

**6** minutes

Learn these phrases, then test yourself, using the cover flap.

**Me manda el contrato, por favor.**
*meh mandah el kontratoh, por fabor*

Please send me the contract.

**¿Hemos acordado un programa?**
*ehmos akordadoh oon programah*

Have we agreed a schedule?

**¿Cuándo puede hacer la entrega?**
*kwandoh pwedeh ahther lah entregah*

When can you make the delivery?

**¿Cuál es el presupuesto?**
*kwal es el prehsoopwestoh*

What's the budget?

**¿Me puede mandar la factura?**
*meh pwedeh mandar lah faktoorah*

Can you send me the invoice?

---

**6** minutes

**el cliente**
*el klyainteh*
client

**el informe**
*el informeh*
report

## 4 SAY IT

**2** minutes

Can you send me the estimate?

Have we agreed on a price?

What are the profits?

# Repase y repita
## REVIEW AND REPEAT

### At the office

**❶ el reloj de pared**
*el rrelokh deh pareh*

**❷ el portátil**
*el portateel*

**❸ la lámpara**
*lah lamparah*

**❹ la impresora**
*lah impresorah*

**❺ la grapadora**
*lah grapadorah*

**❻ el bolígrafo**
*el boleegrafoh*

**❼ el bloc**
*el blok*

**❽ la mesa de escritorio**
*lah mesah deh eskreetoryoh*

### Jobs

**❶ el/la médico/-a**
*el/lah medeekoh/-ah*

**❷ el/la fontanero/-a**
*el/lah fontanairoh/-ah*

**❸ el/la comerciante**
*el/lah komerthyanteh*

**❹ el/la contable**
*el/lah kontableh*

**❺ el/la estudiante**
*el/lah estoodyanteh*

**❻ el/la abogado/-a**
*el/lah abogadoh/-ah*

---

## 1 AT THE OFFICE

Name these items in Spanish.

❶ wall clock ❷ laptop ❸ lamp

❺ stapler ❻ pen ❼ notepad ❽ desk

---

## 2 JOBS

**3** minutes

Name these jobs in Spanish.

❶ doctor
❷ plumber
❸ shopkeeper
❹ accountant
❺ student
❻ lawyer

**4** minutes

 printer

## 3 WORK

 **4** minutes

Answer these questions, following the numbered English prompts.

**¿Para qué empresa trabaja?**
❶ I am self-employed.
**¿En qué universidad está?**
❷ I'm at the University of Salamanca.
**¿Cuál es su especialidad?**
❸ I'm doing research in medicine.
**¿Hemos acordado un programa?**
❹ Yes, my secretary has the schedule.

### Work

❶ **Soy autónomo.**
*soy aootonomoh*

❷ **Estoy en la Universidad de Salamanca.**
*estoy en lah ooneeberseedad deh salamankah*

❸ **Hago investigación en medicina.**
*ahgoh inbesteegathyon en medeetheenah*

❹ **Sí, mi secretaria tiene el programa.**
*see, mee sekretareeah tyeneh el programah*

## 4 HOW MUCH?

**4** minutes

Answer these questions in Spanish, using the amounts given in brackets.

❶ **¿Cuánto cuesta el café? (€2.50)**
❷ **¿Cuánto cuesta la habitación? (€80)**
❸ **¿Cuánto cuesta un kilo de tomates? (€3.25)**
❹ **¿Cuánto cuesta un plaza para cuatro noches? (€200)**

### How much?

❶ **Son dos euros cincuenta.**
*son dos eh-ooros theenkwentah*

❷ **Son ochenta euros.**
*son ochentah eh-ooros*

❸ **Son tres euros veinticinco.**
*son tres eh-ooros beynteetheenkoh*

❹ **Son doscientos euros.**
*son dostheeentos eh-ooros*

<table>
<tr><td>1</td><td>**WARM UP** <br>**1** minute</td></tr>
</table>

Say "**I'm allergic to nuts**" (pp22–23).

Say the verb "**tener**" (*to have*) in all its forms: yo, tú, él/ella, nosotros(-as), vosotros(-as), ellos (-as) (pp14–15).

# El cuerpo
## *THE BODY*

You are most likely to need to refer to parts of the body in the context of illness—for example, when describing aches and pains to a doctor. The most common phrases for talking about aches and pains are **tengo un dolor en la/el...** (*I have a pain in the...*) and **me duele la/el...** (*my... hurts*).

<table>
<tr><td>2</td><td></td><td>**MATCH AND REPEAT**: BODY</td><td>**6** minutes</td></tr>
</table>

Match the numbered parts of the body to the list, then test yourself, using the cover flap.

❶ **la mano**
*lah manoh*

❷ **el codo**
*el kodoh*

❸ **el pelo**
*el peloh*

❹ **la cabeza**
*lah kabethah*

❺ **el brazo**
*el brathoh*

❻ **el cuello**
*el kweyoh*

❼ **el hombro**
*el ombroh*

❽ **el pecho**
*el pechoh*

❾ **el estómago**
*el estomagoh*

❿ **la pierna**
*lah pyairnah*

⓫ **la rodilla**
*lah rrodeeyah*

⓬ **el pie**
*el pee-eh*

hand ❶
❷ elbow
❸ hair
head ❹
❺ arm
❻ neck
shoulder ❼
❽ chest
stomach ❾
leg ❿
knee ⓫
foot ⓬

# 3 — MATCH AND REPEAT: FACE

**3** minutes

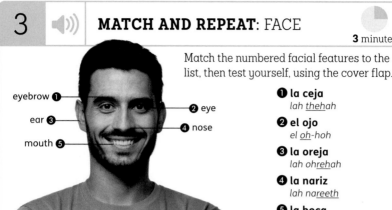

Match the numbered facial features to the list, then test yourself, using the cover flap.

eyebrow **1**
**2** eye
ear **3**
**4** nose
mouth **5**

**1 la ceja**
*lah thehah*

**2 el ojo**
*el oh-hoh*

**3 la oreja**
*lah ohrehah*

**4 la nariz**
*lah nareeth*

**5 la boca**
*lah bokah*

# 4 — USEFUL PHRASES

**3** minutes

Learn these phrases, then test yourself, using the cover flap.

My back hurts. **Me duele la espalda.**
*meh dweleh lah espaldah*

I have a rash on my arm. **Tengo un sarpullido en el brazo.**
*tengoh oon sarpooyeedoh en el brathoh*

I don't feel good. **No me encuentro bien.**
*noh meh enkwentroh byen*

# 5 — PUT INTO PRACTICE

**2** minutes

Complete this dialogue, then test yourself, using the cover flap.

**¿Cuál es el problema?** **No me encuentro bien.**
*kwal es el problemah* *noh meh enkwentroh byen*

What's the problem?

Say: I don't feel good.

**¿Dónde le duele?** **Me duele el hombro.**
*dondeh leh dweleh* *meh dweleh el ombroh*

Where does it hurt?

Say: My shoulder hurts.

# En la farmacia
## *AT THE PHARMACY*

**1**  **WARM UP**

1 minute

Say "**I have a rash**" and "**I don't feel good**" (pp88–89).

Say the Spanish for "**red**", "**green**", "**black**", and "**yellow**" (pp74–75).

Spanish pharmacists study for five to seven years before qualifying. They can give advice about minor health problems and are permitted to dispense prescription medicines as well as over-the-counter medicines. There is a **farmacia de guardia** (*24-hour pharmacy*) in most towns.

---

**2** 🔊 **MATCH AND REPEAT**

**3** minutes

Match the numbered items to the list, then test yourself, using the cover flap.

❶ **la venda**
   lah <u>ben</u>dah

❷ **el jarabe**
   el ha<u>ra</u>beh

❸ **las gotas**
   las <u>go</u>tas

❹ **la crema**
   lah <u>kre</u>mah

❺ **la tirita**
   lah tee<u>ree</u>tah

❻ **la jeringuilla**
   lah hereen<u>ghee</u>yah

❼ **el supositorio**
   el sooposee<u>to</u>ryoh

❽ **la pastilla**
   lah pas<u>tee</u>yah

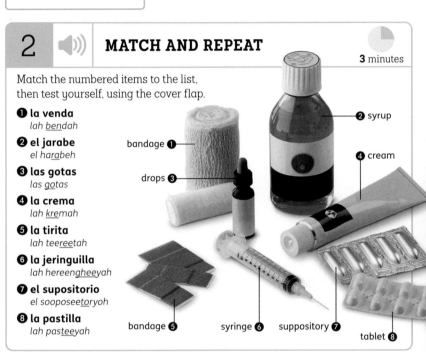

bandage ❶

drops ❸

bandage ❺    syringe ❻    suppository ❼

❷ syrup

❹ cream

tablet ❽

---

**3** 🔊 **IN CONVERSATION**

**Buenos días, señora. ¿Qué desea?**
<u>bwe</u>nos <u>dee</u>yas, sen<u>yo</u>rah. keh de<u>se</u>hah

Good morning, madam. What would you like?

**Tengo dolor de estómago.**
<u>ten</u>goh do<u>lor</u> deh es<u>to</u>magoh

I have a stomachache.

**¿Tiene diarrea?**
<u>tye</u>neh deeah<u>rre</u>hah

Do you have diarrhea?

## 4  WORDS TO REMEMBER

**2** minutes

Familiarize yourself with these words, then test yourself, using the cover flap.

**Tengo dolor de cabeza.**
*tengoh dolor deh kabethah*
I have a headache.

| | |
|---|---|
| headache | **el dolor de cabeza** *el dolor deh kabethah* |
| stomachache | **el dolor de estómago** *el dolor deh estomagoh* |
| diarrhea | **la diarrea** *lah deeahrrehah* |
| cold | **el resfriado** *el rresfreeahdoh* |
| cough | **la tos** *lah tos* |
| sunstroke | **la insolación** *lah eensolatheeyon* |
| toothache | **el dolor de muelas** *el dolor deh mwelas* |

## 5  USEFUL PHRASES

**4** minutes

Learn these phrases, then test yourself, using the cover flap.

| | |
|---|---|
| Do you have face masks? | **¿Tiene mascarillas?** *tyeneh maskareeyas* |
| Do you have that as a syrup? | **¿Lo tiene en jarabe?** *loh tyeneh en harabeh* |
| I'm allergic to penicillin. | **Soy alérgico a la penicilina.** *soy alerheekoh ah lah peneetheeleenah* |

## 6 SAY IT

**2** minutes

I have a cold.

Do you have that as a cream?

He has a toothache.

---

**3** minutes

**No, pero tengo dolor de cabeza.**
*noh, peroh tengoh dolor deh kabethah*

No, but I have a headache.

**Aquí tiene.**
*ahkee tyeneh*

Here you are.

**¿Lo tiene en jarabe?**
*loh tyeneh en harabeh*

Do you have this as a syrup?

## 1 WARM UP

**1** minute

Say "**I need some tablets**" and "**He needs some cream**" (pp60–61 and pp90–91).

What is the Spanish for "**I don't have a son**" (pp14–15)?

# En el médico
## *AT THE DOCTOR*

In an emergency, dial 112 for an ambulance. If it isn't urgent, book an appointment with the doctor and pay when you leave. You can usually be reimbursed if you have comprehensive travel and medical insurance. You can find the names and addresses of local doctors at the town hall, tourist office, or pharmacy.

## 2 USEFUL PHRASES YOU MAY HEAR

**3** minutes

Learn these phrases, then test yourself, using the cover flap.

**No es grave.** It's not serious.
*noh es graveh*

**¿Está tomando alguna medicación?** Are you taking any medications?
*estah tomandoh algoonah medeekathyon*

**Tiene una infección de riñón.** You have a kidney infection.
*tyeneh oonah infekthyon deh rreenyon*

**Necesita ir al hospital.** You need to go to the hospital.
*netheseetah eer al ospeetal*

**Abra la boca por favor.** Please open your mouth.
*ahbrah lah bokah por fabor*

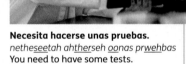

**Necesita hacerse unas pruebas.**
*netheseetah ahtherseh oonas prwehbas*
You need to have some tests.

## 3 IN CONVERSATION

**¿Cuál es el problema?**
*kwal es el problemah*

What's the problem?

**Tengo un dolor en el pecho.**
*tengoh oon dolor en el pechoh*

I have a pain in my chest.

**Déjeme que la examine.**
*dehhehmeh keh lah eksameeneh*

Let me examine you.

## 4  USEFUL PHRASES YOU MAY NEED TO SAY

**4** minutes

Learn these phrases, then test yourself, using the cover flap.

**Estoy embarazada.**
*estoy embarathadah*
I'm pregnant.

| I'm diabetic. | **Soy diabético/-a.** *soy deeahbeteekoh/-ah* |
| I'm epileptic. | **Soy epiléptico/-a.** *soy epeelepteekoh/-ah* |
| I'm asthmatic. | **Soy asmático/-a.** *soy asmateekoh/-ah* |
| I have a heart condition. | **Tengo un problema de corazón.** *tengoh oon problemah deh korathon* |
| I feel faint. | **Estoy mareado.** *estoy mareh-ahdoh* |
| I have a fever. | **Tengo fiebre.** *tengoh fyehbreh* |
| It's urgent. | **Es urgente.** *es oorhenteh* |
| I'm here for my vaccination. | **Vengo a vacunarme.** *bengoh ah vakoonarmeh* |

**Cultural tip** EU nationals can get free emergency medical treatment in Spain with a European Health Insurance Card (EHIC) or E111 form. For UK nationals, the Global Health Insurance Card (GHIC) has replaced the EHIC. Travelers from all other countries should make sure they have comprehensive travel and medical insurance.

## 5 SAY IT

**2** minutes

Do I need tests?

My son needs to go to the hospital.

It's not urgent.

**5** minutes

**¿Es grave?**
*es graveh*

Is it serious?

**No, solo tiene indigestión.**
*noh, soloh tyeneh indeehestyon*

No, you only have indigestion.

**¡Menos mal!**
*mehnos mal*

What a relief!

# En el hospital
## *AT THE HOSPITAL*

### 1 WARM UP
**1** minute

Ask "**How long is the journey?**" (pp42–43).

Ask "**Is it serious?**" (pp92–93).

What is the Spanish for "**mouth**" and "**head**" (pp88–89)?

The main hospitals in Spain are attached to universities and are known as **Hospitales Universitarios**. Most Spanish hospital rooms are en suite, with only two beds. It is useful to know a few basic phrases relating to hospitals for use in an emergency or in case you need to visit a friend or colleague in the hospital.

### 2  USEFUL PHRASES

**5** minutes

Learn these phrases, then test yourself, using the cover flap.

| | |
|---|---|
| **¿Cuáles son las horas de visita?** *kwales son las oras deh beeseetah* | What are the visiting hours? |
| **¿Hay disponible un bucle de inducción magnética?** *ah-ee disponeebleh oon book-leh deh eendookthyon magneteekah* | Is a hearing loop available? |

**¿Dónde está la sala de espera?**
*dondeh estah lah salah deh esperah*
Where is the waiting room?

| | |
|---|---|
| **¿Cuánto tiempo va a tardar?** *kwantoh tyempoh bah ah tardar* | How long will it take? |
| **¿Me va a doler?** *meh bah ah doler* | Will it hurt? |
| **Túmbese aquí por favor.** *toombeseh ahkee por fabor* | Please lie down here. |
| **No puede comer nada.** *noh pwedeh komer nadah* | You can't eat anything. |
| **No mueva la cabeza.** *noh mwebah lah kabethah* | Don't move your head. |
| **Necesita un análisis de sangre.** *netheseetah oon analeesees deh sangreh* | You need a blood test. |

**el gotero**
*el gotehroh*
intravenous drip

**¿Se encuentra mejor?**
*seh enkwentrah mehor*
Are you feeling better?

## 3  WORDS TO REMEMBER

**4** minutes

Familiarize yourself with these words, then test yourself, using the cover flap.

**Su radiografía es normal.**
*soo rradyografeeah es normal*
Your x-ray is normal.

| | |
|---|---|
| emergency department | **el servicio de urgencias**<br>*el serbeethyoh deh oorhentheeas* |
| x-ray department | **el servicio de radiología**<br>*el serbeethyoh deh rradyoloheeah* |
| children's ward | **la sala de pediatría**<br>*lah salah deh pedeeatreeah* |
| operating room | **el quirófano**<br>*el keerofanoh* |
| waiting room | **la sala de espera**<br>*lah salah deh esperah* |
| elevator | **el ascensor**<br>*el asthensor* |

## 4  PUT INTO PRACTICE

**3** minutes

Complete this dialogue, then test yourself, using the cover flap.

**Tiene una infección.**
*tyeneh oonah infekthyon*
You have an infection.
Ask: Do I need tests?

**¿Necesito hacerme pruebas?**
*netheseetoh ahthermeh prwehbas*

**Primero necesita un análisis de sangre.**
*preemeroh netheseetah oon analeesees deh sangreh*
First, you will need a blood test.
Ask: Will it hurt?

**¿Me va a doler?**
*meh bah ah doler*

## 5 SAY IT

**2** minutes

Does he need a blood test?

Where is the children's ward?

Do I need an x-ray?

**No, no se preocupe.**
*noh, noh seh preh-okoopeh*
No, don't worry.
Ask: How long will it take?

**¿Cuánto tiempo va a tardar?**
*kwantoh tyempoh bah ah tardar*

# Repase y repita
## REVIEW AND REPEAT

**Respuestas** *Answers*
(Cover with flap)

## The body

❶ **la cabeza**
*lah kabethah*

❷ **el brazo**
*el brathoh*

❸ **el pecho**
*el pechoh*

❹ **el estómago**
*el estomagoh*

❺ **la pierna**
*lah pyairnah*

❻ **la rodilla**
*lah rrodeeyah*

❼ **el pie**
*el pee-eh*

## On the phone

❶ **Quisiera hablar
con Ana Flores.**
*keesyairah hablar
kon annah flores*

❷ **Luis Cortés de
Don Frío.**
*looees kortes deh
don free-oh*

❸ **¿Puedo dejar
un mensaje?**
*pwedoh dehar
oon mensaheh*

❹ **La cita el lunes a
las once está bien.**
*lah theetah el loones ah
las ontheh estah byen*

❺ **Gracias, adiós.**
*grathyas, addy-os*

---

## 1  THE BODY
**4** minutes

Name these body
parts in Spanish.

❶ head

❷ arm

chest ❸

stomach ❹

leg ❺

knee ❻

❼ foot

---

## 2  ON THE PHONE
**4** minutes

You are arranging an appointment. Join in the
conversation, replying in Spanish, following
the numbered English prompts.

**Dígame, Apex Finanzas.**
❶ I'd like to speak to
Ana Flores.

**¿De parte de quién?**
❷ Luis Cortés, of Don Frío.

**Lo siento, está
comunicando.**
❸ Can I leave a message?

**Sí, dígame.**
❹ The appointment on
Monday at 11am is fine.

**Muy bien, adiós.**
❺ Thank you, goodbye.

## 3  CLOTHING
**3** minutes

Name these items of clothing in Spanish.

tie ❶

❷ jacket

❸ skirt

trousers ❹

❺ tights

shoes ❻

---

## 4  AT THE DOCTOR'S
**4** minutes

Say these sentences in Spanish.

❶ I don't feel good.

❷ Do I need tests?

❸ I have a heart condition.

❹ Do I need to go to the hospital?

❺ I'm pregnant.

❻ I'm here for my vaccination.

---

**Respuestas** *Answers*
(Cover with flap)

### Clothing

❶ **la corbata**
*lah korbatah*

❷ **la chaqueta**
*lah chaketah*

❸ **la falda**
*lah faldah*

❹ **el pantalón**
*el pantalon*

❺ **las medias**
*las medeeas*

❻ **los zapatos**
*los thapatos*

### At the doctor's

❶ **No me encuentro bien.**
*noh meh enkwentroh byen*

❷ **¿Necesito hacerme pruebas?**
*netheseetoh ahthermeh prwehbas*

❸ **Tengo un problema de corazón.**
*tengoh oon problemah deh korathon*

❹ **¿Necesito ir al hospital?**
*netheseetoh eer al ospeetal*

❺ **Estoy embarazada.**
*estoy embarathadah*

❻ **Vengo a vacunarme.**
*bengoh ah vakoonarmeh*

## 1 WARM UP
**1** minute

Say the months of the year in Spanish (pp28–29).

Ask "**Is there a car park?**" (pp48–49) and "**Are there toilets?**" (pp14–15).

# En casa
## *AT HOME*

Many city dwellers live in apartment blocks (**los bloques de piso**), but in rural areas, houses tend to be detached (**los chalets**). If you ask "**¿cuántos dormitorios hay?**," you will be told the number of bedrooms, whereas if you ask "**¿cuántas habitaciones hay?**," the answer will include all the main rooms. If you want to know how big the house is, you will need to ask in square meters.

## 2 🔊 MATCH AND REPEAT

Match the numbered items to the list, then test yourself, using the cover flap.

❶ **la terraza**
*lah terrathah*

❷ **la chimenea**
*lah cheemenehah*

❸ **el tejado**
*el tehadoh*

❹ **las persianas**
*las perseeanahs*

❺ **el garaje**
*el garaheh*

❻ **la ventana**
*lah bentanah*

❼ **el muro**
*el mooroh*

❽ **la puerta**
*lah pwertah*

terrace ❶    chimney ❷    roof ❸    shutters ❹

garage ❺    ❻ window

**Cultural tip** Most Spanish houses have shutters (**las persianas**) at each window. These are closed at night and in the heat of the day. Curtains, where they are present, tend to be more for decoration. Carpets are not popular in Spanish homes; ceramic tiles or parquet floors with rugs are a more common flooring solution.

**¿Cuánto es el alquiler al mes?**
*kwantoh es el alkeeler al mes*
What is the monthly rent?

**5** minutes

wall **7**    **8** door

---

## 3 🔊 USEFUL PHRASES
**3** minutes

Learn these phrases, then test yourself, using the cover flap.

**¿Hay un garaje?**
*ah-ee oon garaheh*

Is there a garage?

**¿Cuándo está disponible?**
*kwandoh estah deesponeebleh*

When is it available?

**¿Está amueblado?**
*estah amwebladoh*

Is it furnished?

---

## 4 🔊 WORDS TO REMEMBER
**4** minutes

Familiarize yourself with these words, then test yourself, using the cover flap.

| | |
|---|---|
| room | **la habitación** *lah abeetathyon* |
| floor | **el suelo** *el sweloh* |
| ceiling | **el techo** *el techoh* |
| cellar | **el sótano** *el sotahnoh* |
| attic | **el ático** *el ahteekoh* |
| bedroom | **el dormitorio** *el dormeetoreeoh* |
| bathroom | **el cuarto de baño** *el kwartoh deh banyoh* |
| living room | **el cuarto de estar** *el kwartoh deh estar* |
| dining room | **el comedor** *el komedor* |
| kitchen | **la cocina** *lah kotheenah* |

---

## 5 SAY IT
**2** minutes

Is there a dining room?

Is it large?

Is it available in July?

# 1 WARM UP

1 minute

What is the Spanish for "**table**" (pp20–21), "**chair**" (pp80–81), "**toilet(s)**" (pp52–53), and "**curtains**" (pp60–61)?

How do you say "**soft**," "**beautiful**," and "**big**" (pp64–65)?

# En la casa
## *IN THE HOUSE*

When you rent a house or villa in Spain, the most common option is to take it for a full month or, if not, for a **quincena**, the first or last fifteen days of the month. You will need to check in advance whether utilities, such as electricity and gas, are included in the rent. Be aware that, occasionally, rentals may not have a cell phone signal or a landline, although many will offer Wi-Fi.

# 2 ◀)) MATCH AND REPEAT

3 minutes

Match the numbered items to the list, then test yourself, using the cover flap.

❶ **el frigorífico**
*el freego*ree*feekoh*

❷ **la cocina**
*lah ko*thee*nah*

❸ **el fregadero**
*el frega*der*oh*

❹ **la encimera**
*lah enthee*mer*ah*

❺ **el microondas**
*el meekro-*on*das*

❻ **el horno**
*el* or*noh*

❼ **la mesa**
*lah* me*sah*

❽ **la silla**
*lah* see*yah*

fridge ❶  stove ❷  sink ❸  ❹ counter

microwave ❺  oven ❻  table ❼  ❽ chair

# 3 ◀)) IN CONVERSATION

**Este es el horno.**
*esteh es el* or*noh*

This is the oven.

**¿Hay también un lavavajillas?**
*ah-ee tamb*yen *oon lababa*hee*yas*

Is there a dishwasher as well?

**Sí, y hay un congelador grande.**
*see, ee ah-ee oon konhela*dor *grandeh*

Yes, and there's a big freezer.

## 4  WORDS TO REMEMBER

**2** minutes

Familiarize yourself with these words, then test yourself, using the cover flap.

**El sofá es nuevo.**
*el sofah es nweboh*
The sofa is new.

| | |
|---|---|
| wardrobe | **el armario** *el armaryoh* |
| armchair | **el sillón** *el seeyon* |
| fireplace | **la chimenea** *lah cheemenehah* |
| carpet | **la moqueta** *lah moketah* |
| bathtub | **la bañera** *lah banyerah* |
| toilet | **el váter** *el bater* |
| wash basin | **el lavabo** *el lababoh* |

## 5  USEFUL PHRASES

**4** minutes

Learn these phrases, then test yourself, using the cover flap.

| | |
|---|---|
| Is electricity included? | **¿Está incluida la electricidad?** *estah eenklooeedah lah ehektreetheedad* |
| I don't like the curtains. | **No me gustan las cortinas.** *noh meh goostan las korteenas* |
| The stove is broken. | **La cocina no funciona.** *lah kotheenah noh foonthyonah* |

## 6 SAY IT

**2** minutes

Is there a microwave?

I don't like the fireplace.

What a soft sofa!

---

**3** minutes

**Todo está muy nuevo.**
*todoh estah mwee nweboh*

Everything is very new.

**Sí. Y aquí está la lavadora.**
*see. ee ahkee estah lah labadorah*

Yes. And here's the washing machine.

**¡Qué azulejos más bonitos!**
*keh ah-thoolehhos mas boneetos*

What beautiful tiles!

# El jardín
## *THE YARD*

**1** | **WARM UP** — **1** minute

Say "**I need**" and "**you need**" (pp64–65 and pp94–95).

What is the Spanish for "**day**" and "**month**" (pp28–29)?

Ask "**Is the wardrobe included?**" (pp100–101).

The courtyard of a block of apartments may be communal, while houses generally have their own private yards. In some cases, a charge for the upkeep of the yard may be included with the rent for an apartment. Make sure that you check the position carefully with the estate agent or homeowner in advance before signing the agreement.

---

**2**  | **WORDS TO REMEMBER**

**3** minutes

Familiarize yourself with these words, then test yourself, using the cover flap.

| | |
|---|---|
| **la máquina cortacésped** *lah makeenah kortathesped* | lawn mower |
| **la horca** *lah orkah* | fork |
| **la pala** *lah palah* | spade |
| **el rastrillo** *el rrastreeyoh* | rake |
| **el vivero** *el beeberoh* | garden center |

---

**3**  | **MATCH AND REPEAT**

Match the numbered items to the list, then test yourself, using the cover flap.

tree **1**

lawn **2**

path **3**   weeds **4**   patio **5**

## 4  USEFUL PHRASES

**4** minutes

Learn these phrases, then test yourself, using the cover flap.

| | |
|---|---|
| Is the yard private? | **¿Es el jardín privado?**<br>*es el hardeen preebadoh* |

| | |
|---|---|
| The gardener comes once a week. | **El jardinero viene una vez a la semana.**<br>*el hardeenairoh byaineh oonah beth ah lah semanah* |
| Can you mow the lawn? | **¿Puede cortar el césped?**<br>*pwedeh kortar el thesped* |
| The yard needs watering. | **Hay que regar el jardín.**<br>*ah-ee keh rregar el hardeen* |

## 5 SAY IT

**2** minutes

The lawn needs watering.

Are there any flowers?

The gardener comes on Fridays.

---

**5** minutes

- 6 hedge
- 7 flowers
- 8 flowerbed
- 9 plants
- 10 soil

**1** el árbol
*el arbol*

**2** el césped
*el thesped*

**3** el camino
*el kameenoh*

**4** las malas hierbas
*las malas yerbas*

**5** la terraza
*lah terrathah*

**6** el seto
*el setoh*

**7** las flores
*las flores*

**8** el parterre
*el partairreh*

**9** las plantas
*las plantas*

**10** la tierra
*lah tyairrah*

# Los animales de compañía
## *PETS*

<table>
<tr><td>

**1** **WARM UP**

**1** minute

Say "**My name is John**" (pp8–9).

How do you say "**Don't worry**" (pp94–95)?

What is "**your**" in Spanish (pp12–13)?

</td><td>

About half of all Spanish households include at least one pet, which is often treated like a member of the family. Pet passports may be available to allow travelers to take their pets with them to Spain. Consult your vet for details of how to obtain the necessary vaccinations and paperwork.

</td></tr>
</table>

**2** 🔊 **MATCH AND REPEAT**

Match the numbered items to the list, then test yourself, using the cover flap.

❶ **el conejo**
  el ko*ne*hoh

❷ **el pez**
  el peth

❸ **el pájaro**
  el *pa*haroh

❹ **el gato**
  el *ga*toh

❺ **el perro**
  el *pe*rroh

❻ **el hámster**
  el *ham*ster

❷ fish

❶ rabbit

dog ❺

❹ cat

**3** 🔊 **USEFUL PHRASES**

**4** minutes

Learn these phrases, then test yourself, using the cover flap.

**¿Es bueno el perro?**   Is the dog friendly?
*es bwenoh el perroh*

**¿Puedo llevar a mi perro guía?**   Can I bring my guide dog?
*pwedoh yebar ah mee perroh guee-ah*

**Me dan miedo los gatos.**   I'm frightened of cats.
*meh dan myehdoh los gatos*

**Este gato está lleno de pulgas.**
*esteh gatoh estah yenoh deh poolgas*
This cat is full of fleas.

**Mi perro no muerde.**   My dog doesn't bite.
*mee perroh noh mwedeh*

**Cultural tip** Many dogs in Spain are working or guard dogs, and you may encounter them tethered or roaming free. Approach farms and rural houses with care and keep away from the dog's territory. Look out for warning notices, such as **¡cuidado con el perro!** (beware of the dog).

¡CUIDADO CON EL PERRO!

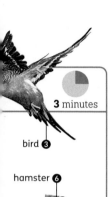

bird **3**

hamster **6**

## 4 WORDS TO REMEMBER

**4** minutes

Familiarize yourself with these words, then test yourself, using the cover flap.

**Mi perro no está bien.**
mee *perroh* noh *estah* byen
My dog is not well.

| | |
|---|---|
| vet | **el veterinario** *el betereenaryoh* |
| vaccination | **la vacuna** *lah bakoonah* |
| pet passport | **el pasaporte de animales** *el pasaporteh deh aneemales* |
| basket | **la cesta** *lah thestah* |
| cage | **la jaula** *lah haoolah* |
| bowl | **el bol** *el bol* |
| collar | **el collar** *el koyar* |
| leash | **la correa** *lah korreh-ah* |
| fleas | **las pulgas** *las poolgas* |

## 5 PUT INTO PRACTICE

**3** minutes

Complete this dialogue, then test yourself, using the cover flap.

**¿Es suyo este perro?**
es *sooyoh* *esteh* *perroh*
Is this your dog?

Say: Yes, he's named Sandy.

**Sí, se llama Sandy.**
see, seh *yamah* sandy

**Me dan miedo los perros.**
meh dan *myehdoh* los perros
I'm frightened of dogs.

Say: Don't worry. He's friendly.

**No se preocupe. Es bueno.**
noh seh prehohkoopeh. es *bwe*noh

# Repase y repita
## REVIEW AND REPEAT

## Colors

**❶ negra**
_negrah_

**❷ blanca**
_blankah_

**❸ rojo**
_rrohoh_

**❹ verde**
_berdeh_

**❺ amarillos**
_amareeyos_

## 1  COLORS

**4** minutes

Fill in the blanks with the correct Spanish masculine or feminine form of the color given in brackets.

**❶ Quisiera la camisa _____ .** (black)
**❷ Me llevo la falda _____ .** (white)
**❸ ¿Tiene este traje en _____ ?** (red)
**❹ No, pero lo tengo en _____ .** (green)
**❺ Quiero los zapatos _____ .** (yellow)

## Kitchen

**❶ el frigorífico**
_el freegoreefeekoh_

**❷ la cocina**
_lah kotheenah_

**❸ el horno**
_el ornoh_

**❹ el fregadero**
_el fregaderoh_

**❺ el microondas**
_el meekro-ondas_

**❻ la mesa**
_lah mesah_

**❼ la silla**
_lah seeyah_

## 2  KITCHEN

Name these items in Spanish.

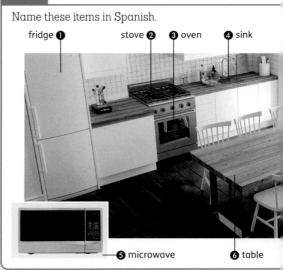

fridge ❶     stove ❷     ❸ oven     ❹ sink

❺ microwave     ❻ table

## 3 HOUSE

4 minutes

You are visiting a house in Spain. Join in the conversation, replying in Spanish, following the numbered English prompts.

**Este es el cuarto de estar.**
❶ What a lovely fireplace.

**Sí, y tiene una cocina muy grande.**
❷ How many bedrooms are there?

**Hay tres dormitorios.**
❸ Do you have a garage?

**Sí, pero no hay un jardín.**
❹ When is it available?

**En julio.**
❺ What is the monthly rent?

---

4 minutes

## 4 AT HOME

3 minutes

Name these things in Spanish.

❶ washing machine
❷ sofa
❸ attic
❹ dining room
❺ tree
❻ yard

❼ chair

---

### House

❶ **¡Qué chimenea más bonita!**
*keh cheemenehah mas boneetah*

❷ **¿Cuántos dormitorios hay?**
*kwantos dormeetoreeos ah-ee*

❸ **¿Tiene garaje?**
*tyeneh garaheh*

❹ **¿Cuándo está disponible?**
*kwandoh estah deesponeebleh*

❺ **¿Cuánto es el alquiler al mes?**
*kwantoh es el alkeeler al mes*

### At home

❶ **la lavadora**
*lah labadorah*

❷ **el sofá**
*el sofah*

❸ **el ático**
*el ahteekoh*

❹ **el comedor**
*el komedor*

❺ **el árbol**
*el arbol*

❻ **el jardín**
*el hardeen*

# Los servicios financieros y postales
## *FINANCIAL AND POSTAL SERVICES*

You can exchange one currency for another at a bureau de change. You can also get cash at a bank ATM but may be charged a fee. The post office also serves as a bank. Stamps are sold at the post office as well as at **el estanco** (p68). Banks and post offices are usually open only on weekdays until lunchtime.

---

**2**  **WORDS TO REMEMBER:** MAIL  *3 minutes*

Familiarize yourself with these words, then test yourself, using the cover flap.

| | |
|---|---|
| **el buzón** *el boothon* | mailbox |
| **la postal** *lah postal* | postcard |
| **el paquete** *el paketeh* | package |
| **por avión** *por abyon* | air mail |
| **el correo certificado** *el korreoh therteefeekadoh* | registered post |
| **el código postal** *el kodeegoh postal* | zip code |
| **el/la cartero/-a** *el/lah kartairoh/-ah* | mailman/ mailwoman |

**los sellos**
*los seyos*
stamps

**el sobre**
*el sobreh*
envelope

¿Cuánto es para el Reino Unido?
*kwantoh es parah el rreheenoh ooneedoh*
How much is it for the United Kingdom?

---

**3**  **IN CONVERSATION:** BUREAU DE CHANGE

**Quisiera cambiar dinero.**
*keesyairah kambyar deeneroh*

I would like to change some money.

**¿Qué quiere cambiar?**
*keh kee-ehreh kambeear*

What would you like to exchange?

**Quisiera quinientos dólares en euros.**
*keesee-ehrah keenee-entos dolares en eh-ooros*

I would like to buy euros for five hundred dollars.

# 4  **WORDS TO REMEMBER**: BANK

**2** minutes

Familiarize yourself with these words, then test yourself, using the cover flap.

**la tarjeta de débito**
*lah tarhetah deh debeetoh*
debit card

**¿Cómo puedo pagar?**
*komoh pwedoh pagar*
How can I pay?

| | |
|---|---|
| bank | **el banco** *el bankoh* |
| ATM/ cashpoint | **el cajero automático** *el kaheroh aootomateekoh* |
| PIN | **el pin** *el peen* |
| cash | **el efectivo** *el efekteeboh* |
| notes | **los billetes** *los beeyetes* |
| credit card | **la tarjeta de crédito** *lah tarhetah deh kredeetoh* |
| contactless payment | **el pago sin contacto** *el pagoh seen kontaktoh* |

# 5  **USEFUL PHRASES**

**4** minutes

Learn these phrases, then test yourself, using the cover flap.

| | |
|---|---|
| I'd like to change some money. | **Quisiera cambiar dinero.** *keesyairah kambyar deeneroh* |
| What is the exchange rate? | **¿A cuánto está el cambio?** *ah kwantoh estah el kambyoh* |
| What would you like to exchange? | **¿Qué quiere cambiar?** *keh kee-ehreh kambeear* |

# 6 **SAY IT**

**2** minutes

I'd like a stamp for the United States.

Can I pay by credit card?

Do I need my PIN?

**3** minutes

| | | |
|---|---|---|
| **Sí, claro. ¿Tiene identificación?** *see, klaroh. tyeneh eedenteefeekathyon* | **Sí, aquí tiene mi pasaporte.** *see, ahkee tyeneh mee pasaporteh* | **Gracias, aquí tiene los euros.** *grathyas, akee tyeneh los eh-ooros* |
| Yes, of course. Do you have any identification? | Yes, here's my passport. | Thank you, here are your euros. |

## 1 WARM UP

**1** minute

What's the Spanish for "**It doesn't work**" (pp60–61)?

Say "**today**" and "**tomorrow**" in Spanish (pp28–29).

# Los servicios
## SERVICES

You can combine the Spanish words on these pages with the vocabulary you learned in week 10 to help you explain basic problems and arrange most repairs. When organizing building work or a repair, it's a good idea to agree on the price and method of payment in advance.

## 2  WORDS TO REMEMBER:
### SERVICES

**4** minutes

Familiarize yourself with these words, then test yourself, using the cover flap. The feminine form is also shown.

| | |
|---|---|
| **el/la fontanero/-a**<br>*el/lah fontanairoh/-ah* | plumber |
| **el/la electricista**<br>*el/lah ehlektreetheestah* | electrician |
| **el/la mecánico/-a**<br>*el/lah mekaneekoh/-ah* | mechanic |
| **el/la constructor/-a**<br>*el/lah konstrooktor/-ah* | builder |
| **el/la pintor/-a**<br>*el/lah peentor/-ah* | decorator |
| **el/la carpintero/-a**<br>*el/lah karpeenteroh/-ah* | carpenter |
| **el/la albañil**<br>*el/lah albanyeel* | bricklayer |
| **la persona de la limpieza**<br>*lah personah deh lah leempee-ethah* | cleaning staff |

**No necesito un mecánico.**
*noh netheseetoh oon mekaneekoh*
I don't need a mechanic.

## 3  IN CONVERSATION

**La lavadora no funciona.**
*lah labadorah noh foothyonah*

The washing machine's not working.

**Sí, la manguera está rota.**
*see, lah mangherah estah rrotah*

Yes, the hose is broken.

**¿La puede arreglar?**
*lah pwedeh arreglar*

Can you repair it?

# 4  USEFUL PHRASES

**3** minutes

Learn these phrases, then test yourself, using the cover flap.

**¿Dónde me pueden arreglar la plancha?**
*dondeh meh pweden arreglar lah planchah*
Where can I get the iron repaired?

Can you clean the bathroom?
**¿Puede limpiar el cuarto de baño?**
*pwedeh leempyar el kwartoh deh banyoh*

Can you repair the boiler?
**¿Puede arreglar la caldera?**
*pwedeh arreglar lah kalderah*

Do you know a good electrician?
**¿Conoce a un buen electricista?**
*konotheh ah oon bwen ehlektreetheestah*

# 5  PUT INTO PRACTICE

**4** minutes

Complete this dialogue, then test yourself, using the cover flap.

**Su verja está rota.**
*soo berhah estah rrotah*

Your gate is broken.

Ask: Do you know a good bricklayer?

**¿Conoce a un buen albañil?**
*konotheh ah oon bwen albanyeel*

**Sí, hay uno en el pueblo.**
*see, ah-ee oonoh en el pwebloh*

Yes, there is one in the village.

Ask: Do you have his phone number?

**¿Tiene su número de teléfono?**
*tyeneh soo noomeroh deh telefonoh*

**3** minutes

**No, va a necesitar una nueva.**
*noh, bah ah netheseetar oonah nwebah*

No, you'll need a new one.

**¿Lo puede hacer hoy?**
*loh pwedeh ahther oy*

Can you do it today?

**No, volveré mañana.**
*noh, bolbereh manyanah*

No, I'll come back tomorrow.

# 1  WARM UP
**1** minute

Ask "**How do I get to the library?**" (pp48–49).

How do you say "**cleaning staff**" (pp110–111)?

Say "**It's 9:30**," "**10:45**," and "**12:00**" (pp10–11 and pp30–31).

# Venir
## TO COME

The verb **venir** (*to come*) is another important verb. As well as the main verb (below), it is worth knowing the instruction **¡ven!/¡venga!** (*come here!* informal/formal). Remember that *with me* becomes **conmigo** and *with you* **contigo**: **ven conmigo** (*come with me*); **vengo contigo** (*I'm going with you*).

---

# 2    **VENIR:** TO COME

**6** minutes

Practice **venir** (*to come*) and the sample sentences, then test yourself, using the cover flap.

| | |
|---|---|
| **yo vengo** *yoh bengoh* | I come |
| **tú vienes/usted viene** *too byenes/oosted byeneh* | you come (informal/formal singular) |
| **él/ella viene** *el/eh-yah byeneh* | he/she comes |
| **nosotros(-as) venimos** *nosotros(-as) beneemos* | we come (m/f) |
| **vosotros(-as) venís** *bosotros(-as) benees* | you come (informal plural m/f) |
| **ustedes vienen** *oostedes byenen* | you come (formal plural) |
| **ellos/ellas vienen** *eh-yos/eh-yas byenen* | they come (m/f) |

| | |
|---|---|
| **Vengo ahora.** *bengoh ah-orah* | I'm coming now. |
| **Venimos todos los martes.** *beneemos todos los martes* | We come every Tuesday. |
| **Vienen en muchos colores.** *beehnen en moochos kolores* | They come in many colors. |

**Vienen en tren.**
*byenen en trenñ*
They come by train.

---

**Conversational tip** To say *I come from the United States* in Spanish, you have to use the verb *to be*, as in **soy de los Estados Unidos** (*I am from the United States*). When you use the verb *to come*, as in **vengo de New York,** it means you have just arrived from New York.

## 3  USEFUL PHRASES

**4** minutes

Learn these phrases, then test yourself, using the cover flap.

**La persona de la limpieza viene todos los lunes.**
*lah per<u>so</u>nah deh lah leempee-ethah <u>by</u>eneh <u>to</u>dos los <u>loo</u>nes*
The cleaning staff comes every Monday.

| | |
|---|---|
| When can I come? | **¿Cuándo puedo venir?**<br>*<u>kwa</u>ndoh <u>pwe</u>doh be<u>neer</u>* |
| Does it come in size 44? | **¿Viene en la talla 44?**<br>*<u>by</u>eneh en lah <u>te</u>hah kwa<u>ren</u>tah ee <u>kwa</u>troh* |
| Can you come on Friday? | **¿Puede venir el viernes?**<br>*<u>pwe</u>deh be<u>neer</u> el <u>by</u>airnes* |
| Come with me.<br>(informal/formal) | **Ven conmigo/<br>Venga conmigo.**<br>*ben kon<u>mee</u>goh/<br><u>ben</u>gah kon<u>mee</u>goh* |

## 4  PUT INTO PRACTICE

**4** minutes

Complete this dialogue, then test yourself, using the cover flap.

**Peluquería Cristina, dígame.**
*pelooke<u>ree</u>ah kris<u>tee</u>nah, <u>dee</u>gameh*

Christine's hair salon. How can I help you?

Say: I'd like an appointment.

**Quisiera una cita.**
*kee<u>sya</u>irah <u>oo</u>nah <u>thee</u>tah*

**¿Cuándo quiere venir?**
*<u>kwa</u>ndoh <u>kya</u>ireh be<u>neer</u>*

When do you want to come?

Say: Today, if possible.

**Hoy, si es posible.**
*oy, see es po<u>see</u>bleh*

**Sí, claro. ¿A qué hora?**
*see <u>kla</u>roh, ah keh <u>o</u>rah*

Yes, of course. What time?

Say: At 10:30.

**A las diez y media.**
*ah las <u>dye</u>th ee <u>me</u>deeah*

# 1 WARM UP

**1** minute

What's the Spanish for "**big**" and "**small**" (pp64–65)?

Say "**The room is big**" and "**The bed is small**" (pp64–65).

# La policía y el delito
## POLICE AND CRIME

If you are the victim of a crime while in Spain, you should go to a police station to report it. In an emergency, you can dial 112. You may have to explain your complaint in Spanish, so some basic vocabulary is useful. In the event of a burglary, the police will usually come to the house.

# 2  **WORDS TO REMEMBER**: CRIME

**4** minutes

Familiarize yourself with these words, then test yourself, using the cover flap.

| | |
|---|---|
| **el robo** *el rroboh* | burglary |
| **la denuncia** *lah denoontheeah* | police report |
| **el/la ladrón/-rona** *el/lah ladron/-ronah* | thief |
| **la policía** *lah poleetheeah* | police |
| **la declaración** *lah deklarathyon* | statement |
| **el/la testigo** *el/lah testeegoh* | witness |
| **el/la abogado/-a** *el/lah abogadoh/-ah* | lawyer |

**Necesito un abogado.**
*netheseetoh oon abogadoh*
**I need a lawyer.**

# 3  **USEFUL PHRASES**

**3** minutes

Learn these phrases, then test yourself, using the cover flap.

| | |
|---|---|
| **Me han robado.** *meh an rrobadoh* | I've been robbed. |
| **¿Qué han robado?** *keh an rrobadoh* | What was stolen? |
| **¿Vió quién lo hizo?** *byoh kyain loh eethoh* | Did you see who did it? |
| **¿Cuándo ocurrió?** *kwandoh okoorryoh* | When did it happen? |

**la cámara de fotos**
*lah kamarah deh fotos*
camera

**la cartera**
*lah karterah*
purse

## 4  WORDS TO REMEMBER: APPEARANCE

**5** minutes

Familiarize yourself with these words, then test yourself, using the cover flap. Remember, some adjectives have a feminine form.

| | |
|---|---|
| man | **el hombre** <br> *el ombreh* |
| woman | **la mujer** <br> *lah moo-hair* |
| tall | **alto/alta** <br> *altoh/altah* |
| short | **bajo/baja** <br> *bahoh/bahah* |
| young | **joven** <br> *hoben* |
| old | **viejo/vieja** <br> *byehhoh/byehhah* |
| fat | **gordo/gorda** <br> *gordoh/gordah* |
| thin | **delgado/delgada** <br> *delgadoh/delgadah* |
| long/short hair | **el pelo largo/corto** <br> *el peloh largoh/kortoh* |
| glasses | **las gafas** <br> *las gafas* |
| beard | **la barba** <br> *lah barbah* |

**Tiene el pelo largo y negro.**
*tyeneh el peloh largoh ee negroh*
She has long black hair.

**Es calvo y tiene barba.**
*es kalboh ee tyeneh barbah*
He is bald and has a beard.

## 5  PUT INTO PRACTICE

**2** minutes

Complete this dialogue, then test yourself, using the cover flap.

**¿Cómo era?**    **Bajo y gordo.**
*komoh ehrah*    *bahoh ee gordoh*
What did he look like?
Say: Short and fat.

**¿Y el pelo?**    **Largo y con barba.**
*ee el peloh*    *largoh ee kon barbah*
And his hair?
Say: Long, with a beard.

**Cultural tip** In Spain, there is a difference between **la guardia civil** and **la policía**. **La policía** are the local police, while **la guardia civil** operates in airports and patrols the national road system. The uniforms of **la policía** are blue, while those of **la guardia civil** are green.

# Repase y repita
## *REVIEW AND REPEAT*

### To come

❶ **vienen**
   *byenen*

❷ **viene**
   *byeneh*

❸ **venimos**
   *beneemos*

❹ **venís**
   *benees*

❺ **vengo**
   *bengoh*

---

## 1 TO COME

**3** minutes

Fill in the blanks with the correct form of **venir** (*to come*).

❶ Mis padres _____ a las cuatro.

❷ La persona de la limpieza _____ una vez a la semana.

❸ Nosotros _____ todos los martes.

❹ ¿ _____ vosotros con nosotros?

❺ Yo _____ en taxi.

---

### Bank and mail

❶ **los sellos**
   *los seyos*

❷ **el paquete**
   *el paketeh*

❸ **las postales**
   *las postales*

❹ **la tarjeta de débito**
   *lah tarhetah deh debeetoh*

---

## 2 BANK AND MAIL

**4** minutes

Name these items in Spanish.

stamps ❶

❷ package

❸ postcards

debit card ❹

## 3 APPEARANCE

**4** minutes

What do these sentences mean?

❶ Es un hombre alto y delgado.
❷ Ella tiene el pelo corto y gafas.
❸ Soy baja y tengo el pelo largo.
❹ Ella es vieja y gorda.
❺ Él tiene los ojos azules y barba.

## 4 THE PHARMACY

**4** minutes

You are asking a pharmacist for advice.
Join in the conversation, replying in Spanish,
following the numbered English prompts.

**Buenos días, ¿qué desea?**
❶ Say: I have a cough.
**¿Le duele el pecho?**
❷ Say: No, but I have a headache.
**Tiene estas pastillas.**
❸ Ask: Do you have that as a syrup?
**Sí señor. Aquí tiene.**
❹ Say: Thank you. How much is that?
**Seis euros.**
❺ Say: Here you are. Goodbye.

### Appearance

❶ He's a tall,
thin man.
❷ She has short hair
and glasses.
❸ I'm short, and I
have long hair.
❹ She is old and fat.
❺ He has blue eyes
and a beard.

### The pharmacy

❶ **Tengo tos.**
*tengoh tos*

❷ **No, pero me duele
la cabeza.**
*noh, peroh meh
dweleh lah kabethah*

❸ **¿Lo tiene en
jarabe?**
*loh tyeneh en harabeh*

❹ **Gracias. ¿Cuánto
es?**
*grathyas. kwantoh es*

❺ **Aquí tiene. Adiós.**
*ahkee tyeneh. addy-os*

# 1 WARM UP

**1** minute

What is the Spanish for **"museum"** and **"art gallery"** (pp48–49)?

Say **"I don't like the curtains"** (pp100–101).

Ask **"Do you want...?"** informally (pp24–25).

# El ocio
## *LEISURE TIME*

The Spanish pride themselves on their lively nightlife and love of the arts, including theater and film, and it is also not unusual for them to number politics or philosophy among their interests. Be prepared for any of these topics to be the subject of conversation in social situations.

# 2  WORDS TO REMEMBER

Familiarize yourself with these words, then test yourself, using the cover flap.

| | |
|---|---|
| **el teatro** *el te-ahtroh* | theater |
| **la música** *lah mooseekah* | music |
| **el arte** *el arteh* | art |
| **el cine** *el theeneh* | cinema |
| **los videojuegos** *los beedayohhwegos* | video games |
| **el club nocturno** *el kloob noktoornoh* | nightclub |
| **el deporte** *el deporteh* | sport |
| **el turismo** *el tooreesmo* | sightseeing |

**el traje típico**
*el traheh teepeekoh*
traditional costume

**la bailaora**
*lah baeelaorah*
dancer

# 3  IN CONVERSATION

**Hola Lucía, ¿quieres jugar al tenis esta mañana?**
*o-lah loothee-ah. kyaires hoogar al tenis estah manyanah*

Hi Lucia, do you want to play tennis this morning?

**No gracias, tengo otros planes.**
*noh grathyas, tengoh otros plahnes*

No thank you, I have other plans.

**Ah, ¿qué vas a hacer?**
*ah, keh vas ahther*

Oh, what are you going to do?

## 5 SAY IT

2 minutes

I'm interested in music.

I prefer sports.

I don't like video games.

Shopping bores me!

## 4 🔊 USEFUL PHRASES

4 minutes

Learn these phrases, then test yourself, using the cover flap.

| | |
|---|---|
| What are your (formal/informal) interests? | **¿Cuáles son sus/ tus intereses?** *kwales son soos/ toos intereses* |
| What do you (informal) plan to do this morning? | **¿Qué tienes pensado hacer esta mañana?** *keh tyenes pensadoh ahther estah manyanah* |
| I like the theater. | **Me gusta el teatro.** *meh goostah el te-ahtroh* |
| I prefer the cinema. | **Yo prefiero el cine.** *yoh prefyairoh el theeneh* |
| I'm interested in art. | **Me interesa el arte.** *meh interesah el arteh* |
| I hate shopping. | **Odio ir de compras.** *ohdeeoh eer deh kompras* |
| That bores me. | **Eso me aburre.** *ehsoh meh aboorreh* |

**Me encanta el baile.**
*me enkantah el baeeleh*
I love dancing.

**Me encantan los videojuegos.**
*meh enkantan los beedayohhwegos*
I love video games.

---

**Voy a hacer turismo. ¿Quieres venir?**
*boy ah ahther tooreesmoh. kieres venir*

I am going sightseeing! Do you want to join me?

**Eso suena bien, pero quiero jugar a tenis.**
*esoh sooeh-nah byen peroh kieroh hoogar ah tenees*

That sounds nice, but I want to play tennis.

**No pasa nada, disfruta de tu partido!**
*noh pasah nadah, deesfrootah deh tooh parteedoh*

No problem, enjoy your game!

# El deporte y los pasatiempos
## *SPORT AND HOBBIES*

The verb **hacer** (*to do* or *to make*) is a useful verb for talking about hobbies and is also used when describing the weather. **Jugar** (*to play*) is another handy verb for talking about sports and hobbies. When used for sports, it is usually followed by **al**, as in **juego al baloncesto** (*I play basketball*).

## 1 WARM UP
**1** minute

Ask **"Do you** (formal) **want to play tennis?"** (pp118–119).

Say **"I like the theater"** and **"I prefer sightseeing"** (pp118–119).

Say **"That doesn't interest me"** (pp118–119).

## 2  WORDS TO REMEMBER

**5** minutes

Familiarize yourself with these words, then test yourself, using the cover flap.

| | |
|---|---|
| **el fútbol/rugby** <br> el *footbol/roogbee* | football/ rugby |
| **el tenis/baloncesto** <br> el *tenis/balonthestoh* | tennis/ basketball |
| **la natación** <br> lah natath*yon* | swimming |
| **la vela** <br> lah *belah* | sailing |
| **la pesca** <br> lah *peskah* | fishing |
| **el ciclismo** <br> el thee*klees*moh | cycling |
| **el senderismo** <br> el sender*rees*moh | hiking |
| **el golf** <br> el golf | golf |
| **la pintura** <br> lah peen*toorah* | painting |

**la camiseta**
lah kamee*seh*-tah
T-shirt

**los pantalones cortos**
los pantahl*o*nes *kortos*
shorts

**las botas de fútbol**
las *boh*tas deh *footbol*
soccer shoes

**Juego al fútbol todos los días.**
*hwe*goh al *footbol toh*dos los *dee*yas
I play soccer every day.

## 3  USEFUL PHRASES

**2** minutes

Learn these phrases, then test yourself, using the cover flap.

| | |
|---|---|
| **Juego al baloncesto.** <br> *hwe*goh al balon*thes*toh | I play basketball. |
| **Juega al tenis.** <br> *hwe*gah al *tenis* | He plays tennis. |
| **Ella pinta.** <br> *eh*-yah *peentah* | She paints. |

## 4  HACER: TO DO OR TO MAKE

 4 minutes

Practice **hacer** (*to do* or *to make*) and the sample sentences, then test yourself, using the cover flap.

**Hoy hace buen tiempo para el senderismo.**
*oy ahtheh bwen tyempoh parah el sendereesmoh*
It's nice weather for hiking today.

| | |
|---|---|
| I do | **yo hago** *yoh ahgoh* |
| you do (informal/ formal singular) | **tú haces/usted hace** *too ahthes/oosted ahtheh* |
| he/she does | **él/ella hace** *el/eh-yah ahtheh* |
| we do (m/f) | **nosotros(-as) hacemos** *nosotros(-as) ahthemos* |
| you do (informal plural m/f) | **vosotros(-as) hacéis** *bosotros(-as) ahtheh-ees* |
| you do (formal plural) | **ustedes hacen** *oostedes ahthen* |
| they do (m/f) | **ellos/ellas hacen** *eh-yos/eh-yas ahthen* |
| What do you like doing? (informal/ formal singular) | **¿Qué te/le gusta hacer?** *keh teh/leh goostah ahther* |
| I go hiking. | **Yo hago senderismo.** *yoh ahgoh sendereesmoh* |

## 5  PUT INTO PRACTICE

 3 minutes

Complete this dialogue, then test yourself, using the cover flap.

**¿Qué te gusta hacer?**
*keh teh goostah ahther*
What do you like doing?
Say: I like playing tennis.

**Me gusta jugar al tenis.**
*meh goostah hoogar al tenis*

**¿Juegas al fútbol también?**
*hwegas al footbol tambyen*
Do you play soccer as well?
Say: No, I play rugby.

**No, juego al rugby.**
*noh, hwegoh al roogbee*

**¿Cuándo juegas?**
*kwandoh hwegas*
When do you play?
Say: I play every week.

**Juego todas las semanas.**
*hwegoh todas las semanas*

# La vida social
## *SOCIALIZING*

**1** | **WARM UP**
**1** minute

Say "**my husband**" and "**my wife**" (pp10–11).

How do you say "**lunch**" and "**dinner**" in Spanish (pp20–21)?

Say "**Sorry, I'm busy**" (pp32–33).

The dinner table is the center of the Spanish social world, and you can expect to do a lot of your socializing while enjoying good food and wine. In general, it is best to use the more polite **usted** form to talk to older people and **tú** with the younger crowd.

---

**2**  **USEFUL PHRASES**

Learn these phrases, then test yourself, using the cover flap.

**Me gustaría invitarte a cenar.**
*meh goostareeah inbeetarteh ah thenar*
I'd like to invite you to dinner.

**¿Estás libre el miércoles que viene?**
*estas leebreh el myairkoles keh byeneh*
Are you free next Wednesday?

**Quizá otro día.**
*keethah ohtroh deeyah*
Perhaps another day.

**Gracias por invitarnos.**
*grathyas por inbeetarnos*
Thank you for inviting us.

**la anfitriona**
*lah anfeetryonah*
hostess

---

**3**  **IN CONVERSATION**

**¿Quieres venir a comer el martes?**
*kyaires beneer ah komer el martes*

Would you like to come to lunch on Tuesday?

**Lo siento, estoy ocupada.**
*loh syaintoh, estoy okoopadah*

I'm sorry, I'm busy.

**¿Qué tal el jueves?**
*keh tal el hwebes*

What about Thursday?

**Cultural tip** When you visit someone for the first time, it is usual to take flowers or wine. Having seen their house, you can take a more personal gift if invited again.

**3** minutes

**la invitada**
*lah inbeetadah*
guest

## 4 WORDS TO REMEMBER

**3** minutes

Familiarize yourself with these words, then test yourself, using the cover flap.

| | |
|---|---|
| party | **la fiesta** *lah fyehstah* |
| dinner party | **la cena** *lah thenah* |
| cocktail party | **el coctel** *el koktel* |
| reception | **la recepción** *lah rrethepthyon* |
| invitation | **la invitación** *lah inbeetathyon* |

## 5  PUT INTO PRACTICE

**5** minutes

Complete this dialogue, then test yourself, using the cover flap.

**¿Puede venir a una recepción esta noche?**
*pwedeh beneer ah oonah rrethepthyon estah nocheh*

Can you come to a reception tonight?

Say: Yes, I'd love to.

**Sí, encantado/-a.**
*see, enkan-tadoh/-ah*

**Empieza a las ocho.**
*empyehthah ah las ochoh*

It starts at eight o'clock.

Ask: What should I wear?

**¿Qué me pongo?**
*keh meh pongoh*

**3** minutes

**Encantada.**
*enkan-tadah*

I'd be delighted.

**Ven con tu marido.**
*ben kon too mareedoh*

Bring your husband.

**Gracias, ¿a qué hora?**
*grathyas, ah keh orah*

Thank you, at what time?

# Repase y repita
## *REVIEW AND REPEAT*

### Animals

❶ **el gato**
   el *gatoh*

❷ **el hámster**
   el *hamster*

❸ **el pez**
   el *peth*

❹ **el pájaro**
   el *paharoh*

❺ **el conejo**
   el *konehoh*

❻ **el perro**
   el *perroh*

## 1 ANIMALS

Name these animals in Spanish.

❹ bird

❸ fish

❶ cat

❷ hamster

### I like…

❶ **Juego al baloncesto.**
   hwegoh *al* balon*thes*toh

❷ **Me gusta jugar al tenis.**
   meh *goo*stah hoo*gar* al *ten*is

❸ **No me gusta el fútbol.**
   noh meh *goos*tah el *foot*bol

❹ **Me gusta pintar.**
   meh *goos*tah peen*tar*

## 2 I LIKE…

**4** minutes

Say these sentences in Spanish.

❶ I play basketball.
❷ I like playing tennis.
❸ I don't like soccer.
❹ I like painting.

**3 minutes**

**5** rabbit

**6** dog

## 3 HACER

**4 minutes**

Fill in the blanks with the correct form of **hacer** (*to do* or *to make*).

**1** Vosotros _____ senderismo.

**2** Ella _____ eso todos los días.

**3** ¿Qué _____ tú?

**4** Hoy no _____ frío.

**5** ¿Qué _____ ellos esta noche?

**6** Yo _____ natación.

### Hacer

**1** hacéis
*ahtheh-ees*

**2** hace
*ahtheh*

**3** haces
*ahthes*

**4** hace
*ahtheh*

**5** hacen
*ahthen*

**6** hago
*ahgoh*

## 4 AN INVITATION

**4 minutes**

You are invited for dinner. Join in the conversation, replying in Spanish, following the numbered English prompts.

**¿Quieres venir a comer el viernes?**
**1** I'm sorry, I'm busy.

**¿Qué tal el sábado?**
**2** I'd be delighted.

**Ven con los niños.**
**3** Thank you. What time?

**A las doce y media.**
**4** That's good for me.

### An invitation

**1** Lo siento, estoy ocupado/-a.
*loh syentoh, estoy okoopadoh/-ah*

**2** Encantado/-a.
*enkantadoh/-ah*

**3** Gracias. ¿A qué hora?
*grathyas. ah keh orah*

**4** Me viene bien.
*meh byeneh byen*

# Reinforce and progress

Regular practice is the key to maintaining and advancing your language skills. In this section, you will find a variety of suggestions for reinforcing and extending your knowledge of Spanish. Many involve returning to exercises in the book and extending their scope by using the dictionaries. Go back through the lessons in a different order, mix and match activities to make up your own daily 15-minute program, or focus on topics that are of particular relevance to your current needs.

**1** **WARM UP**
**1 minute**

Say "**He is**" and "**They are**" (pp14–15).

Say "**He is not**" and "**They are not**" (pp14–15).

What is Spanish for "**The children**"? (pp10–11).

**Match, repeat, and extend**
Remind yourself of words related to specific topics by returning to the Match and Repeat and Words to Remember exercises. Test yourself, using the cover flap. Discover new words in that area by referring to the dictionary and menu guide.

**Keep warmed up**
Revisit the Warm Up boxes to remind yourself of key words and phrases. Make sure you work your way through all of them on a regular basis.

**2** 🔊 **MATCH AND REPEAT**
**5 minutes**

Match the numbered items to the list, then test yourself using the cover flap.

❶ **la terraza**
lah te*rrathah*

❷ **la chimenea**
lah cheeme*nehah*

❸ **el tejado**
el te*hadoh*

❹ **las persianas**
las perseea*nahs*

❺ **el garaje**
el ga*raheh*

❻ **la ventana**
lah ben*tanah*

❼ **el muro**
el *mooroh*

❽ **la puerta**
lah *pwertah*

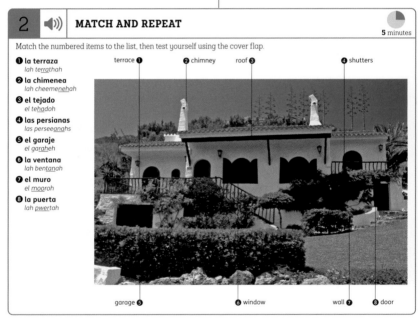

terrace ❶    ❷ chimney    roof ❸    ❹ shutters

garage ❺    ❻ window    wall ❼    ❽ door

**Carry on conversing**
Reread the In Conversation panels. Say both parts of the conversation, paying attention to the pronunciation. Where possible, try incorporating new words from the dictionary.

**3** 🔊 **IN CONVERSATION**

**Hola Lucía, ¿quieres jugar al tenis?**
o-lah loo*thee*-ah. *kyaires* hoo*gar* al *tenis*

Hi Lucia, do you want to play tennis?

**No gracias, tengo otros planes.**
noh *grathyas*, *tengoh* otros *plahnes*

No thank you, I have other plans.

**Ah, ¿qué vas a hacer?**
ah, keh vas a ah*ther*

Oh, what are you going to

**Practice words and phrases**
Return to the Words to Remember, Useful Phrases, and Put into Practice exercises. Test yourself, using the cover flap. When you are confident, devise your own versions of the phrases, using new words from the dictionary.

### 4 ◀))) USEFUL PHRASES: MONTHS

2 minutes

Learn these phrases, then test yourself using the cover flap.

| My children are on holiday in August. | **Mis hijos están de vacaciones en agosto.** mees <u>ee</u>-hos es<u>tan</u> deh baka<u>thyo</u>nes en a<u>gos</u>toh |
|---|---|

| My birthday is in June. | **Mi cumpleaños es en junio.** mee koompleh-<u>anyos</u> es en <u>hoo</u>nee-oh |
|---|---|

### 5 SAY IT

2 minutes

I'm doing research in medicine.

I have a degree in literature.

She's the professor.

**Say it again**
The Say It exercises are a useful instant reminder for each lesson. Practise these, using your own vocabulary variations from the dictionary or elsewhere in the lesson.

### 6 BE OR HAVE

5 minutes

Fill in the blanks with the correct form of **tener** (*to have*) or **ser** (*to be*).

❶ Yo _____ inglesa.

❷ Nosotros _____ cuatro niños.

❸ Yo no _____ feliz.

❹ ¿ _____ tú coche?

❺ Él _____ mi marido.

❻ Yo no _____ teléfono móvil.

❼ Tú no _____ español.

❽ ¿ _____ usted hijos?

**Review and repeat again**
Work through a Review and Repeat lesson as a way of reinforcing words and phrases presented in the course. Return to the main lesson for any topic about which you are no longer confident.

## Using other resources

As well as working with this book, try the following language extension ideas:

**Visit a Spanish-speaking country** and try out your new skills with native speakers. Find out if there is a Spanish community near you. There may be shops, cafés, restaurants, and clubs. Try to visit some of these and use your Spanish to order food and drink and strike up conversations. Most native speakers will be happy to speak Spanish to you.

**Join a language class or club**. There are usually evening and day classes available at a variety of different levels. Or you could start a club yourself if you have friends who are also interested in keeping up their Spanish.

**Look at Spanish magazines** and newspapers. The pictures will help you understand the text. Advertisements are also a useful way of expanding your vocabulary.

**Use the Internet**, where you can find all kinds of websites for learning languages, some of which offer free online help and activities. You can also find Spanish websites for everything from renting a house to shampooing your pet. You can even access Spanish radio and TV stations online. Start by going to a search engine and typing in a subject that interests you or give yourself a challenge, such as finding a two-bedroom house for rent in Madrid.

# Menu guide

This guide lists the most common terms you may encounter on Spanish menus or when shopping for food. If you can't find an exact phrase, try looking up its component parts.

## A

**aceitunas** *olives*
**acelgas** *spinach beet*
**achicoria** *chicory*
**aguacate** *avocado*
**ahumados** *smoked*
**agua mineral** *mineral water*
**ajo** *garlic*
**al ajillo** *with garlic*
**a la parrilla** *grilled*
**a la plancha** *grilled*
**albaricoques** *apricots*
**albóndigas** *meatballs*
**alcachofas** *artichokes*
**alcaparras** *capers*
**al horno** *baked*
**allioli** *garlic mayonnaise*
**almejas** *clams*
**almejas a la marinera** *clams stewed in wine and parsley*
**almejas naturales** *live clams*
**almendras** *almonds*
**almíbar** *syrup*
**alubias** *beans*
**ancas de rana** *frogs' legs*
**anchoas** *anchovies*
**anguila** *eel*
**angulas** *baby eels*
**arenque** *herring*
**arroz a la cubana** *rice with fried eggs, tomato sauce, and often a fried banana*
**arroz a la valenciana** *rice with seafood and meat*
**arroz con leche** *rice pudding*
**asados** *roast meat*
**atún** *tuna*
**azúcar** *sugar*

## B

**bacalao a la vizcaína** *cod served with ham, peppers, and chilies*
**bacalao al pil pil** *cod served with chilies and garlic*
**batido** *milk shake*
**bebidas** *drinks*
**berenjenas** *aubergine*
**besugo al horno** *baked sea bream*
**bistec de ternera** *veal steak*
**bonito** *fish similar to tuna*

**boquerones fritos** *fried, fresh anchovies*
**brazo gitano** *swiss roll*
**brocheta** *meat grilled on a skewer, such as shish kebab*
**brocheta de riñones** *kidney skewer*
**buñuelos** *fried pastries*
**butifarra** *Catalan sausage*

## C

**cabrito asado** *roast kid*
**cacahuetes** *peanuts*
**cachelada** *pork stew with eggs, tomato, and onion*
**café** *coffee*
**café americano** *black coffee*
**café con leche** *coffee with milk*
**café solo** *espresso*
**calabacines** *courgettes*
**calabaza** *pumpkin*
**calamares a la romana** *squid rings in batter*
**calamares en su tinta** *squid cooked in their ink*
**caldeirada** *fish soup*
**caldereta gallega** *vegetable stew*
**caldo de...** *...soup*
**caldo de gallina** *chicken soup*
**caldo de pescado** *clear fish soup*
**caldo gallego** *vegetable soup*
**caldo guanche** *soup of potatoes, tomatoes, onions, and courgettes*
**callos a la madrileña** *tripe cooked with chilies*
**camarones** *baby prawns*
**canela** *cinnamon*
**cangrejos** *crabs*
**caracoles** *snails*
**caramelos** *sweets*
**carnes** *meats*
**castañas** *chestnuts*
**cebolla** *onion*
**cebolletas** *spring onions*
**centollo** *spider crab*
**cerdo** *pork*
**cerezas** *cherries*
**cerveza** *beer*
**cesta de frutas** *selection of fresh fruit*
**champiñones** *mushrooms*

**chanquetes** *fish (similar to whitebait)*
**chipirones** *baby squid*
**chipirones en su tinta** *baby squid cooked in their ink*
**chocos** *cuttlefish*
**chocolate caliente** *hot chocolate*
**chorizo** *spicy sausage*
**chuleta de buey** *beef chop*
**chuleta de cerdo** *pork chop*
**chuleta de cerdo empanada** *breaded pork chop*
**chuleta de cordero** *lamb chop*
**chuleta de cordero empanada** *breaded lamb chop*
**chuleta de ternera** *veal chop*
**chuleta de ternera empanada** *breaded veal chop*
**chuletas de lomo ahumado** *smoked pork chops*
**chuletitas de cordero** *small lamb chops*
**chuletón** *large chop*
**chuletón de buey** *large beef chop*
**churros** *sweet, deep-fried dough sticks*
**cigalas** *Norway lobster*
**cigalas cocidas** *boiled Norway lobster*
**ciruelas** *plums*
**ciruelas pasas** *prunes*
**cochinillo asado** *roast suckling pig*
**cocido** *meat, chickpea, and vegetable stew*
**cocktail de bogavante** *lobster cocktail*
**cococha (de merluza)** *hake stew*
**cóctel de gambas** *shrimp cocktail*
**cóctel de langostinos** *jumbo shrimp cocktail*
**cóctel de mariscos** *seafood cocktail*
**codornices** *quails*
**codornices escabechadas** *marinated quails*
**codornices estofadas** *braised quails*
**col** *cabbage*
**coles de Bruselas** *Brussels sprouts*

**coliflor** *cauliflower*
**coñac** *brandy*
**conejo** *rabbit*
**conejo encebollado** *rabbit with onions*
**congrio** *conger eel*
**consomé con yema** *consommé with egg yolk*
**consomé de ave** *fowl consommé*
**contra de ternera con guisantes** *veal stew with peas*
**contrafilete de ternera** *veal fillet*
**copa** *glass (of wine)*
**copa de helado** *ice cream, assorted flavors*
**cordero asado** *roast lamb*
**cordero al chilindrón** *lamb stew with onion, tomato, peppers, and eggs*
**cortado** *espresso with a bit of milk*
**costillas de cerdo** *pork ribs*
**crema catalana** *crème brûlée*
**cremada** *dessert made with egg, sugar, and milk*
**crema de...** *cream of...soup*
**crema de legumbres** *cream of vegetable soup*
**crepe imperiale** *crêpe suzette*
**criadillas de tierra** *truffles*
**crocante** *ice cream with chopped nuts*
**croquetas** *croquettes*
**cuajada** *curds*

## D, E

**dátiles** *dates*
**embutidos** *sausages*
**embutidos de la tierra** *local sausages*
**empanada gallega** *fish pie*
**empanada santiaguesa** *fish pie*
**empanadillas** *small pies*
**endivia** *endive*
**en escabeche** *marinated*
**ensalada** *salad*
**ensalada de arenque** *fish salad*
**ensalada mixta** *mixed salad*
**ensalada simple** *green salad*
**ensaladilla rusa** *Russian salad (potatoes, carrots, peas, and other vegetables in mayonnaise)*
**entrecot a la parrilla** *grilled entrecôte*
**entremeses** *hors d'oeuvres, appetizers*
**escalope a la milanesa** *breaded veal with cheese*
**escalope a la parrilla** *grilled veal*
**escalope a la plancha** *grilled veal*

**escalope de lomo de cerdo** *escalope of pork fillet*
**escalope de ternera** *veal escalope*
**escalope empanado** *breaded escalope*
**escalopines al Marsala** *veal escalopes cooked in Marsala wine*
**escalopines de ternera** *veal escalopes*
**espadín a la toledana** *kebab*
**espaguetis** *spaghetti*
**espárragos** *asparagus*
**espárragos trigueros** *wild green asparagus*
**espinacas** *spinach*
**espinazo de cerdo con patatas** *stew of pork ribs with potatoes*
**estofado** *braised; stew*
**estragón** *tarragon*

## F

**fabada (asturiana)** *bean stew with sausage*
**faisán** *pheasant*
**faisán trufado** *pheasant with truffles*
**fiambres** *cold meats*
**fideos** *thin pasta, noodles*
**filete a la parrilla** *grilled beef steak*
**filete de cerdo** *pork steak*
**filete de ternera** *veal steak*
**flan** *crème caramel*
**frambuesas** *raspberries*
**fresas** *strawberries*
**fritos** *fried*
**fruta** *fruit*

## G

**gallina en pepitoria** *chicken stew with peppers*
**gambas** *shrimp*
**gambas cocidas** *boiled shrimp*
**gambas en gabardina** *shrimp in batter*
**gambas rebozadas** *shrimp in batter*
**garbanzos** *chickpeas*
**garbanzos a la catalana** *chickpeas with sausage, boiled eggs, and pine nuts*
**gazpacho andaluz** *cold tomato soup*
**gelatina de...** *...jelly*
**gratén de...** *...au gratin (baked in a cream and cheese sauce)*
**granizada** *crushed ice drink*
**gratinada/o** *au gratin*
**grelo** *turnip*

**grillado** *grilled*
**guisantes** *peas*
**guisantes salteados** *sautéed peas*

## H

**habas** *broad beans*
**habichuelas** *white beans*
**helado** *ice cream*
**helado de vainilla** *vanilla ice cream*
**helado de turrón** *nougat ice cream*
**hígado** *liver*
**hígado de ternera** *calf's liver*
**hígado estofado** *braised liver*
**higos con miel y nueces** *figs with honey and nuts*
**higos secos** *dried figs*
**horchata (de chufas)** *cold drink made from chufa nuts*
**huevo hilado** *egg yolk garnish*
**huevos** *eggs*
**huevos a la flamenca** *fried eggs with ham, tomato, and vegetables*
**huevos cocidos** *hard-boiled eggs*
**huevos con patatas fritas** *fried eggs and chips*
**huevos con picadillo** *eggs with minced meat*
**huevos duros** *hard-boiled eggs*
**huevos escalfados** *poached eggs*
**huevos pasados por agua** *soft-boiled eggs*
**huevos revueltos** *scrambled eggs*

## J, K

**jamón** *ham*
**jamón con huevo hilado** *ham with egg yolk garnish*
**jamón serrano** *cured ham*
**jarra de vino** *wine jug*
**jerez** *sherry*
**jeta** *pigs' cheeks*
**judías verdes** *green beans*
**judías verdes a la española** *bean stew*
**judías verdes al natural** *plain green beans*
**kebab** *grilled meat, pressed and cut in slices, most often put inside bread*

## L

**langosta** *lobster*
**langosta a la americana** *lobster with brandy and garlic*
**langosta a la catalana** *lobster with mushrooms and ham in white sauce*

**langosta fría con mayonesa** cold lobster with mayonnaise
**langostinos** king shrimp
**langostinos dos salsas** king shrimp cooked in two sauces
**laurel** bay leaves
**leche** milk
**leche frita** pudding made from milk and eggs
**leche merengada** milk shake with cinnamon
**lechuga** lettuce
**lengua de buey** ox tongue
**lengua de cordero** lamb's tongue
**lenguado a la romana** sole in batter
**lenguado meuniere** sole meunière (floured sole fried in butter)
**lentejas** lentils
**lentejas aliñadas** lentils in vinaigrette dressing
**licores** spirits, liqueurs
**liebre estofada** stewed hare
**lima** lime
**limón** lemon
**lombarda** red cabbage
**lomo curado** pork loin sausage
**lonchas de jamón** sliced, cured ham
**longaniza** cooked Spanish sausage
**lubina** sea bass
**lubina a la marinera** sea bass in a parsley sauce

# M

**macedonia de fruta** fruit salad
**mahonesa** or **mayonesa** mayonnaise
**Málaga** a sweet wine
**mandarinas** tangerines
**manitas de cordero** lamb shank
**manos de cerdo** pig's feet
**manos de cerdo a la parrilla** grilled pig's feet
**mantecadas** small sponge cakes
**mantequilla** butter
**manzanas** apples
**mariscada** cold mixed shellfish
**mariscos del día** fresh shellfish
**mariscos del tiempo** seasonal shellfish
**medallones** steaks
**media botella de agua** half bottle of mineral water
**mejillones** mussels
**mejillones a la marinera** mussels in a wine sauce
**melocotón** peach
**melón** melon
**menestra de legumbres** vegetable stew
**menú de la casa** set menu
**menú del día** set menu
**merluza** hake

**merluza a la cazuela** stewed hake
**merluza al ajo arriero** hake with garlic and chilies
**merluza a la riojana** hake with chilies
**merluza a la romana** hake steaks in batter
**merluza a la vasca** hake in a garlic sauce
**merluza en salsa** hake in sauce
**merluza en salsa verde** hake in a green (parsley and wine) sauce
**merluza fría** cold hake
**merluza frita** fried hake
**mermelada** jam
**mero** grouper (fish)
**mero en salsa verde** grouper in green (garlic and parsley) sauce
**mollejas de ternera fritas** fried sweetbreads
**morcilla** blood sausage
**morcilla de carnero** mutton blood sausage
**morros de cerdo** pig's cheeks
**morros de vaca** cow's cheeks
**mortadela** salami-type sausage
**morteruelo** kind of pâté

# N, O

**nabo** turnip
**naranjas** oranges
**nata** cream
**natillas** cold custard
**níscalos** wild mushrooms
**nueces** walnuts
**orejas de cerdo** pig's ears

# P

**paella** fried rice with seafood and/or meat
**paella castellana** meat paella
**paella valenciana** shellfish, rabbit, and chicken paella
**paleta de cordero lechal** shoulder of lamb
**pan** bread
**pan con jamón** bread with ham
**pan con tomate** bread with tomato
**panache de verduras** vegetable stew
**panceta** bacon
**parrillada de caza** mixed grilled game
**parrillada de mariscos** mixed grilled shellfish
**pasas** raisins
**pastel de ternera** veal pie
**pasteles** cakes
**patatas a la pescadora** potatoes with fish
**patatas asadas** baked potatoes

**patatas bravas** potatoes in spicy tomato sauce
**patatas fritas** chips
**patitos rellenos** stuffed duckling
**pato a la naranja** duck in orange sauce
**pavo** turkey
**pavo trufado** turkey stuffed with truffles
**pecho de ternera** breast of veal
**pechuga de pollo** breast of chicken
**pepinillos** gherkins
**pepino** cucumber
**peras** pears
**percebes** edible barnacle
**perdices a la campesina** partridges with vegetables
**perdices a la manchega** partridges in red wine, garlic, herbs, and pepper
**perdices escabechadas** marinated partridges
**perejil** parsley
**perritos calientes** hot dogs
**pescaditos fritos** fried fish
**pestiños** sugared pastries flavored with aniseed
**pez espada** swordfish
**picadillo de ternera** minced veal
**pimienta** black pepper
**pimientos** bell peppers
**pimientos a la riojana** baked red peppers fried in oil and garlic
**pimientos morrones** a type of bell pepper
**pimientos verdes** green peppers
**piña al gratín** pineapple au gratin
**piña fresca** fresh pineapple
**pinchitos/pinchos** meat grilled on a skewer, such as shish kebab; snacks served in bars
**pinchos morunos** pork kebabs
**piñones** pine nuts
**pisto** ratatouille
**pisto manchego** vegetable marrow with onion and tomato
**plátanos** bananas
**plátanos flameados** flambéed bananas
**pollo** chicken
**pollo a la riojana** chicken with peppers and chilies
**pollo al ajillo** fried chicken with garlic
**pollo asado** roast chicken
**pollo braseado** braised chicken
**pollo en cacerola** chicken casserole
**pollo en pepitoria** chicken in wine with saffron, garlic, and almonds
**pollos tomateros con zanahorias** young chicken with carrots

**pomelo** *grapefruit*
**porrusalda** *rustic soup with leeks, potatoes, carrots, and sometimes cod*
**potaje castellano** *thick broth*
**potaje de...** *...stew*
**puchero canario** *casserole of meat, chickpeas, and corn*
**pulpitos con cebolla** *baby octopus with onions*
**pulpo** *octopus*
**puré de patatas** *mashed potatoes, potato purée*

## Q

**queso con membrillo** *cheese with quince jelly*
**queso de bola** *Dutch cheese*
**queso de Burgos** *soft white cheese*
**queso del país** *local cheese*
**queso de oveja** *sheep's cheese*
**queso gallego** *a creamy cheese*
**queso manchego** *a hard, strong cheese*
**quisquillas** *shrimp*

## R

**rábanos** *radishes*
**ragout de ternera** *veal ragoût*
**rape a la americana** *monkfish with brandy and herbs*
**rape a la cazuela** *stewed monkfish*
**raya** *skate*
**rebozado** *in batter*
**redondo al horno** *roast filet of beef*
**rellenos** *stuffed*
**remolacha** *beetroot*
**repollo** *cabbage*
**repostería de la casa** *cakes baked on the premises*
**requesón** *cream cheese, cottage cheese*
**revuelto de...** *scrambled eggs with...*
**revuelto de ajos tiernos** *scrambled eggs with spring garlic*
**revuelto de trigueros** *scrambled eggs with asparagus*
**revuelto mixto** *scrambled eggs with mixed vegetables*
**riñones** *kidneys*
**rodaballo** *turbot (fish)*
**romero** *rosemary*
**ron** *rum*
**roscas** *sweet pastries*

## S

**sal** *salt*
**salchichas** *sausages*
**salchichas de Frankfurt** *hot dogs*
**salchichón** *sausage similar to salami*
**salmón ahumado** *smoked salmon*
**salmonetes** *red mullet*
**salmonetes en papillote** *red mullet cooked in foil*
**salmón frío** *cold salmon*
**salmorejo** *sauce of bread, tomatoes, oil, vinegar, green pepper, and garlic*
**salpicón de mariscos** *shellfish in vinaigrette*
**salsa bechamel** *white sauce*
**salsa holandesa** *hollandaise sauce*
**sandía** *watermelon*
**sardinas a la brasa** *barbecued sardines*
**seco** *dry*
**semidulce** *medium-sweet*
**sesos** *brains*
**sesos a la romana** *fried brains in batter*
**sesos rebozados** *brains in batter*
**setas** *mushrooms*
**sidra** *cider*
**sobreasada** *sausage with cayenne pepper*
**solomillo** *fillet steak*
**solomillo con patatas** *fillet steak with chips*
**solomillo de ternera** *fillet of veal*
**solomillo de vaca** *filet of beef*
**solomillo frío** *cold roast beef*
**sopa** *soup*
**sopa castellana** *vegetable soup*
**sopa de almendras** *almond soup*
**sopa de cola de buey** *oxtail soup*
**sopa de gallina** *chicken soup*
**sopa del día** *soup of the day*
**sopa de legumbres** *vegetable soup*
**sopa de marisco** *fish and shellfish soup*
**sopa de rabo de buey** *oxtail soup*
**sopa mallorquina** *soup of tomato, meat, and eggs*
**sopa sevillana** *fish and mayonnaise soup*
**soufflé de fresones** *strawberry soufflé*

## T

**tallarines** *noodles*
**tallarines a la italiana** *tagliatelle*
**tarta** *cake*
**tarta de la casa** *cake baked on the premises*
**tarta de manzana** *apple tart*

**té** *tea, usually black but can also refer to green, red, herbal, or fruit tea*
**té con leche** *tea with milk*
**té con limón** *tea with lemon*
**té negro** *black tea*
**tencas** *tench*
**ternera asada** *roast veal*
**tocinillos del cielo** *a very sweet crème caramel*
**tomates** *tomatoes*
**tomillo** *thyme*
**torrijas** *sweet pastries*
**tortilla a la paisana** *vegetable omelet*
**tortilla a su gusto** *omelet made to the customer's wishes*
**tortilla de escabeche** *fish omelet*
**tortilla española** *Spanish omelet with potato, onion, and garlic*
**tortilla sacromonte** *vegetable, brains, and sausage omelet*
**tortillas variadas** *assorted omelets*
**tostada con mantequilla y mermelada** *toast with butter and jam*
**tournedó** *fillet steak*
**trucha** *trout*
**trucha ahumada** *smoked trout*
**trucha escabechada** *marinated trout*
**truchas a la marinera** *trout in wine sauce*
**truchas molinera** *trout meunière (floured trout fried in butter)*
**trufas** *truffles*
**turrón** *nougat*

## U, V

**uvas** *grapes*
**verduras** *vegetables*
**vieiras** *scallops*
**vino de mesa/blanco/rosado/ tinto** *table/white/rosé/red wine*

## Z

**zanahorias a la crema** *creamed carrots*
**zarzuela de mariscos** *seafood stew*
**zarzuela de pescados y mariscos** *fish and shellfish stew*
**zumo de...** *...juice*

# Dictionary
## ENGLISH TO SPANISH

The gender of a Spanish noun is indicated by the word for *the*: **el** and **la** (masculine and feminine singular) or their plural forms **los** (masculine) and **las** (feminine). Spanish adjectives (adj) vary according to the gender and number of the word they describe, and the masculine form is shown here. In general, adjectives that end in **-o** adopt an **-a** ending in the feminine form, and those that end in **-e** usually stay the same. For the plural form, an **-s** is added.

## A

*a* **un/una**
*able* (verb): *to be able* **poder**
*about: about sixteen* **alrededor de dieciséis**
*accelerator* **el acelerador**
*accident* **el accidente**
*accommodations* **el alojamiento**
*accountant* **el/la contable**
*ache* **el dolor**
*across from the hotel* **enfrente del hotel**
*adaptor* **el adaptador**
*address* **la dirección**
*adhesive* **el pegamento**
*admission charge* **el precio de entrada**
*after…* **después de…**
*aftershave* **el after-shave**
*afternoon snack* **merienda**
*again* **otra vez**
*against* **contra**
*agenda* **el orden del día**
*agency* **la agencia**
*AIDS* **el sida**
*air* **el aire**
*air conditioning* **el aire acondicionado**
*aircraft* **el avión**
*airline* **la compañía aérea**
*air mail* **por avión**
*air mattress* **la colchoneta**
*airport* **el aeropuerto**
*airport bus* **el autobús del aeropuerto**
*aisle* **el pasillo**
*alarm clock* **el despertador**
*alcohol* **el alcohol**
*Algeria* **Argelia** (f)
*all* **todo;** *all the streets* **todas las calles;** *that's all* **eso es todo**
*allergic* (adj) **alérgico**
*almost* **casi**
*alone* (adj) **solo**
*already* **ya**
*always* **siempre**
*am: I am* **soy/estoy**
*ambulance* **la ambulancia**
*America* **América**
*American* **el americano/ la americana**

*and* **y;** (after "i" or "h") **e**
*angle-poise lamp* **el flexo**
*ankle* **el tobillo**
*another* **otro**
*answering machine* **el contestador automático**
*antifreeze* **el anticongelante**
*antiques shop* **el anticuario**
*antiseptic* **el antiséptico**
*apartment* (flat) **el apartamento, el piso**
*aperitif* **el aperitivo**
*appetite* **el apetito**
*apple* **la manzana**
*application form* **el impreso de solicitud**
*appointment* (business) **la cita;** (at hairdresser's) **hora**
*apricot* **el albaricoque**
*April* **abril**
*are: you are* (informal singular) **eres/estás;** (formal singular) **es/está;** (informal plural) **sois/ estáis;** (formal plural) **son/están;** *we are* **somos/ estamos;** *they are* **son/están**
*arm* **el brazo**
*armchair* **el sillón**
*arrive* (verb) **llegar**
*art* **el arte**
*art gallery* **la galería de arte**
*artichoke* **la alcachofa**
*artist* **el/la artista**
*as: as soon as possible* **lo antes posible**
*ashtray* **el cenicero**
*asleep: he's asleep* **está dormido**
*aspirin* **la aspirina**
*asthmatic* (adj) **asmático**
*at: at the post office* **en Correos;** *at night* **por la noche;** *at 3 o'clock* **a las tres**
*Atlantic Ocean* **el Océano Atlántico**
*ATM* **el cajero automático**
*attic* **el ático**
*attractive* (adj: person) **guapo;** (object) **bonito;** (adj: offer) **atractivo**

*audio guide* **la audioguía**
*August* **agosto**
*aunt* **la tía**
*Australia* **Australia**
*Australian* **el australiano/ la australiana;** (adj) **australiano**
*automatic* **automático**
*available* (adj) **disponible**
*away: is it far away?* **¿está lejos?;** *go away!* **¡váyase!**
*awful* (adj) **horrible**
*ax* **el hacha**
*axle* **el eje**

## B

*baby* **el niño pequeño, el bebé**
*baby wipes* **las toallitas para bebé**
*back* (not front) **la parte de atrás;** (body) **la espalda**
*backpack* **la mochila**
*bachelor's degree* **un grado**
*bacon* **el bacon;** *bacon and eggs* **los huevos fritos con bacon**
*bad* (adj) **malo**
*bag* **la bolsa**
*bait* **el cebo**
*bake* (verb) **cocer al horno**
*bakery* **la panadería**
*balcony* **el balcón**
*bald* (adj) **calvo**
*Balearic Islands* **las (Islas) Baleares**
*ball* (soccer, etc.) **el balón;** (tennis, etc.) **la pelota**
*ballpoint pen* **el bolígrafo**
*banana* **el plátano**
*band* (musicians) **la banda**
*bandage* **la venda**
*bangs* (hair) **el flequillo**
*bank* **el banco**
*bank card* **la tarjeta de banco**
*banknote* **el billete de banco**
*bar* (drinks) **el bar, la taberna**
*barbecue* **la barbacoa**
*barber* **la peluquería de caballeros (barbero)**

*bargain* **la ganga**
*basement* **el sótano**
*basin* (sink) **el lavabo**
*basket* **el cesto**
*basketball* **el baloncesto**
*bath* **el baño;** *to have a bath*
(verb) **darse un baño**
*bathroom* **el cuarto de baño**
*battery* (car) **la batería;**
(torch) **la pila**
*Bay of Biscay* **el Golfo
de Vizcaya**
*be* (verb) **ser/estar**
*beach* **la playa**
*beach ball* **el balón de playa**
*beans* **las judías**
*beard* **la barba**
*beautiful* (object) **precioso;**
(adj: person) **guapo**
*beauty products* **los
productos de belleza**
*because* **porque**
*bed* **la cama**
*bed linen* **la ropa de cama**
*bedroom* **el dormitorio**
*bedside lamp* **la lamparilla
de noche**
*bedside table* **la mesilla
de noche**
*bedspread* **la colcha**
*beef* **la carne de vaca**
*beer* **la cerveza**
*before…* **antes de…**
*beginner* **el/la principiante**
*behind…* **detrás de…**
*beige* **beige**
*bell* (church) **la campana;**
(door) **el timbre**
*below…* **debajo de…**
*belt* **el cinturón**
*beside* **al lado de**
*best* **el/la mejor**
*better* **mejor**
*between* **entre**
*bicycle* **la bicicleta**
*big* (adj) **grande**
*bill* **la cuenta**
*bin* **el contendor de
basura**
*bin liner* **la bolsa de
basura**
*binoculars* **los gemelos**
*bird* **el pájaro**
*birthday* **el cumpleaños;**
*happy birthday!*
**¡felicidades!**
*birthday present* **el regalo
de cumpleaños**
*biscuit* **la galleta**
*bite* (by dog) **la mordedura;**
(by insect) **la picadura;**
(verb: by dog) **morder;**
(verb: by insect) **picar**
*black* (adj) **negro**
*blackberries* **las moras**
*black currants* **las grosellas
negras**

*blanket* **la manta**
*bleach* **la lejía;** (verb:
hair) **teñir**
*blind* (adj) (cannot see)
**ciego**
*blinds* **las persianas**
*blister* **la ampolla**
*blizzard* **la ventisca**
*blond(e)* (adj) **el rubio/
la rubia**
*blood* **la sangre**
*blood test* **el análisis
de sangre**
*blouse* **la blusa**
*blue* (adj) **azul**
*boarding pass* **la tarjeta
de embarque**
*boat* **el barco;** (small)
**la barca**
*body* **el cuerpo**
*boil* (verb: water) **hervir;**
(egg, etc.) **cocer**
*boiled* (adj) **hervido**
*bolt* (on door) **el cerrojo;**
(verb) **echar el cerrojo**
*bone* **el hueso**
*book* **el libro;** (verb) **reservar**
*bookshop* **la librería**
*boot* (footwear) **la bota**
*border* **el borde;** (between
countries) **la frontera**
*boring* (adj) **aburrido**
*born: I was born in…*
**nací en…**
*both: both of them* **los dos;**
*both of us* **los dos;** *both…
and…* **tanto…como…**
*bottle* **la botella**
*bottle opener* **el
abrebotellas**
*bottom* **el fondo;** (part of
body) **el trasero**
*bowl* **el cuenco**
*box* **la caja**
*box office* (theater, etc.) **la
taquilla**
*boy* **el chico**
*boyfriend* **el novio**
*bra* **el sostén**
*bracelet* **la pulsera**
*braces* (clothing) **los
tirantes**
*brake* **el freno;** (verb) **frenar**
*branch* (of company) **la
oficina**
*brandy* **el coñac**
*bread* **el pan;** *bread with
ham* **el pan con jamón;**
*bread with tomato* **el pan
con tomate**
*breakdown* (car) **la avería;**
(nervous) **la crisis
nerviosa;** *I've had
a breakdown* (car)
**he tenido una avería**
*breakfast* **el desayuno**
*breathe* (verb) **respirar**

*bricklayer* **el/la albañil**
*bridge* **el puente;** (game)
**el bridge**
*briefcase* **la cartera**
*British* **británico**
*brochure* **el folleto**
*broken* (adj) **roto**
*brooch* **el broche**
*brother* **el hermano**
*brown* (adj) **marrón;** (hair)
**castaño;** (skin) **moreno**
*bruise* **el cardenal**
*brush* (paint) **la brocha;**
(cleaning) **el cepillo;**
(hair) **el cepillo del pelo;**
(verb: hair) **cepillar el pelo**
*budget* **el presupuesto**
*bucket* **el cubo**
*builder* **el constructor/la
constructora**
*building* **el edificio**
*bull* **el toro**
*bullfight* **la corrida de
toros**
*bullfighter* **el torero**
*bullring* **la plaza de
toros**
*burglar* **el ladrón**
*burn* **la quemadura;**
(verb) **quemar**
*bus* **el autobús**
*business* **el negocio;** *business
proposal* **la propuesta;**
*it's none of your business*
**no es asunto suyo**
*business card* **la tarjeta
de vista**
*bus station* **la estación
de autobús**
*busy* (adj) (bar) **concurrido;**
(engaged) **ocupado**
*but* **pero**
*butcher's* **la carnicería**
*butter* **la mantequilla**
*button* **el botón**
*buy* (verb) **comprar**
*by: by the window* **junto a la
ventana;** *by Friday* **para el
viernes;** *by myself* **yo solo;**
*written by* **escrito por**

# C

*cabbage* **la col**
*cable car* **el teleférico**
*cable TV* **la televisión
por cable**
*cafeteria* **el café**
*cage* **la jaula**
*cake* (small) **el pastel;**
(large) **la tarta;**
*sponge cake* **el bizcocho**
*cake shop* **la pastelería**
*calculator* **la calculadora**
*call: what's it called?* **¿cómo
se llama?**
*camcorder* **la videocámara**

*camera* **la máquina de fotos, la cámara de fotos**
*camper van* **la autocaravana**
*campfire* **la hoguera**
*camping gas* **el camping gas**
*campsite* **el camping**
*campsite office* **la oficina del camping**
*camshaft* **el árbol de levas**
*can* (tin) **la lata;** (verb: to be able) **poder;** *can you...?* **¿puede...?;** *I can't...* **no puedo...**
*Canada* **Canadá**
*Canadian* **canadiense**
*canal* **el canal**
*Canaries* **las (Islas) Canarias**
*candle* **la vela**
*can opener* **el abrelatas**
*cap* (bottle) **el tapón;** (hat) **la gorra**
*car* **el coche**
*caravan* **la caravana**
*carburetor* **el carburador**
*card* **la tarjeta**
*cardigan* **la rebeca**
*careful* (adj) **prudente;** *be careful!* **¡cuidado!**
*caretaker* **el portero, el encargado**
*carpenter* **el carpintero/la carpintera**
*carpet* **la alfombra**
*carriage* (train) **el vagón**
*carrot* **la zanahoria**
*carry-on bag* **el equipaje de mano**
*car seat* (for a baby) **la silla de bebé**
*case* (suitcase) **la maleta**
*cash* **el efectivo;** *to cash* (verb) **cobrar;** *to pay cash* (verb) **pagar al contado**
*cashier* **el cajero**
*cashpoint* **el cajero automático**
*castanets* **las castañuelas**
*Castile* **Castilla**
*Castilian* **castellano**
*castle* **el castillo**
*cat* **el gato**
*Catalonia* **Cataluña**
*catch* (verb) (bus, etc.) **coger**
*cathedral* **la catedral**
*Catholic* (adj) **católico**
*cauliflower* **la coliflor**
*cave* **la cueva**
*ceiling* **el techo**
*cellar* **la bodega**
*cell phone* **el móvil, el celular**
*cemetery* **el cementerio**
*center* **el centro**
*central heating* **la calefacción central**

*certificate* **el certificado**
*chair* **la silla**
*change* (money) **el cambio;** (verb: money) **cambiar;** (clothes) **cambiarse;** (trains, etc.) **hacer transbordo**
*charger* **el cargador**
*charging cable* **el cable de carga**
*charging point/station* **el punto/la estación de carga**
*check* **el cheque**
*checkbook* **el talonario de cheques**
*check in* (verb) **facturar**
*check-in* (desk) **la (el mostrador de) facturación**
*checkout* (supermarket) **la caja**
*cheers!* (toast) **¡salud!**
*cheese* **el queso**
*cherry* **la cereza**
*chess* **el ajedrez**
*chest* (part of body) **el pecho;** (furniture) **el arcón**
*chest of drawers* **la cómoda**
*chewing gum* **el chicle**
*chicken* **el pollo**
*child* **el niño/la niña**
*children* **los niños/las niñas**
*children's ward* **la sala de pediatría**
*chimney* **la chimenea**
*china* **la porcelana**
*chips* **las patatas fritas**
*chocolate* **el chocolate;** *box of chocolates* **la caja de bombones;** *chocolate bar* **la tableta de chocolate;** *hot chocolate* **chocolate caliente**
*chop* (food) **la chuleta;** (verb: cut) **cortar**
*Christmas* **la Navidad**
*church* **la iglesia**
*cigar* **el puro**
*cigarette* **el cigarrillo**
*cinema* **el cine**
*city* **la ciudad**
*city center* **el centro de la ciudad**
*class* **la clase**
*classical music* **la música clásica**
*clean* (adj) **limpio;** (verb) **limpiar**
*cleaning staff* **la persona de la limpieza**
*clear* (obvious) **evidente;** (adj: water) **claro**
*clever* (adj) **listo**
*client* **el cliente**

*clock* **el reloj;** *wall clock* **el reloj de pared**
*close* (near) **cerca;** (stuffy) **sofocante;** (verb) **cerrar**
*closed* (adj) **cerrado**
*clothes* **la ropa**
*clubs* (cards) **tréboles**
*coat* **el abrigo**
*coat hanger* **la percha**
*cockroach* **la cucaracha**
*cocktail party* **el coctel**
*coffee* **el café**
*coin* **la moneda**
*cold* (illness) **el resfriado;** (adj) **frío;** *I have a cold* **tengo un resfriado;** *I'm cold* **tengo frío**
*collar* **el cuello;** (of animal) **el collar**
*collection* (stamps, etc.) **la colección;** (postal) **la recogida**
*color* **el color**
*color film* **la película en color**
*comb* **el peine;** (verb) **peinar**
*come* (verb) **venir;** *I come from...* **soy de...;** *we came last week* **llegamos la semana pasada;** *come here!* **¡venga aquí!**
*come back* **volver**
*compact disc* **el disco compacto**
*compartment* **el compartimento**
*complicated* (adj) **complicado**
*computer* **el ordenador**
*computer games* **los videojuegos**
*concert* **el concierto**
*conditioner* (hair) **el acondicionador**
*condom* **el condón**
*conductor* (bus) **el cobrador;** (orchestra) **el director**
*conference* **la conferencia**
*conference room* **la sala de conferencias**
*congratulations!* **¡enhorabuena!**
*consulate* **el consulado**
*consultant* **el consultor/la consultora**
*contact lenses* **las lentes de contacto**
*contraceptive* **el anticonceptivo**
*contract* **el contrato**
*cook* **el cocinero/la cocinera;** (verb) **guisar**
*cooking utensils* **los utensilios de cocina**
*cool* (adj) **fresco**
*cork* **el corcho**
*corkscrew* **el sacacorchos**
*corner* (of street) **la esquina;** (of room) **el rincón**

*corridor* **el pasillo**
*cosmetics* **los cosméticos**
*cost* (verb) **costar;** *what does it cost?* **¿cuánto cuesta?**
*cot* **la cuna**
*cotton* **el algodón**
*cotton wool* **el algodón**
*cough* **la tos;** (verb) **toser**
*cough drops* **las pastillas para la garganta**
*country* (state) **el país**
*countryside* **el campo**
*cousin* **el primo/la prima**
*crab* **el cangrejo**
*cramp* **el calambre**
*crayfish* **el cangrejo de río**
*cream* (dairy) **la nata;** (lotion) **la crema**
*credit card* **la tarjeta de crédito**
*crib* **el capazo**
*crowded* (adj) **lleno**
*cruise* **el crucero**
*crutches* **las muletas**
*cry* (verb) (weep) **llorar;** (shout) **gritar**
*cucumber* **el pepino**
*cuff links* **los gemelos**
*cup* **la taza**
*cupboard* **el armario**
*curlers* **los rulos**
*curls* **los rizos**
*curry* **el curry**
*curtain* **la cortina**
*cushion* **el cojín**
*customs* **la aduana**
*cut* **la cortadura;** (verb) **cortar**
*cycling* **el ciclismo**

# D

*dad* **papá**
*dairy products* **los productos lácteos**
*damp* (adj) **húmedo**
*dance* **el baile;** (verb) **bailar**
*dangerous* (adj) **peligroso**
*dark* **oscuro;** *dark blue* **azul oscuro**
*daughter* **la hija**
*day* **el día**
*dead* (adj) **muerto**
*deaf* (adj) **sordo**
*dear* (adj) (person) **querido**
*debit card* **la tarjeta de débito**
*December* **diciembre**
*deck of cards* **la baraja**
*decorator* **el pintor/la pintora**
*deep* (adj) **profundo**
*delayed* (adj) **retrasado**
*deliberately* **a propósito**
*delicatessen* **la charcutería**
*delivery* **la entrega**

*dentist* **el/la dentista**
*dentures* **la dentadura postiza**
*deny* (verb) **negar**
*deodorant* **el desodorante**
*department* **el departamento**
*department store* **los grandes almacenes**
*departure* **la salida**
*departures* (airport, etc.) **las salidas**
*deposit* **la señal**
*designer* **el diseñador/la diseñadora**
*desk* **la mesa de escritorio**
*dessert* **el postre**
*develop* (verb) (film) **revelar**
*diabetic* (adj) **diabético**
*diamonds* (jewels) **los diamantes;** (cards) **los diamantes**
*diaper* **el pañal**
*diarrhea* **la diarrea**
*diary* **la agenda**
*dictionary* **el diccionario**
*die* (verb) **morir**
*diesel* (oil) **el gasoil;** (adj: engine) **diésel**
*different* (adj) **diferente;** *that's different!* **¡eso es distinto!;** *I'd like a different one* **quisiera otro distinto**
*difficult* (adj) **difícil**
*dining room* **el comedor**
*dinner* **la cena**
*dinner party* **la cena**
*dirty* **sucio**
*disabled* (adj) **minusválido**
*discount* **el descuento**
*dish towel* **el paño de cocina**
*dishwasher* **el lavavajillas**
*dishwashing liquid* **el líquido lavavajillas**
*disposable nappies* **los pañales desechables**
*divorced* (adj) **divorciado**
*do* (verb) **hacer**
*dock* **el muelle**
*doctor* **el médico/la médica**
*document* **el documento**
*dog* **el perro**
*doll* **la muñeca**
*dollar* **el dólar**
*door* **la puerta**
*double room* **la habitación doble**
*doughnut* **el dónut**
*down* **hacia abajo**
*dress* **el vestido**
*drink* **la bebida;** (verb) **beber;** *would you like something to drink?* **¿quiere beber algo?**

*drinking water* **agua potable**
*drive* (verb: car) **conducir**
*driver* **el conductor/la conductora**
*driver's license* **el carnet de conducir**
*drops* **las gotas**
*drugstore* **droguería**
*drunk* (adj) **borracho**
*dry* (adj) **seco;** (sherry) **fino**
*dry cleaner* **la tintorería**
*during* **durante**
*duster* **el trapo del polvo**
*duty-free* **libre de impuestos;** *duty-free shop* **el duty-free**
*duvet* **el edredón**

# E

*each* (every) **cada;** *20 euros each* **veinte euros cada uno**
*ear* (inner) **el oído;** (outer) **la oreja;** *ears* **las orejas**
*earbuds* **los auriculares**
*early* **temprano**
*earrings* **los pendientes**
*east* **este;** *the East* **el Este**
*easy* (adj) **fácil**
*eat* (verb) **comer**
*egg* **el huevo**
*eggplants* **las berenjenas**
*eight* **ocho**
*eighteen* **dieciocho**
*eighty* **ochenta**
*either: either of them* **cualquiera de ellos;** *either... or* **bien... o...**
*elastic* **elástico**
*elbow* **el codo**
*electric* **eléctrico**
*electric car* **el coche eléctrico**
*electrician* **el/la electricista**
*electricity* **la electricidad**
*eleven* **once**
*else: something else* **algo más;** *someone else* **alguien más;** *somewhere else* **en otro sitio**
*email* **el email, el correo electrónico**
*email address* **la dirección de email**
*embarrassing* (adj) **embarazoso**
*embassy* **la embajada**
*embroidery* **el bordado**
*emergency* **la emergencia**
*emergency brake* (train) **el freno de emergencia**
*emergency department* **el servicio de urgencias**
*emergency exit* **la salida de emergencia**

employee **el empleado/ la empleada**
empty (adj) **vacío**
end **el final**
engaged (marriage) **prometido/prometida;** (telephone) **ocupado**
engine (car) **el motor**
engineering **la ingeniería**
England **Inglaterra** (f)
English **inglés**
Englishman **el inglés**
Englishwoman **la inglesa**
enlargement **la ampliación**
enough **bastante**
entertainment **las diversiones**
entrance **la entrada**
envelope **el sobre**
epileptic (adj) **epiléptico**
eraser **la goma de borrar**
escalator **la escalera mecánica**
especially **sobre todo**
espresso **el café solo;** espresso with a bit of milk **el cortado**
estimate **el presupuesto**
evening **la tarde**
every **cada;** every day **todos los días**
everyone **todos**
everything **todo**
everywhere **por todas partes**
example **el ejemplo;** for example **por ejemplo**
excellent (adj) **excelente**
excess baggage **exceso de equipaje**
exchange (verb) **cambiar**
exchange rate **el cambio**
excursion **la excursión**
excuse me! (verb) (to get attention) **¡oiga, por favor!;** (when sneezing etc) **¡perdón!;** excuse me, please (to get past) **¿me hace el favor?**
executive (in company) **el ejecutivo**
exhaust (car) **el tubo de escape**
exhibition **la exposición**
exit **la salida**
expensive (adj) **caro**
extension cord **el cable alargador**
eye **el ojo**
eyebrow **la ceja**

# F

face **la cara**
face mask **la mascarilla**
faint (unclear) **tenue;** (verb) **desmayarse;** I feel faint **estoy mareado**

fair (adj: just) **la feria;** it's not fair **no hay derecho**
false teeth **la dentadura postiza**
family **la familia**
fan (enthusiast) **el fan;** (soccer) **el hincha;** (ventilator) **el ventilador;** (handheld) **el abanico**
fantastic **fantástico**
far **lejos;** how far is it to...? **¿qué distancia hay a...?**
fare **el billete, la tarifa**
farm **la granja**
farmer **el granjero**
fashion **la moda**
fast (adj) **rápido**
fat (adj: person) **gordo;** (on meat, etc.) **la grasa**
father **el padre**
fax (verb) **enviar por fax**
February **febrero**
feel (verb) (touch) **tocar;** I feel hot **tengo calor;** I feel like... **me apetece...;** I don't feel well **no me encuentro bien**
felt-tip pen **el rotulador**
fence **la cerca**
ferry **el ferry**
fiancé **el prometido**
fiancée **la prometida**
field (of grass, etc.) **el campo;** (of study) **la especialidad**
fifteen **quince**
fifty **cincuenta**
fig **el higo**
figures **los números**
filling (in tooth) **el empaste;** (in sandwich, cake) **el relleno**
film **la película**
filter **el filtro**
filter papers **los papeles de filtro**
finger **el dedo**
fire **el fuego;** (blaze) **el incendio**
fire extinguisher **el extintor**
fireplace **la chimenea**
fireworks **los fuegos artificiales**
first **primero**
first aid **primeros auxilios**
first class **de primera**
first floor **el primer piso**
first name **el nombre de pila**
fish **el pez;** (food) **el pescado**
fishing **la pesca;** to go fishing (verb) **ir a pescar**
fishmonger's **la pescadería**
five **cinco**
fizzy water **el agua con gas**

flash (camera) **el flash**
flat (apartment) **el apartamento, el piso;** (adj.) (level) **plano**
flat tire **la rueda pinchada**
flavor **el sabor**
flea **la pulga**
flea spray **el spray antipulgas**
flight **el vuelo;** flight number **el número de vuelo**
floor (ground) **el suelo;** (story) **el piso**
flour **la harina**
flower **la flor**
flowerbed **el parterre**
flute **la flauta**
fly (insect) **la mosca;** (verb: of plane, insect) **volar;** (verb: of person) **viajar en avión**
flyover **el paso elevado**
fog **la niebla**
folk music **la música folclórica**
food **la comida**
food poisoning **la intoxicación alimenticia**
foot **el pie**
for: for me **para mí;** what for? **¿para qué?;** for a week **(para) una semana**
foreigner **el extranjero/ la extranjera**
forest **el bosque;** (tropical) **la selva**
forget (verb) **olvidar**
fork **el tenedor;** (garden) **la horca**
forty **cuarenta**
fountain **la fuente**
fountain pen **la (pluma) estilográfica**
four **cuatro**
fourteen **catorce**
fourth **cuarto**
France **Francia**
free (not engaged) **libre;** (adj: no charge) **gratis**
freezer **el congelador**
French **francés**
Friday **viernes**
fridge **el frigorífico**
fried (adj) **frito**
friend **el amigo/la amiga**
friendly (adj) **simpático**
front: in front of... **delante de...**
frost **la escarcha**
frozen foods **los congelados**
fruit **la fruta**
fruit juice **el zumo de frutas**
fry (verb) **freír**
frying pan **la sartén**
full (verb) **lleno;** I'm full (up) **estoy lleno**

*full board* **pensión completa**
*funny* (adj) **divertido**; (odd)
  **raro**
*furniture* **los muebles**

# G

*garage* (for parking) **el
  garage**; (for repairs)
  **el taller**
*garden* **el jardín**
*garden center* **el vivero**
*garlic* **el ajo**
*gas* **la gasolina**
*gas-permeable lenses*
  **las lentes de contacto
  semirígidas**
*gas station* **la gasolinera**
*gate* **la puerta, la verja**;
  (at airport) **la puerta
  de embarque**
*gay* (homosexual) **gay**
*gear stick* **la palanca
  de velocidades**
*gel* (hair) **el gel**
*German* **alemán**
*Germany* **Alemania** (f)
*get* (verb) (fetch) **traer**; *have
  you got...?* **¿tiene...?**; *to
  get the train* (verb) **coger
  el tren** *get back: we get
  back tomorrow* **nos
  volvemos mañana**; *to get
  something back* (verb)
  **recobrar algo**
*get in* (verb) (train, etc.)
  **subirse**; (of person) **llegar**
*get off* (verb) (bus, etc.)
  **bajarse**
*get on* (verb) (bus, etc.)
  **subirse**
*get out* (verb) **bajarse**;
  (bring out) **sacar**
*get up* (verb) (rise)
  **levantarse**
*Gibraltar* **Gibraltar**
*gift* **el regalo**
*gin* **la ginebra**
*ginger* (spice) **el jengibre**
*girl* **la chica**
*girlfriend* **la novia**
*give* (verb) **dar**
*give way* (verb) **el ceda el
  paso**
*glad* (adj) **alegre**
*glass* (material) **el cristal**;
  (for drinking) **el vaso,
  la copa**
*glasses* (spectacles) **las
  gafas**
*glossy prints* **las copias
  con brillo**
*gloves* **los guantes**
*glue* **el pegamento**
*go* (verb) **ir**
*gold* **el oro**
*good* **bueno**; *good!* **¡bien!**

*good afternoon* **buenas
  tardes**
*goodbye* **adiós**
*good evening* **buenas
  noches**
*good morning* **buenos días**
*government* **el gobierno**
*granddaughter* **la nieta**
*grandfather* **el abuelo**
*grandmother* **la abuela**
*grandparents* **los abuelos**
*grandson* **el nieto**
*grapes* **las uvas**
*grass* **la hierba**
*gray* (adj) **gris**
*Great Britain* **Gran Bretaña**
*green* **verde**
*grill* **la parrilla**
*grilled* **a la plancha**
*grocer's* **el ultramarinos,
  la tienda de alimentación**
*grocery* **la frutería**
*ground floor* **la planta baja**
*ground sheet* **la lona
  impermeable,
  el suelo aislante**
*guarantee* **la garantía**;
  (verb) **garantizar**
*guest* **la invitada**
*guide* **el/la guía**
*guidebook* **la guía turística**
*guided tour* **la visita con
  guía**
*guitar* **la guitarra**
*gun* (rifle) **la escopeta**;
  (pistol) **la pistola**

# H

*hair* **el pelo**
*haircut* **el corte de pelo**
*hairdresser's* **la peluquería**
*hairdryer* **el secador
  (de pelo)**
*hairspray* **la laca**
*half* **medio**; *half an
  hour* **media hora**
*half board* **media pensión**
*ham* **el jamón**
*hamburger* **la hamburguesa**
*hammer* **el martillo**
*hamster* **el hámster**
*hand* **la mano**
*handbag* **el bolso**
*handbrake* **el freno de mano**
*handle* (door) **el picaporte**
*hand sanitizer* **el
  desinfectante de manos**
*handshake* **el apretón
  de manos**
*handsome* (adj) **guapo**
*hangover* **la resaca**
*happy* (adj) **contento, feliz**
*harbor* **el puerto**
*hard* (adj) **duro**; (difficult)
  **difícil**
*hardware store* **la ferretería**

*hat* **el sombrero**; (woollen)
  **el gorro**
*have* **tener**; *I don't have...*
  **no tengo...**; *do you have...?*
  **¿tiene...?**; *I have to go*
  **tengo que irme**; *can I
  have...?* **¿me pone...?**
*hay fever* **la fiebre del heno**
*he* **él**
*head* **la cabeza**
*headache* **el dolor de
  cabeza**
*headlights* **los faros**
*headphones* **los cascos**
*hear* (verb) **oír**
*hearing aid* **el audífono**
*heart* **el corazón**
*hearts* (cards) **los corazones**
*heater* **la estufa**
*heating* **la calefacción**
*heavy* (adj) **pesado**
*hedge* **el seto**
*heel* **el talón**; (shoe) **el
  tacón**
*hello* **hola**; (on phone)
  **dígame**
*help* **la ayuda**; (verb) **ayudar**
*hepatitis* **la hepatitis**
*her: it's for her* **es para ella**;
  *her book* **su libro**; *her
  shoes* **sus zapatos**;
  *it's hers* **es suyo**; *give
  it to her* **déselo**
*high* (adj) **alto**
*highway* **la autopista**
*hiking* **el senderismo**
*hill* **el monte**
*him: it's for him* **es para
  él**; *give it to him*
  **déselo**
*hire* (verb) **alquilar**
*his: his book* **su libro**; *his
  shoes* **sus zapatos**; *it's
  his* **es suyo**
*history* **la historia**
*hitchhike* (adj) **hacer
  autostop**
*HIV-positive* **seropositivo**
*hobby* **el hobby**
*home* **la casa**; *at home*
  **en casa**
*homeopathy* **la homeopatía**
*honest* (adj) **honrado**;
  (sincere) **sincero**
*honey* **la miel**
*honeymoon* **el viaje de
  novios**
*horn* (car) **el claxon**;
  (animal) **el cuerno**
*horrible* (adj) **horrible**
*hospital* **el hospital**
*hostess* **la anfitriona**
*hot chocolate* **el chocolate
  caliente**
*hour* **la hora**
*house* **la casa**; *small house*
  **la casa pequeña**

*household products* **los productos de limpieza**
*housekeeping* (at a hotel) **el servicio de limpieza**
*hovercraft* **el aerodeslizador**
*how?* **¿cómo?**
*how are you?* **¿qué tal?**
*hundred* **cien**
*hungry: I'm hungry* **tengo hambre**
*hurry: I'm in a hurry* **tengo prisa**
*husband* **el marido**
*hydrofoil* **la hidroaleta**

# I

*I* **yo**
*ice* **el hielo**
*ice cream* **el helado**
*ice skates* **los patines para hielo**
*if* **si**
*ignition* **el encendido**
*immediately* **inmediatamente**
*impossible* **imposible**
*in* **en**; *in English* **en inglés**; *in the hotel* **en el hotel**; *in Barcelona* **en Barcelona**; *he's not in* **no está**
*included* **incluido**
*indicator* **el intermitente**
*indigestion* **la indigestión**
*inexpensive* (adj) **barato**
*infection* **la infección**
*information* **la información**
*inhaler* (for asthma, etc.) **el spray, el inhalador**
*injection* **la inyección**
*injury* **la herida**
*ink* **la tinta**
*inn* **la fonda**
*inner tube* **la cámara (neumática)**
*insect* **el insecto**
*insect repellent* **la loción antimosquitos**
*insomnia* **el insomnio**
*instant coffee* **el café instantáneo**
*insurance* **el seguro**
*interesting* (adj) **interesante**
*Internet* **el internet**
*interpret* (verb) **interpretar**
*interpreter* **el/la intérprete**
*intravenous drip* **el gotero**
*invitation* **la invitación**
*invoice* **la factura**
*Ireland* **Irlanda** (f)
*Irish* **irlandés/irlandesa**
*iron* (metal) **el hierro**; (for clothes) **la plancha**; (verb) **planchar**
*is* **es/está**
*island* **la isla**
*it* **lo/la**

*Italian* (adj) **italiano/ italiana** (m/f)
*Italy* **Italia** (f)
*its* **su**

# J

*jacket* **la chaqueta**
*jam* **la mermelada**
*January* **enero**
*jazz* **el jazz**
*jeans* **los tejanos, los vaqueros**
*jellyfish* **la medusa**
*jeweler's* **la joyería**
*job* **el trabajo**
*jog* (verb) **hacer footing**
*joke* **la broma**; (funny story) **el chiste**
*journey* **el viaje**
*juice* **el zumo**
*July* **julio**
*June* **junio**
*just* (only) **solo**; *it's just arrived* **acaba de llegar**

# K

*kettle* **el hervidor de agua**
*key* **la llave**
*keyboard* **el teclado**
*kidney* **el riñón**
*kilo* **el kilo**
*kilometer* **el kilómetro**
*kitchen* **la cocina**
*knee* **la rodilla**
*knife* **el cuchillo**
*knit* (verb) **hacer punto**
*knitwear* **los artículos de punto**
*know* (verb) **saber**; (person, place) **conocer**; *I don't know* **no sé**

# L

*label* **la etiqueta**
*lace* **el encaje**
*laces* (shoe) **los cordones (de los zapatos)**
*lady* **la señora**
*lake* **el lago**
*lamb* **el cordero**
*lamp* **la lámpara, el flexo**
*lampshade* **la pantalla**
*land* **la tierra**; (verb) **aterrizar**
*language* **el idioma**
*laptop* **el portátil**
*large* (adj) **grande**
*last* (final) **último**; *at last!* **¡por fin!**; *last week* **la semana pasada**
*late: it's getting late* **se está haciendo tarde**; *the bus is late* **el autobús se ha retrasado**

*later* **más tarde**
*laugh* (verb) **reír**
*laundry* (dirty) **la ropa sucia**; (washed) **la colada**
*law* (subject) **el derecho**
*lawn* **el césped**
*lawn mower* **la máquina cortacésped**
*lawyer* **el abogado/ la abogada**
*laxative* **el laxante**
*lazy* (adj) **perezoso**
*lead* **la correa**
*leaf* **la hoja**
*leaflet* **el folleto**
*learn* (verb) **aprender**
*leather* **el cuero**
*lecture hall* **el anfiteatro**
*lecturer* (university) **el profesor/la profesora**
*left* (not right) **izquierdo**; *there's nothing left* **no queda nada**
*leg* **la pierna**
*lemon* **el limón**
*lemonade* **la limonada**
*length* **la longitud**
*lens* (camera) **la lente**
*less* **menos**
*lesson* **la clase**
*letter* (mail) **la carta**; (of alphabet) **la letra**
*lettuce* **la lechuga**
*library* **la biblioteca**
*license* **el permiso**
*license plate* **la matrícula**
*life* **la vida**
*lift* **el ascensor**
*light* **la luz**; (adj) (not heavy) **ligero**; (not dark) **claro**
*light bulb* **la bombilla**
*lighter* **el encendedor**
*lighter fluid* **el gas para el encendedor**
*light meter* **el fotómetro**
*like* (verb): *I like…* **me gusta…**; *I like swimming* **me gusta nadar**; *it's like…* **es como…**; *like this one* (similar to) **como este**
*lime* (fruit) **la lima**
*line* **la cola**; (phone, etc.) **línea**; (verb) **hacer cola**
*lipstick* **la barra de labios**
*liqueur* **el licor**
*list* **la lista**
*liter* **el litro**
*literature* **la literatura**
*litter* **la basura**
*little* (adj) (small) **pequeño**; *it's a little big* **es un poco grande**; *just a little* **solo un poquito**
*liver* **el hígado**

*living room* **el cuarto de estar**
*lobster* **la langosta**
*lollipop* **el chupa-chups**
*long* (adj) **largo**
*lost property office* **la oficina de objetos perdidos**
*lot: a lot* **mucho**
*loud* (adj) **alto**
*lounge* (in house) **el cuarto de estar;** (in hotel etc) **el salón**
*love* **el amor;** (verb) **querer;** *I love Spain* **me encanta España**
*lover* **el/la amante**
*low* (adj) **bajo**
*low hill* **la colina baja**
*luck: good luck!* **¡suerte!**
*luggage* **el equipaje**
*luggage rack* **la rejilla de equipajes**
*lunch* **la comida**

# M

*mad* **loco**
*madam* **señora**
*magazine* **la revista**
*mail* **el correo**
*mailbox* **el buzón**
*mailman* **el cartero**
*mailwoman* **la cartera**
*main course* **el plato principal**
*main road* **la calle principal**
*Majorca* **Mallorca**
*make* (verb) **hacer**
*makeup* **el maquillaje**
*man* **el hombre**
*manager* **el/la gerente, el jefe/la jefa;** (hotel) **el director/la directora**
*many* **muchos/muchas;** *many thanks* **muchas gracias;** *many people* **mucha gente;** *how many* **¿cuántos?;** *too many* **demasiados;** *not many* **no muchos**
*map* **el mapa;** *town map/plan* **el plano de la ciudad;** *online map* **los mapas en línea**
*marble* **el mármol**
*March* **marzo**
*margarine* **la margarina**
*market* **el mercado**
*marmalade* **la mermelada de naranja**
*married* (adj) **casado**
*mascara* **el rímel**
*mask* (face) **la mascarilla**
*mass* (church) **la misa**
*master's degree* **un máster**

*match* (light) **la cerilla;** (sport) **el partido**
*material* (cloth) **la tela**
*matter: it doesn't matter* **no importa**
*mattress* **el colchón**
*May* **mayo**
*maybe* **quizás**
*me: it's for me* **es para mí;** *give it to me* **démelo**
*meal* **la comida**
*mean: what does this mean?* **¿qué significa esto?**
*meat* **la carne;** *grilled meat* (on a skewer) **la brocheta, el pinchitos/pinchos;** *grilled meat* (pressed and cut in slices) **el kebab**
*mechanic* **el mecánico/la mecánica**
*medicine* (subject) **la medicina**
*Mediterranean* **el Mediterráneo**
*medium* (sherry) **amontillado**
*medium-dry* (wine) **semiseco**
*meeting* **la reunión**
*melon* **el melón**
*menu* **la carta;** *set menu* **el menú (del día)**
*message* **el recado, el mensaje**
*metro station* **la estación de metro**
*microwave* **el microondas**
*midday* **el mediodía**
*middle: in the middle* **en el centro**
*midnight* **la medianoche**
*milk* **la leche;** *milkshake with cinnamon* **la leche merengada**
*mine: it's mine* **es mío**
*mineral water* **el agua mineral**
*minute* **el minuto**
*mirror* **el espejo**
*Miss* **Señorita**
*mistake* **la equivocación**
*modem* **el módem**
*Monday* **lunes**
*money* **el dinero**
*monitor* (computer) **el monitor**
*month* **el mes**
*monument* **el monumento**
*moon* **la luna**
*moped* **el ciclomotor**
*more* **más**
*morning* **la mañana;** *in the morning* **por la mañana**
*Morocco* **Marruecos**
*mosaic* **el mosaico**
*mosquito* **el mosquito**
*mother* **la madre**
*motorboat* **la motora**

*motorcycle* **la motocicleta**
*mountain* **la montaña;** *high mountain* **la montaña alta**
*mountain bike* **la bicicleta de montaña**
*mouse* **el ratón**
*mousse* (hair) **la espuma moldeadora**
*moustache* **el bigote**
*mouth* **la boca**
*move* (verb) (something) **mover;** (oneself) **moverse;** (house) **mudarse de casa;** *don't move!* **¡no se mueva!**
*movie* **la película**
*Mr.* **Señor**
*Mrs.* **Señora**
*much: much better* **mucho mejor;** *much slower* **mucho más despacio**
*mug* **la jarrita**
*mom* **mama**
*museum* **el museo**
*mushrooms* **los champiñones, las setas**
*music* **la música**
*musical instrument* **el instrumento musical**
*musician* **el músico**
*music system* **el equipo de música**
*mussels* **los mejillones**
*must* (verb) (to have to) **tener que** *I must...* **tengo que...**
*mustard* **la mostaza**
*my: my book* **mi libro;** *my keys* **mis llaves**

# N

*nail* (metal) **el clavo;** (finger) **la uña**
*nail clippers* **el cortauñas**
*nailfile* **la lima de uñas**
*nail polish* **el esmalte de uñas**
*name* **el nombre;** *what's your name?* **¿cómo se llama usted?;** *my name is...* **me llamo...**
*nap* **la siesta**
*napkin* **la servilleta**
*narrow* (adj) **estrecho**
*near: near the door* **junto a la puerta;** *near New York* **cerca de New York**
*necessary* (adj) **necesario**
*neck* **el cuello**
*necklace* **el collar**
*need* (verb) **necesitar;** *I need...* **necesito...;** *there's no need* **no hace falta**
*needle* **la aguja**

negative (photo) **el negativo**
neither: neither of them **ninguno de ellos;** neither...nor... **ni...ni...**
nephew **el sobrino**
never **nunca**
new (adj) **nuevo**
news **las noticias**
newsagent's **el kiosko de periódicos**
newspaper **el periódico**
New Zealand **Nueva Zelanda**
New Zealander **el neozelandés/la neozelandesa**
next **próximo, siguiente;** next week **la semana que viene;** what next? **¿y ahora qué?**
nice (adj) **bonito;** (pleasant) **agradable;** (verb) (to eat) **bueno**
niece **la sobrina**
night **la noche**
nightclub **el club nocturno**
nightgown **el camisón**
night porter **el vigilante nocturno**
nine **nueve**
nineteen **diecinueve**
ninety **noventa**
no (response) **no;** I have no money **no tengo dinero;** no entry **la entrada prohibida**
nobody **nadie**
noisy (adj) **ruidoso**
noon **mediodía**
north **el norte**
Northern Ireland **Irlanda del Norte**
Norway lobster **las cigalas;** boiled Norway lobster **las cigalas cocidas**
nose **la nariz**
not **no;** he's not... **no es/está...**
notebook **el cuaderno**
notepad **el bloc**
nothing **nada**
novel **la novela**
November **noviembre**
now **ahora**
nowhere **en ninguna parte**
nudist **el/la nudista**
number **el número**
nurse **el enfermo/la enfermera**
nut (fruit) **la nuez;** (for bolt) **la tuerca**

# O

oars **los remos**
occasionally **de vez en cuando**
occupied (adj) **ocupado**

October **octubre**
octopus **el pulpo**
of **de**
office (place) **la oficina;** (room) **el despacho**
office block **el bloque de oficinas**
often **a menudo**
oil **el aceite**
ointment **la pomada**
OK **vale**
old (adj) **viejo;** how old are you? **¿cuántos años tiene?**
olive **la aceituna**
olive oil **el aceite de oliva**
olive tree **el olivo**
omelet (egg) **la tortilla**
on... **en...**
one **uno;** one way **el sentido obligatorio**
onion **la cebolla**
only **solo**
open (adj) **abierto;** (verb) **abrir**
opening times **el horario de apertura**
operating room **el quirófano**
operation **la operación**
operator (phone) **la operadora**
optician **el/la oculista**
or **o**
orange (fruit) **la naranja;** (color) **naranja**
orchestra **la orquesta**
order **el pedido**
organ (music) **el órgano**
other: the other (one) **el otro**
our **nuestro;** it's ours **es nuestro**
out: he's out **no está**
outside **fuera;** external **externa**
oven **el horno**
over... **encima de...;** (more than) **más de...;** it's over the road **está al otro lado de la calle;** when the party is over **cuando termine la fiesta;** over there **allí**
overtake (adj) (in a car) **adelantar**
oyster **la ostra**

# P

package **el paquete**
packet **el paquete;** (cigarettes) **la cajetilla;** (candy, chips) **la bolsa**
padlock **el candado**
page **la página**

pain **el dolor**
paint **la pintura**
pair **el par**
pajamas **el pijama**
palace **el palacio**
pale (adj) **pálido**
pancakes **las crepes**
pandemic **pandemia**
paper **el papel;** (newspaper) **el periódico**
paraffin **la parafina**
pardon? **¿cómo dice?**
parents **los padres**
park **el parque;** (verb) **aparcar;** no parking **estacionamiento prohibido, prohibido aparcar, prohibido estacionar**
parking lot **el aparcamiento**
parsley **el perejil**
part (in hair) **la raya**
party (celebration) **la fiesta;** (group) **el grupo;** (political) **el partido**
passenger **el pasajero**
passport **el pasaporte**
password **la contraseña**
pasta **la pasta**
path **el camino**
pavement **la acera**
pay (verb) **pagar**
payment **el pago;** contactless payment **el pago sin contacto**
peach **el melocotón**
peanuts **los cacahuetes**
pear **la pera**
pearl **la perla**
peas **los guisantes**
pedestrian **el peatón**
pedestrian zone **la zona peatonal**
peg **la pinza**
pen **la pluma**
pencil **el lápiz**
pencil sharpener **el sacapuntas**
penknife **la navaja**
pen pal **el amigo/la amiga por correspondencia**
people **la gente**
pepper (and salt) **la pimienta;** (red, green bell pepper) **el pimiento**
peppermints **las pastillas de menta**
per: per night **por noche**
perfect (adj) **perfecto**
perfume **el perfume**
perhaps **quizás**
perm **la permanente**
pet passport **el pasaporte de animales**
pets **los animales de compañía; los animales domésticos**
pharmacy **farmacia** (f)

*PhD* **un doctorado**
*phone book* **la guía telefónica**
*phone booth* **la cabina telefónica**
*phonecard* **la tarjeta telefónica**
*photocopier* **la fotocopiadora**
*photograph* **la foto** (grafía); (verb) **fotografiar**
*photographer* **el fotógrafo/ la fotógrafa**
*phrase book* **el libro de frases**
*piano* **el piano**
*pickpocket* **el/la carterista**
*picnic* **el pícnic**
*piece* **el pedazo**
*pill* **la pastilla**
*pillow* **la almohada**
*pilot* **el piloto**
*PIN* **el pin**
*pin* **el alfiler**
*pine* (tree) **el pino**
*pineapple* **la piña**
*pink* (adj) **rosa**
*pipe* (for smoking) **la pipa**; (for water) **la tubería**
*piston* **el pistón**
*pizza* **la pizza**
*place* **el lugar**; *at your place* **en su casa**
*plans* **los planos**
*plant* **la planta**
*plaster* **la tirita**
*plastic* **el plástico**
*plastic bag* **la bolsa de plástico**
*plastic wrap* **el plástico para envolver**
*plate* **el plato**
*platform* (train) **el andén**
*play* (theater) **la obra de teatro**; (verb) **jugar**
*please* **por favor**
*pleased to meet you* **encantado/encantada**
*plug* (electrical) **el enchufe**; (sink) **el tapón**
*plumber* **el fontanero/ la fontanera**
*pocket* **el bolsillo**
*poison* **el veneno**
*police* **la policía**
*police officer* **el policía**
*police report* **la denuncia**
*police station* **la comisaría**
*politics* **la política**
*poor* (adj) **pobre**; (bad quality) **malo**
*pop music* **la música pop**
*pork* **la carne de cerdo**
*port* (harbor) **el puerto**; (drink) **el oporto**
*porter* (hotel) **el conserje**
*Portugal* **Portugal**
*Portuguese* **portugués**
*possible* **posible**
*post* **el correo**; (verb) **echar al correo**

*postcard* **la postal**
*postcode* **el código postal**
*poster* **el póster**
*post office* **(la oficina de) Correos**
*potato* **la patata**
*potato chips* **las patatas fritas**
*poultry* **las aves**
*pound* (sterling) **la libra**
*powder* **el polvo**; (cosmetic) **los polvos**
*powdered detergent* **el detergente en polvo**
*prefer* **preferir**
*pregnant* **embarazada**
*prescription* **la receta**
*pretty* (adj) **bonito**; (quite) **bastante**
*price* **el precio**
*priest* **el cura**
*printer* **la impresora**
*private* (adj) **privado**
*problem* **el problema**
*profession* **la profesión**
*professor* **el catedrático/ la catedrática**
*profits* **los beneficios**
*prohibited* **prohibido**
*protection factor* (SPF) **el factor de protección**
*public* **público**
*public holiday* **el día de fiesta**
*public swimming pool* **la piscina municipal**
*pull* (verb) **tirar de**
*puncture* **el pinchazo**
*purple* **morado**
*purse* **la cartera, el monedero**
*push* (verb) **empujar**
*put* (verb) **poner**
*Pyrenees* **los Pirineos**

# Q

*quality* **la calidad**
*quarantine* **la cuarentena**
*quarter* **el cuarto**
*question* **la pregunta**
*quick* (adj) **rápido**
*quiet* **tranquilo**; (adj: person) **callado**
*quite* (fairly) **bastante**; (fully) **completamente**
*quotation* **el presupuesto**

# R

*rabbit* **el conejo**
*radiator* **el radiador**
*radio* **la radio**
*radish* **el rábano**
*rake* **el rastrillo**
*railway* **el ferrocarril**
*rain* **la lluvia**
*raincoat* **la gabardina**
*rainforest* **la selva**
*raisins* **las pasas**

*raspberry* **la frambuesa**
*rare* (adj) (uncommon) **raro**; (steak) **poco hecho, poco pasado**
*rat* **la rata**
*razor blades* **las cuchillas de afeitar**
*read* (verb) **leer**
*ready* (adj) **listo**
*ready meals* **los platos preparados**
*receipt* **el recibo**
*reception* **la recepción**
*receptionist* **el/ la recepcionista**
*record* (music) **el disco**; (verb) **grabar**; (sports, etc.) **el récord**
*record player* **el tocadiscos**
*record store* **la tienda de discos**
*red* **rojo**; (wine) **tinto**
*refreshments* **los refrescos**
*refrigerator* **el frigorífico**
*registered mail* **el correo certificado**
*relative* **el pariente**
*relax* **relajarse**; (verb: rest) **descansar**
*religion* **la religión**
*remember* (verb): *I remember* **me acuerdo**; *I don't remember* **no me acuerdo**
*repair* **arreglar**
*report* **el informe**
*reservation* **la reserva**
*rest* (remainder) **el resto**; (verb: relax) **descansar**
*restaurant* **el restaurante**
*restaurant car* **el vagónrestaurante**
*return* (come back) **volver**; (give back) **devolver**
*return ticket* **el billete de ida y vuelta**
*rice* **el arroz**; *rice with fried eggs, tomato sauce, and often a fried banana* **el arroz a la cubana**
*rich* (adj) **rico**
*right* (adj) (correct) **correcto**; (not left) **derecho**
*ring* (jewelry) **el anillo**
*ripe* (adj) **maduro**
*river* **el río**
*road* **la carretera**; *priority road* **la calzada con prioridad**
*roasted* (adj) **asado**
*robbery* **el robo**
*rock* (stone) **la roca**
*roll* (bread) **el bollo**
*roof* **el tejado**
*room* (usually in a hotel) **la habitación**; (space) **el sitio**

*room service* **el servicio de habitaciones**
*rope* **la cuerda**
*rose* **la rosa**
*round* (adj) (circular) **redondo**
*roundabout* **la rotonda**
*row* (verb) **remar**
*rowing boat* **la barca de remos**
*rubber* (material) **la goma**
*rubber band* **la goma**
*rubbish* **la basura**
*ruby* (stone) **el rubí**
*rug* (mat) **la alfombra**; (blanket) **la manta**
*rugby* **el rugby**
*ruins* **las ruinas**
*ruler* (for measuring) **la regla**
*rum* **el ron**
*run* (verb) **correr**
*runway* **la pista**

# S

*sad* (adj) **triste**
*safe* (adj) (not dangerous) **seguro**
*safety pin* **el imperdible**
*sailboard* **la tabla de windsurfing**
*sailing* **la vela**
*salad* **la ensalada**
*sale* (at reduced prices) **las rebajas**
*sales* **las ventas**
*saline solution* (for contact lenses) **la solución limpiadora**
*salmon* **el salmón**
*salt* **la sal**
*same: the same dress* **el mismo vestido**; *the same people* **la misma gente**; *same again, please* **lo mismo otra vez, por favor**
*sand* **la arena**
*sandals* **las sandalias**
*sand dunes* **las dunas**
*sandwich* **el bocadillo**
*sanitary napkins* **las compresas**
*Saturday* **sábado**
*sauce* **la salsa**
*saucepan* **el cazo**
*saucer* **el platillo**
*sauna* **la sauna**
*sausage* **la salchicha**
*say* (verb) **decir**; *what did you say?* **¿qué ha dicho?**; *how do you say...?* **¿cómo se dice...?**
*scampi* **las gambas**
*scarf* **la bufanda**; (head) **el pañuelo**
*schedule* **el programa**
*school* **la escuela**

*science* **las ciencias**
*scissors* **las tijeras**
*Scotland* **Escocia** (f)
*Scottish* **escocés/escocesa**
*screen* **la pantalla**
*screw* **el tornillo**
*screwdriver* **el destornillador**
*sea* **el mar**
*seafood* **los mariscos**
*seat* **el asiento**
*seat belt* **el cinturón de seguridad**
*second* **el segundo**
*second class* **de segunda**
*see* (verb) **ver**; *I can't see* **no veo**; *I see* **comprendo**
*self-employed* (person) el **autónomo/la autónoma**
*self-service laundry* **la lavandería automática**
*sell* (verb) **vender**
*seminar* **el seminario**
*send* (verb) **mandar**
*separate* (adj) **distinto**
*separated* **separado**
*September* **septiembre**
*serious* (adj) **serio**
*server* (waiter/waitress) **el camarero/la camarera**; *waiter!* **¡camarero!**; *waitress!* **¡Oiga, por favor!**
*seven* **siete**
*seventeen* **diecisiete**
*seventy* **setenta**
*several* **varios**
*sew* (verb) **coser**
*shampoo* **el champú**
*shake* (verb) **agitar**
*shave* **el afeitado**; *to have a shave* (verb) **afeitarse**
*shaving cream* **la espuma de afeitar**
*shawl* **el chal**
*she* **ella**
*sheet* **la sábana**; (of paper) **la hoja**
*shell* **la concha**
*shellfish* **los mariscos**
*sherry* **el jerez**
*ship* **el barco**
*shirt* **la camisa**
*shoelaces* **los cordones de los zapatos**
*shoe polish* **la crema de zapatos**
*shoes* **los zapatos**
*shoe store* **la zapatería**
*shop* **la tienda**
*shopping* **la compra**; *to go shopping* (verb) **ir de compras**
*shopping center* **el centro comercial**
*short* (adj) **corto**; (height) **bajo**
*shorts* **los pantalones cortos**

*shoulder* **el hombro**
*shower* (bath) **la ducha**; (rain) **el chaparrón**
*shower gel* **el gel de ducha**
*shrimp* **las gambas**
*shrimp* **las quisquillas**
*shutter* (camera) **el obturador**; (window) **el postigo**
*sick* (adj) **náuseas**; *I feel sick* **tengo náuseas**; *to be sick* (verb) (vomit) **vomitar**
*side* (edge) **el borde**
*side lights* **las luces de posición**
*sights: the sights of...* **los lugares de interés de...**
*sightseeing* **el turismo**
*silk* **la seda**
*silver* (metal) **la plata**; (color) **plateado**
*SIM card* **la tarjeta SIM**
*simple* (adj) **sencillo**
*sing* (verb) **cantar**
*single* (ticket) **de ida**; (only) **único**; (adj) (unmarried) **soltero/soltera**
*single room* **la habitación individual**
*sink* **el fregadero**
*sister* **la hermana**
*site* (for camping) **la plaza**
*six* **seis**
*sixteen* **dieciséis**
*sixty* **sesenta**
*skid* (verb) **patinar**
*ski resort* **la estación de esquí**
*skiing: to go skiing* (verb) **ir a esquiar**
*skin cleanser* **la leche limpiadora**
*skirt* **la falda**
*skis* **los esquís**
*sky* **el cielo**
*sleep* **el sueño**; (verb) **dormir**
*sleeper car* **el coche cama**
*sleeping bag* **el saco de dormir**
*sleeping pill* **el somnífero**
*sleeve* **la manga**
*slip* (underwear) **la combinación**
*slippers* **las zapatillas**
*slow* (adj) **lento**
*small* (adj) **pequeño**
*smell* **el olor**; (verb) **oler**
*smile* **la sonrisa**; (verb) **sonreír**
*smoke* **el humo**; (verb) **fumar**
*snack* **la comida ligera**
*sneakers* **los zapatos de deporte**
*snow* **la nieve**
*so: so good* **tan bueno**; *not so much* **no tanto**

*soap* **el jabón**
*soccer* **el fútbol**; *(ball)* **el balón**; *soccer shoes* **las botas de fútbol**
*socks* **los calcetines**
*soda water* **la soda**
*sofa* **el sofá**
*soft (adj)* **blando**
*soil* **la tierra**
*somebody* **alguien**
*somehow* **de algún modo**
*something* **algo**
*sometimes* **a veces**
*somewhere* **en alguna parte**
*son* **el hijo**
*song* **la canción**
*sorry!* **¡perdón!**; *I'm sorry* **perdón/lo siento**; *sorry? (pardon)* **¿cómo dice?**
*soup* **la sopa**
*south* **el sur**
*South America* **Sudamérica**
*souvenir* **el recuerdo**
*spade* **la pala**
*spades (cards)* **las picas**
*Spain* **España** (f)
*Spaniard* **el español/ la española**
*speak (verb)* **hablar**; *do you speak...?* **¿habla...?**; *I don't speak...* **no hablo...**
*speed* **la velocidad**
*speed limit* **el límite de velocidad**
*spider* **la araña**
*spinach* **las espinacas**
*spoon* **la cuchara**
*sport* **el deporte**
*sports center* **el centro deportivo**
*spring (mechanical)* **el muelle**; *(season)* **la primavera**
*square (in town)* **la plaza**; *(adj: shape)* **cuadrado**
*staircase* **la escalera**
*stairs* **las escaleras**
*stamp* **el sello**
*stapler* **la grapadora**
*star* **la estrella**
*start (beginning)* **el principio**; *(verb)* **empezar**
*starters* **los entrantes**
*statement* **la declaración**
*station* **la estación**
*statue* **la estatua**
*steak* **el filete**
*steal (verb)* **robar**; *it's been stolen* **lo han robado**
*steamed (adj)* **al vapor**
*steamer (boat)* **el vapor**
*stepdaughter* **la hijastra**
*stepfather* **el padrastro**
*stepmother* **la madrastra**
*stepson* **el hijastro**
*still water* **el agua sin gas**
*stockings* **las medias**
*stomach* **el estómago**

*stomachache* **el dolor de estómago**
*stop (bus)* **la parada**; *(verb)* **parar**; *stop!* **¡alto!**
*storm* **la tormenta**
*stove* **la cocina**
*strawberries* **las fresas**
*stream (small river)* **el arroyo**
*street* **la calle**
*string* **la cuerda**
*stroller* **el carrito**
*stroller* **el cochecito**
*stroller* **la silla de paseo**
*strong (adj)* **fuerte**
*student* **el/la estudiante**
*stupid (adj)* **estúpido**
*suburbs* **las afueras**
*sugar* **el azúcar**
*suit (clothing)* **el traje**; *it suits you* **te sienta bien**
*suitcase* **la maleta**
*sun* **el sol**
*sunbathe (verb)* **tomar el sol**
*sunburn* **la quemadura de sol**
*Sunday* **domingo**
*sunglasses* **las gafas de sol**
*sunny (adj): it's sunny* **hace sol**
*sunshade* **la sombrilla**
*sunstroke* **la insolación**
*suntan: to get a suntan (verb)* **broncearse**
*suntan lotion* **la loción bronceadora**
*suntanned* **bronceado**
*supermarket* **el supermercado**
*supper* **la cena**
*supplement* **el suplemento**
*suppository* **el supositorio**
*sure* **seguro**
*surname* **el apellido**
*sweat* **el sudor**; *(verb)* **sudar**
*sweater* **el jersey**
*sweatshirt* **la sudadera**
*sweet (adj: not sour)* **dulce**; *sweets* **los caramelos**
*swim (verb)* **nadar**
*swimming* **la natación**
*swimming pool* **la piscina**
*swimming trunks* **el bañador**
*swimsuit* **el bañador, el traje de baño**
*switch* **el interruptor**
*synagogue* **la sinagoga**
*syringe* **la jeringuilla**
*syrup* **el jarabe**

# T

*T-shirt* **la camiseta**
*table* **la mesa**
*tablet* **la pastilla**
*take (verb)* **tomar**
*take off* **el despegue**
*talcum powder* **los polvos de talco**

*talk* **la charla**; *(verb)* **hablar**
*tall (adj)* **alto**
*tampons* **los tampones**
*tangerine* **la mandarina**
*tap (water)* **el grifo**
*tapas (food)* **tapas**
*tapestry* **el tapiz**
*taxi* **el taxi**
*taxi stand* **la parada de taxis**
*tea (usually black but can also refer to green, red, herbal, or fruit tea)* **el té**; *tea with milk* **el té con leche**; *tea with lemon* **el té con limón**; *el té negro* *black tea*
*teacher* **el profesor/ la profesora**
*technician* **el técnico/la técnica**
*telephone* **el teléfono**; *(verb)* **llamar por teléfono**
*television* **la televisión**
*temperature* **la temperatura**; *(fever)* **la fiebre**
*ten* **diez**
*tennis* **el tenis**
*tent* **la tienda (de campaña)**
*tent peg* **la estaquilla, la estaca**
*tent pole* **el mástil**
*terminal* **la terminal**
*terrace* **la terraza**
*test* **la prueba**
*than* **que**
*thank (verb)* **agradecer**; *thank you/thanks* **gracias**
*that* **ese/esa, eso**; *that bus* **ese autobús**; *that man* **ese hombre**; *that woman* **esa mujer**; *what's that?* **¿qué es eso?**; *I think that...* **creo que...**; *that one* **ese/esa**
*the* **el/la**; *(plural)* **los/las**
*theater* **el teatro**
*their: their room* **su habitación**; *their books* **sus libros**; *it's theirs* **es suyo**
*them: it's for them* **es para ellos/ellas**; *give it to them* **déselo**
*then* **entonces**; *(after)* **después**
*there* **allí**; *there is/are...* **hay...**; *is/are there...?* **¿hay...?**
*these: these men* **estos hombres**; *these women* **estas mujeres**; *these are mine* **estos son míos**

they **ellos/ellas**
thick (adj) **grueso**
thief **el ladrón/la ladrona**
thin (adj) **delgado**
think (verb) **pensar;**
I think so **creo que sí;**
I'll think about it **lo pensaré**
third **tercero**
thirsty: (adj) I'm thirsty **tengo sed**
thirteen **trece**
thirty **treinta**
this: this one **este/esta;**
this man **este hombre;**
this woman **esta mujer;**
what's this? **¿qué es esto?;**
this is Mr.... **este es el señor...**
those: those men **esos hombres;** those women **esas mujeres**
thousand **mil**
throat **la garganta**
through **por**
three **tres**
thumbtack **la chincheta**
thunderstorm **la tormenta**
Thursday **jueves**
ticket (train, etc.) **el billete;** (theater, etc.) **la entrada**
ticket office **la taquilla**
tide **la marea**
tie **la corbata;** (verb) **atar**
tight (adj) **ajustado**
tights **las medias, los pantis**
time **tiempo;** what's the time? **¿qué hora es?**
timetable **el horario**
tin **la hojalata**
tip (end) **la punta;** (money) **la propina**
tire **el neumático**
tired (adj) **cansado**
tissues **los pañuelos de papel**
to: to America **a América;** to the station **a la estación;** to the doctor **al médico**
toast **la tostada;** toast with butter and jam **la tostada con mantequilla y mermelada**
tobacco **el tabaco**
tobacconist **el estanco**
today **hoy**
together **juntos**
toilet (room in house) **el baño;** (bathroom item) **el váter;** (in public establishment) **los servicos**
toilet paper **el papel higiénico**

toilets (men) **los servicios de caballeros;** (women) **los servicios de señoras**
tomato **el tomate**
tomato juice **el zumo de tomate**
tomorrow **mañana**
tongue **la lengua**
tonic **la tónica**
tonight **esta noche**
too (also) **también;** (excessively) **demasiado**
tooth **el diente;** back tooth **la muela**
toothache **el dolor de muelas**
toothbrush **el cepillo de dientes**
toothpaste **la pasta dentífrica**
torch **la linterna**
tortilla (flatbread) **la tortilla**
tour **la excursión**
tourist **el/la turista**
tourist office **la oficina de información turística**
towel **la toalla**
tower **la torre**
town **el pueblo**
town hall **el ayuntamiento**
toy **el juguete**
trade fair **la feria**
track suit **el chándal**
tractor **el tractor**
tradition **la tradición**
traffic **el tráfico**
traffic laws **el código de la circulación**
traffic lights **el semáforo**
trailer **el remolque**
train **el tren**
trainee **el/la aprendiz**
translate (verb) **traducir**
translator **el traductor/ la traductora**
transmission **la caja de cambios**
trash can **el cubo de la basura**
travel agency **la agencia de viajes**
tray **la bandeja**
tree **el árbol**
trolley **el carrito**
trousers **el pantalón**
truck **el camión**
true **cierto;** it's true **es verdad**
trunk (car) **el maletero**
try (verb) **intentar**
Tuesday **martes**
tunnel **el túnel**
turn (left/right) **gire (a la izquierda/a la derecha)**
turn: it's my turn **me toca a mí**

tweezers **las pinzas**
twelve **doce**
twenty **veinte**
twins (identical) **los gemelos**
two **dos**
typewriter **la máquina de escribir**

# U

ugly (adj) **feo**
umbrella **el paraguas**
uncle **el tío**
under... **debajo de...**
underground (railway) **el metro**
understand (verb) **entender;** I don't understand **no entiendo**
underwear **la ropa interior**
underwear **los calzoncillos**
United States **Estados Unidos**
university **la universidad**
unleaded **sin plomo**
until **hasta**
unusual (adj) **poco común**
up **arriba;** (upward) **hacia arriba**
urgent (adj) **urgente**
us: it's for us **es para nosotros/nosotras;** give it to us **dénoslo**
use (verb) **el uso, usar;** it's no use **no sirve de nada**
useful (adj) **útil**
usual (adj) **corriente**
usually **en general**

# V

vacancies (rooms) **habitaciones libres**
vacation **las vacaciones**
vaccinate (verb) **vacunar**
vaccination **la vacuna**
vaccine **la vacuna**
vacuum cleaner **la aspiradora**
valley **el valle**
valve **la válvula**
vanilla **la vainilla**
vase **el jarrón**
veal **la (carne de) ternera**
vegetables **la verdura**
vegetarian (adj) **vegetariano**
vehicle **el vehículo**
very **muy;** very much **mucho**
vest **la camiseta**
vet **el veterinario**
video (tape) **la cinta de vídeo;** (film) **el vídeo**

*video games* **los videojuegos**
*video recorder* **el (aparato de) vídeo**
*view* **la vista**
*viewfinder* **el visor de imagen**
*villa* **el chalet**
*village* **el pueblo**
*vinegar* **el vinagre**
*violin* **el violín**
*visit* **la visita**; (verb: place) **visitar**
*visiting hours* **las horas de visita**
*visitor* **el/la visitante**
*vitamin pills* **las vitaminas**
*vodka* **el vodka**
*voice* **la voz**
*voicemail* **la mensajería de voz**

# W

*wait* (verb) **esperar**; *wait!* **¡espere!**
*waiter* (server) **el camarero**; *waiter!* **¡camarero!**
*waiting room* **la sala de espera**
*waitress* (server) **la camarera**; *waitress!* **¡Oiga, por favor!**
*Wales* **Gales**
*walk* (stroll) **el paseo**; (verb) **andar**; *to go for a walk* (verb) **ir de paseo**
*wall* **la pared**; (outside) **el muro**
*wallet* **la cartera**
*want* (verb) **querer**
*war* **la guerra**
*wardrobe* **el armario**
*warm* **caliente**; (weather) **caluroso**
*was* **estaba/era**
*washing machine* **la zapatilla**
*wasp* **la avispa**
*watch* **el reloj**; (verb) **mirar**
*water* **el agua**
*waterfall* **la cascada**
*water heater* **el calentador** (de agua)
*wave* **la ola**; (verb) **saludar con la mano**
*wavy* (adj: hair) **ondulado**
*we* **nosotros/nosotras**
*weather* **el tiempo**
*website* **el sitio web**, **la página web**
*wedding* **la boda**
*Wednesday* **miércoles**
*weeds* **las malas hierbas**
*week* **la semana**

*welcome* (adj) **bienvenido**; (verb) **dar la bienvenida**; *you're welcome* **no hay de qué**
*Wellington boots* **las botas de agua**
*Welsh* **galés/galesa**
*were: you were* (informal singular) **eras/estabas**; (formal singular) **era/estaba**; (informal plural) **erais/estabais**; (formal plural) **eran/estaban**; *we were* **éramos/estábamos**; *they were* **eran/estaban**
*west* **el oeste**
*wet* (adj) **mojado**
*what?* **¿qué?**
*wheel* **la rueda**
*wheel brace* **la llave de las tuercas**
*wheelchair* **la silla de ruedas**
*when?* **¿cuándo?**
*where?* **¿dónde?**
*whether* **si**
*which?* **¿cuál?**
*whisky* **el whisky**
*white* (adj) **blanco**
*white coffee* **el café con leche**
*who?* **¿quién?**
*why?* **¿por qué?**
*wide* (adj) **ancho**; *3 meters wide* **de tres metros de anchura**
*wife* **la mujer**
*wind* **el viento**
*window* **la ventana**
*windshield* **el parabrisas**
*wine* **el vino**
*wine list* **la carta de vinos**
*wine merchant* **el vinatero**
*wing* **el ala**
*with* **con**
*without* **sin**
*witness* **el/la testigo**
*woman* **la mujer**
*wood* (material) **la madera**
*wool* **la lana**
*word* **la palabra**
*work* **el trabajo**; (verb) **trabajar**; (verb) (to function) **funcionar**
*worktop* **el mostrador**
*worse* **peor**
*worst* **(el) peor**
*wrapping paper* **el papel de envolver**; (for presents) **el papel de regalo**

*wrench* **la llave inglesa**
*wrist* **la muñeca**
*writing paper* **el papel de escribir**
*wrong* (adj) **equivocado**

# X, Y, Z

*x-ray department* **el servicio de radiología**
*year* **el año**
*yellow* (adj) **amarillo**
*yes* **sí**
*yesterday* **ayer**
*yet* **todavía**; *not yet* **todavía no**
*yogurt* **el yogur**
*you* (informal singular) **tú**; (formal singular) **usted**; (informal plural, m/f) **vosotros/ vosotras**; (formal plural) **ustedes**
*young* (adj) **joven**
*your: your book* (informal singular) **tu libro**; (formal singular) **su libro**; *your shoes* (informal singular) **tus zapatos**; (formal singular) **sus zapato**
*yours: is this yours?* (informal) **¿es tuyo esto?**; (formal) **¿es suyo esto?**
*youth hostel* **el albergue juvenil**
*zip* **la cremallera**
*zoo* **el zoo**

# Dictionary
## SPANISH TO ENGLISH

The gender of Spanish nouns listed here is indicated by the abbreviations (m) and (f) for masculine and feminine nouns. Plural nouns are indicated by (m pl) or (f pl). Spanish adjectives (adj) vary according to the gender and number of the word they describe; the masculine form is shown here. Certain endings use a different rule: masculine adjectives that end in **-o** adopt an **-a** ending in the feminine form, while those that end in -e usually stay the same. For the plural form, an **-s** is added.

## A

**a** to; **a América** to America; **a la estación** to the station; **al médico** to the doctor; **a las tres** at 3 o'clock

**abanico** (m) fan (handheld)

**abierto** (adj) open

**abogado/abogada** (m/f) lawyer

**abrebotellas** (m) bottle opener

**abrelatas** (m) can opener

**abrigo** (m) coat

**abril** April

**abrir** (verb) to open

**abuela** (f) grandmother

**abuelo** (m) grandfather

**abuelos** (m pl) grandparents

**aburrido** (adj) boring

**acaba de llegar** it's just arrived

**accidente** (m) accident

**aceite** (m) oil; **el aceite de oliva** olive oil

**aceituna** (f) olive

**acelerador** (m) accelerator

**acera** (f) pavement

**acondicionador** (m) conditioner (hair)

**acuerdo** (verb) **me acuerdo** I remember; **no me acuerdo** I don't remember

**adaptador** (m) adaptor

**adelantar** (adj) overtake (car)

**adiós** goodbye

**aduana** (f) customs

**aerodeslizador** (m) hovercraft

**aeropuerto** (m) airport

**afeitado** (m) shave

**afeitarse** (verb) to have a shave

**after-shave** (m) aftershave

**afueras** (f pl) suburbs

**agencia** (f) agency

**agencia de viajes** (f) travel agency

**agenda** (f) diary

**agitar** (verb) to shake

**agosto** August

**agradable** pleasant

**agradecer** (verb) to thank

**agua** (m) water; **el agua con gas** fizzy water; **el agua mineral** mineral water; **el agua potable** drinking water; **el agua sin gas** still water

**aguja** (f) needle

**ahora** now; **¿y ahora qué?** what next?

**aire** (m) air

**aire acondicionado** (m) air conditioning

**ajedrez** (m) chess

**ajo** (m) garlic

**ajustado** (adj) tight

**ala** (m) wing

**albañil** (m/f) bricklayer

**albaricoque** (m) apricot

**albergue juvenil** (m) youth hostel

**alcachofa** (f) artichoke

**alcohol** (m) alcohol

**alegre** (adj) glad

**alemán** German

**Alemania** (f) Germany

**alérgico** (adj) allergic

**alfiler** (m) pin

**alfombra** (f) carpet; rug

**algo** something

**algodón** (m) cotton, cotton wool

**alguien** somebody

**alguna: en alguna parte** somewhere

**allí** there, over there

**almohada** (f) pillow

**alojamiento** (m) accommodations

**alquilar** (verb) to hire

**alto** (adj) high, tall, loud

**¡alto!** stop!

**amante** (m/f) lover

**amargo** bitter

**amarillo** (adj) yellow

**ambulancia** (f) ambulance

**América** America

**americano/americana** (m/f) American

**amigo/amiga** (m/f) friend; **amigo/amiga por correspondencia** (m/f) pen pal

**amontillado** medium (sherry)

**amor** (m) love

**ampliación** (f) enlargement

**ampolla** (f) blister

**análisis de sangre** (m) blood test

**andar** (verb) to walk

**andén** (m) platform

**anfiteatro** (m) lecture hall

**anfitriona** (f) hostess

**anillo** (m) ring (jewelry)

**animal** (m) animal; **los animales de compañía/ los animales domésticos** pets

**año** (m) year

**antes de...** before...

**anticonceptivo** (m) contraceptive

**anticongelante** (m) antifreeze

**anticuario** (m) antiques shop

**antiséptico** (m) antiseptic

**aparcamiento** (m) parking lot

**aparcar** (verb) to park; **prohibido aparcar** no parking

**apartamento** (m) apartment (flat)

**apellido** (m) surname

**aperitivo** (m) aperitif

**apetito** (m) appetite

**aprender** (verb) to learn

**aprendiz** (m/f) trainee

**apretón de manos** (m) handshake

**araña** (f) spider

**árbol** (m) tree

**árbol de levas** (m) camshaft

**arcón** (m) chest (furniture)

**arena** (f) sand

**Argelia** Algeria (f)

**armario** (m) cupboard, wardrobe

**arreglar** repair

**arriba** up; **hacia arriba** upward

**arroyo** (m) stream (small river)

**arroz** (m) rice; **arroz a la cubana** rice with fried eggs, tomato sauce, and often a fried banana

**arte** (m) *art*
**artículos de punto** (m pl) *knitwear*
**artista** (m/f) *artist*
**asado** (adj) *roasted*
**ascensor** (m) *lift*
**asiento** (m) *seat*
**asmático** (adj) *asthmatic*
**aspiradora** (f) *vacuum cleaner*
**aspirina** (f) *aspirin*
**atar** (verb) *to tie*
**atasco** (m) *traffic jam*
**aterrizar** (verb) *to land*
**ático** (m) *attic*
**atractivo** (adj) *attractive (offer)*
**audífono** (m) *hearing aid*
**audioguía** (f) *audio guide*
**auriculares** (m pl) *earbuds*
**Australia** *Australia*
**australiano/australiana** (m/f) *Australian*
**autobús** (m) *bus*
**autobús del aeropuerto** *airport bus*
**autocaravana** (f) *camper van*
**automático** *automatic*
**autónomo/autónoma** (m/f) *self-employed*
**autopista** (f) *highway*
**avería** (f) *(car) breakdown;* **he tenido una avería** *I've had a breakdown*
**aves** (f pl) *poultry*
**avión** (m) *aircraft*
**avispa** (f) *wasp*
**ayer** *yesterday*
**ayuda** (f) *help*
**ayudar** (verb) *to help*
**ayuntamiento** (m) *town hall*
**azúcar** (m) *sugar*
**azul** *blue*

# B

**bacon** (m) *bacon*
**bailar** (verb) *to dance*
**baile** (m) *dance*
**bajarse** (verb) *to get off (bus etc); to get out*
**bajo** (adj) *low, short*
**balandro** (m) *sailing boat*
**balcón** (m) *balcony*
**Baleares: las (Islas) Baleares** *Balearic Islands*
**balón** (m) *soccer (ball);* **el balón de playa** *beach ball*
**baloncesto** (m) *basketball*
**bañador** (m) *swimsuit, swimming trunks*
**banco** (m) *bank*
**banda** (f) *band (musicians)*
**bandeja** (f) *tray*
**bandera** (f) *flag*

**baño** (m) *bath, bathroom, toilet (room in a house);* **darse un baño** (verb) *to have a bath;* **el traje de baño** *swimsuit*
**bar** (m) *bar (drinks)*
**baraja** (f) *deck of cards*
**barato** (adj) *inexpensive*
**barba** (f) *beard*
**barbacoa** (f) *barbecue*
**barca** (f) *small boat;* **la barca de remos** *rowing boat*
**barco** (m) *boat, ship*
**barra de labios** (f) *lipstick*
**bastante** *enough, quite, fairly*
**basura** (f) *litter, rubbish*
**batería** (f) *battery (car)*
**bebé** (m) *baby*
**beber** (verb) *to drink;* **¿quiere beber algo?** *would you like something to drink?*
**bebida** (f) *drink*
**beige** *beige*
**beneficios** (m pl) *profits*
**berenjenas** (f pl) *eggplants*
**biblioteca** (f) *library*
**bicicleta** (f) *bicycle;* **la bicicleta de montaña** *mountain bike*
**bien** *good;* **te sienta bien** *it suits you*
**bienvenido** *welcome*
**bigote** (m) *moustache*
**billete** (m) *fare, ticket (train etc);* **billete de ida y vuelta** (m) *return ticket*
**billete de banco** (m) *banknote*
**bizcocho** (m) *sponge cake*
**blanco** (adj) *white*
**blando** (adj) *soft*
**bloc** (m) *notepad*
**bloque de oficinas** (m) *office block*
**blusa** (f) *blouse*
**boca** (f) *mouth*
**bocadillo** (m) *sandwich*
**boda** (f) *wedding*
**bodega** (f) *cellar*
**bolígrafo** (m) *ballpoint pen*
**bollo** (m) *roll (bread)*
**bolsa** (f) *bag, packet (candy, chips);* **la bolsa de basura** *trash can liner;* **la bolsa de plástico** *plastic bag*
**bolsillo** (m) *pocket*
**bolso** (m) *handbag*
**bombilla** (f) *light bulb*
**bonito** (adj) *nice, pretty, attractive (object)*
**bordado** (m) *embroidery*
**borde** (m) *edge, border, side*
**borracho** (adj) *drunk*
**bosque** (m) *forest*
**bota** (f) *boot*

**botas de agua** (f pl) *Wellington boots*
**botas de fútbol** (f pl) *soccer shoes*
**botella** (f) *bottle*
**botón** (m) *button*
**brazo** (m) *arm*
**bridge** (m) *bridge (game)*
**británico/británica** (m/f) *British*
**brocha** (f) *paint brush*
**broche** (m) *brooch*
**brocheta** (f) *grilled meat (on a skewer)*
**broma** (f) *joke*
**bronceado** *suntanned*
**broncearse** (verb) *suntan: to get a suntan*
**buenas noches** *good evening*
**buenas tardes** *good afternoon*
**bueno** *good, good to eat, tasty*
**buenos días** *good morning*
**bufanda** (f) *scarf*
**buzón** (m) *postbox*

# C

**cabeza** (f) *head*
**cabina telefónica** (f) *phone booth*
**cable alargador** (m) *extension cord*
**cacahuetes** (m pl) *peanuts*
**cada** *every, each;* **viente euros cada uno** *20 euros each*
**café** (m) *cafetería, coffee;* **el café con leche** *white coffee;* **el café instantáneo** *instant coffee;* **el café solo** *espresso*
**caja** (f) *box; checkout;* **la caja de bombones** *box of chocolates;* **la caja de cambios** *transmission*
**cajero** (m) *cashier;* **el cajero automático** *ATM, cashpoint*
**cajetilla** (f) *packet (cigarettes)*
**calambre** (m) *cramp*
**calcetines** (m pl) *socks*
**calculadora** (m) *calculator*
**calefacción** (f) *heating;* **la calefacción central** *central heating*
**calentador** (de agua) (m) *water heater*
**calidad** (f) *quality*
**caliente** *warm*
**callado** *quiet (person)*
**calle** (f) *street;* **la calle principal** *main road*
**caluroso** *warm (weather)*
**calvo** (adj) *bald*
**calzada con prioridad** (f) *priority road*
**calzoncillos** (m pl) *underwear*
**cama** (f) *bed*
**cámara de fotos** (f) *camera*

**cámara neumática** (f) *inner tube*
**camarero/camarera** (m/f) *waiter, waitress (server);*
**¡camarero!** *waiter!*
**cambiar** (verb) *to change (money)*
**cambiarse** (verb) *to change (clothes)*
**cambio** (m) *change (money); exchange rate*
**camino** (m) *path*
**camión** (m) *truck*
**camisa** (f) *shirt*
**camiseta** (f) *vest, T-shirt*
**camisón** (m) *nightgown*
**campana** (f) *bell (church)*
**camping** (m) *campsite*
**camping gas** (m) *camping gas*
**campo** (m) *countryside, field*
**Canadá** *Canada*
**canadiense** *Canadian*
**canal** (m) *canal*
**Canarias: las (Islas) Canarias** *Canaries*
**canción** (f) *song*
**candado** (m) *padlock*
**cangrejo** (m) *crab*
**cangrejo de río** (m pl) *crayfish*
**cansado** (adj) *tired*
**cantar** (verb) *to sing*
**capazo** (m) *crib*
**capó** (m) *hood (car)*
**cara** (f) *face*
**caramelos** *candy*
**caravana** (f) *caravan*
**carburador** (m) *carburetor*
**cardenal** (m) *bruise*
**cargador** (m) *charger;* **punto/estación de carga** *charging point/station;* **cable de carga** *charging cable*
**carne** (f) *meat*
**carne de cerdo** (f) *pork*
**carne de vaca** (f) *beef*
**carnet de conducir** (m) *driver's license*
**carnicería** (f) *butcher's*
**caro** (adj) *expensive*
**carpintero/carpintera** (m/f) *carpenter*
**carretera** (f) *road*
**carrito** (m) *trolley, stroller*
**carta** (f) *letter (mail); menu;* **la carta de vinos** (f) *wine list*
**cartera** (f) *purse, briefcase, wallet*
**carterista** (m/f) *pickpocket*
**cartero/cartera** (m/f) *mailman, mailwoman*
**casa** (f) *house, home;* **en casa** *at home;* **casa pequeña** *small house*
**casado** (adj) *married*
**cascada** (f) *waterfall*

**cascos** (m pl) *headphones*
**casi** *almost*
**castaño** *brown (hair)*
**castañuelas** (f pl) *castanets*
**castellano** *Castilian*
**Castilla** *Castile*
**castillo** (m) *castle*
**Cataluña** *Catalonia*
**catedral** (f) *cathedral*
**catedrático/catedrática** (m/f) *professor*
**católico** (adj) *Catholic*
**catorce** *fourteen*
**cazo** (m) *saucepan*
**cebo** (m) *bait*
**cebolla** (f) *onion*
**ceda el paso** (f) (verb) *give way*
**ceja** (f) *eyebrow*
**celular** (m) *cell phone*
**cementerio** (m) *cemetery*
**cena** (f) *dinner, supper, dinner party*
**cenicero** (m) *ashtray*
**centro** (m) *center; city center;* **el centro deportivo** *sports center;* **el centro comercial** *shopping center;* **en el centro middle** *in the middle*
**cepillar el pelo** (verb) *to brush hair*
**cepillo** (m) *brush (for cleaning);* **el cepillo del pelo** *hairbrush;* **el cepillo de dientes** *toothbrush*
**cerca** (f) *near, close; fence*
**cereza** (f) *cherry*
**cerilla** (f) *match (light)*
**cerrado** (adj) *closed*
**cerrar** (verb) *to close*
**cerrojo** (m) *bolt (on door)*
**certificado** (m) *certificate*
**cerveza** (f) *beer*
**césped** (m) *lawn*
**cesto** (m) *basket*
**chal** (m) *shawl*
**chalet** (m) *villa*
**champiñones** (m pl) *mushrooms*
**champú** (m) *shampoo*
**chándal** (m) *track suit*
**chaparrón** (m) *shower (rain)*
**chaqueta** (f) *jacket*
**charcutería** (f) *delicatessen*
**charla** (f) *talk*
**cheque** (m) *check*
**chica** (f) *girl*
**chicle** (m) *chewing gum*
**chico** (m) *boy*
**chimenea** (f) *chimney, fireplace*
**chincheta** (f) *thumbtack*
**chiste** (m) *joke (funny story)*
**chocolate** (m) *chocolate;* **chocolate caliente** *hot chocolate*

**chuleta** (f) *chop (food)*
**chupa-chups** (m) *lollipop*
**ciclismo** (m) *cycling*
**ciclomotor** (m) *moped*
**ciego** (adj) *blind (cannot see)*
**cielo** (m) *sky*
**cien** *hundred*
**ciencias** (f pl) *science*
**cierto** *true*
**cigalas** (f) *Norway lobster;* **cigalas cocidas** *boiled Norway lobster*
**cigarrillo** (m) *cigarette*
**cinco** *five*
**cincuenta** *fifty*
**cine** (m) *cinema*
**cinturón** (m) *belt;* **el cinturón de seguridad** *seat belt*
**cita** (f) *appointment*
**ciudad** (f) *city, town;* **el centro de la ciudad** *city center*
**claro** *clear (water); light (adj: not dark)*
**clase** (f) *class; lesson*
**clavo** (m) *nail (metal)*
**claxon** (m) *horn (car)*
**cliente** (m) *client*
**club nocturno** (m) *nightclub*
**cobrador** (m) *conductor (bus)*
**cobrar** (verb) *to cash*
**cocer** (verb) *to cook, boil*
**cocer al horno** (verb) *to bake*
**coche** (m) *car*
**coche cama** (m) *sleeper car*
**coche eléctrico** (m) *electric car*
**cochecito** (m) *stroller*
**cocina** (f) *stove; kitchen*
**cocinero/cocinera** (m/f) *cook*
**coctel** (m) *cocktail party*
**código** *code;* **el código de la circulación** *traffic laws;* **el código postal** *postcode*
**codo** (m) *elbow*
**coger** *catch;* **coger el tren** (verb) *to catch the train*
**cojín** (m) *cushion*
**col** (f) *cabbage*
**cola** (f) *line*
**colada** (f) *laundry (washed)*
**colcha** (f) *bedspread*
**colchón** (m) *mattress*
**colchoneta** (f) *air mattress*
**colección** (f) *collection (stamps, etc.)*
**coliflor** (f) *cauliflower*
**colina baja** (f) *low hill*
**collar** (m) *collar (of animal)*
**collar** (m) *necklace; color*
**combinación** (f) *slip (underwear)*
**comedor** (m) *dining room*
**comer** (verb) *to eat*
**comida** (f) *food, meal; lunch*
**comida ligera** (f) *snack*
**comisaría** (f) *police station*

**como** *like;* **como este** *like this one (similar to)*
**¿cómo?** *how?;* **¿cómo se llama usted?** *what's your name?* **¿cómo dice?** *pardon?, what did you say?*
**cómoda** (f) *chest of drawers*
**compañía aérea** (f) *airline*
**compartimento** (m) *compartment*
**completamente** *completely*
**complicado** (adj) *complicated*
**compra** (f) (verb) *shopping*
**comprar** (verb) *to buy*
**comprendo** *I see*
**compresas** (f pl) *sanitary napkins*
**con** *with*
**coñac** (m) *brandy*
**concha** (f) *shell*
**concierto** (m) *concert*
**concurrido** (adj) *crowded*
**condón** (m) *condom*
**conducir** (verb) *to drive (car)*
**conductor/conductora** (m/f) *driver*
**conejo** (m) *rabbit*
**conferencia** (f) *conference;* **la sala de conferencias** *conference room*
**congelador** (m) *freezer*
**congelados** (m pl) *frozen foods*
**conocer** (verb) *to know (person, place)*
**conserje** (m) *porter (hotel)*
**constructor/constructora** (m/f) *builder*
**consulado** (m) *consulate*
**consultor/consultora** (m/f) *consultant*
**contable** (m/f) *accountant*
**contendor de basura** (m) *bin*
**contento** (adj) *happy*
**contestador automático** (m) *answering machine*
**contra** *against*
**contraseña** (f) *password*
**contrato** (m) *contract*
**copa** (f) *glass (for drinking)*
**corazón** (m) *heart*
**corazones** (m pl) *hearts (cards)*
**corbata** (f) *tie*
**corcho** (m) *cork*
**cordero** (m) *lamb*
**cordones** (de los zapatos) (m pl) (shoe) *laces*
**correa** (f) *lead*
**correcto** (adj) *right (correct)*
**correo** (m) *mail;* **el correo certificado** *registered mail;* **el correo electrónico** *email*
**Correos** (la oficina de) **Correos** (f) *post office*
**correr** (verb) *to run*
**corrida de toros** (f) *bullfight*
**corriente** (adj) *ordinary; usual*

**cortadura** (f) *cut*
**cortar** (verb) *to chop, cut*
**cortauñas** (m) *nail clippers*
**corte de pelo** (m) *haircut*
**cortina** (f) *curtain*
**corto** (adj) *short*
**coser** (verb) *to sew*
**cosméticos** (m pl) *cosmetics*
**costar** (verb) *to cost;* **¿cuánto cuesta?** *what does it cost?*
**crema** (f) *cream (lotion)*
**crema de zapatos** (f) *shoe polish*
**cremallera** (f) *zip*
**creo que...** *I think that...*
**crepes** (f pl) *pancakes*
**crisis nerviosa** (f) *nervous breakdown*
**cristal** (m) *glass (material)*
**crucero** (m) *cruise*
**cuaderno** (m) *notebook*
**cuadrado** (adj) *square*
**¿cuál?** *which?*
**cualquiera de ellos** *either of them*
**¿cuándo?** *when?*
**¿cuánto cuesta?** *what does it cost?, how much is it?*
**¿cuántos años tiene?** *how old are you?*
**cuarenta** *forty*
**cuarentena** (f) *quarantine*
**cuarto** (m) *quarter, room;* (adj) *fourth*
**cuarto de baño** (m) *bathroom*
**cuarto de estar** (m) *living room, lounge*
**cuatro** *four*
**cubo** (m) *bucket;* **el cubo de la basura** *trashcan*
**cucaracha** (f) *cockroach*
**cuchara** (f) *spoon*
**cuchillas de afeitar** (f pl) *razor blades*
**cuchillo** (m) *knife*
**cuello** (m) *neck, collar*
**cuenco** (m) *bowl*
**cuenta** (f) *bill*
**cuerda** (f) *string, rope*
**cuerno** (m) *horn (animal)*
**cuero** (m) *leather*
**cuerpo** (m) *body*
**cueva** (f) *cave*
**¡cuidado!** *be careful!*
**cumpleaños** (m) *birthday*
**cuna** (f) *cot*
**cura** (m) *priest*
**curry** (m) *curry*

# D

**dar** *give;* **dar la bienvenida** (verb) *to welcome*
**de** *of;* **de algún modo** *somehow;* **de ida** *single (ticket)*
**debajo de...** *below..., under...*

**decir** (verb) *to say;* **¿qué ha dicho?** *what did you say?;* **¿cómo se dice...?** *how do you say...?*
**declaración** (f) *statement*
**dedo** (m) *finger*
**delante de** *in front of...*
**delgado** (adj) *thin*
**demasiado** *too (excessively)*
**démelo** *give it to me*
**dentadura postiza** (f) *dentures, false teeth*
**dentista** (m/f) *dentist*
**denuncia** (f) *police report*
**departamento** (m) *department*
**deporte** (m) *sport*
**derecho** (m) *law (subject), justice;* **no hay derecho** *it's not fair;* (adj) *right (not left)*
**desayuno** (m) *breakfast*
**descansar** (verb) *to rest*
**desinfectante de manos** (m) *hand sanitizer*
**descuento** (m) *discount*
**desmayarse** (verb) *to faint*
**desodorante** (m) *deodorant*
**despacho** (m) *office (room)*
**despegue** (m) *take off*
**despertador** (m) *alarm clock*
**después** *then (after);* **después de...** *after...*
**destornillador** (m) *screwdriver*
**detergente en polvo** (m) *powdered detergent*
**detrás de...** *behind...*
**devolver** (verb) *to return (give back); to be sick (vomit, informal)*
**día** (m) *day;* **el día de fiesta** *public holiday*
**diabético** (adj) *diabetic*
**diamantes** (m pl) *diamonds*
**diarrea** (f) *diarrhea*
**diccionario** (m) *dictionary*
**diciembre** *December*
**diecinueve** *nineteen*
**dieciocho** *eighteen*
**dieciséis** *sixteen*
**diecisiete** *seventeen*
**diente** (m) *tooth*
**diésel** *diesel* (adj: *engine*)
**diez** *ten*
**diferente** *different*
**difícil** (adj) *difficult*
**dígame** *hello (on phone)*
**dinero** (m) *money, cash;* **no tengo dinero** *I have no money*
**dirección** (f) *address*
**director/directora** (m/f) *manager (hotel); conductor (orchestra)*
**disco** (m) *record (music)*
**disco compacto** (m) *compact disc*

**diseñador/diseñadora** (m/f) designer
**disponible** (adj) available
**distancia** distance; **¿qué distancia hay a...?** how far is it to...?
**distinto** (adj) separate, different; **¡eso es distinto!** that's different!; **quería otro distinto** I'd like a different one
**diversiones** (f pl) entertainment
**divertido** (adj) odd; **raro** funny
**divorciado** (adj) divorced
**doce** twelve
**documento** (m) document
**doctorado** PhD
**dólar** (m) dollar
**dolor** (m) ache, pain; **el dolor de cabeza** headache; **el dolor de estómago** stomachache; **el dolor de muelas** toothache
**domingo** Sunday
**¿dónde?** where?; **¿dónde está...?** where is...?
**dónut** (m) doughnut
**dormir** (verb) to sleep
**dormitorio** (m) bedroom
**dos** two; **los dos** both
**droguería** drugstore
**ducha** (f) shower (bath)
**dulce** sweet (adj: not sour)
**dunas** (f pl) sand dunes
**durante** during
**duro** (adj) hard (not soft)
**duty-free** (m) duty-free shop

# E

**echar al correo** (verb) to post
**echar el cerrojo** (verb) to bolt
**edificio** (m) building
**edredón** (m) duvet
**efectivo** cash
**eje** (m) axle
**ejecutivo** (m) executive (in company)
**ejemplo** (m) example; **por ejemplo** for example
**él** (m) he, him, the; **es para él** it's for him
**elástico** elastic
**electricidad** (f) electricity
**electricista** (m/f) electrician
**eléctrico** electric
**ella** (f) she, her, the; **es para ella** it's for her
**ellos/ellas** they, them; **es para ellos/ellas** it's for them

**email** (m) email; **la dirección de email** email address
**embajada** (f) embassy
**embarazada** pregnant
**embarazoso** (adj) embarrassing
**emergencia** (f) emergency
**empaste** (m) filling (in tooth)
**empezar** (verb) to start
**empleado/empleada** (m/f) employee
**empujar** (verb) to push
**en** on, at, in; **en inglés** in English; **en el hotel** in the hotel; **en Barcelona** in Barcelona; **en Correos** at the post office; **en su casa** at your place
**encaje** (m) lace
**encantado/encantada** (m/f) pleased to meet you
**encargado** (m) caretaker
**encendedor** (m) lighter
**encendido** (m) ignition
**enchufe** (m) plug (electrical)
**encima de...** over...
**encuentro** (m) meeting; **no me encuentro bien** I don't feel well
**enero** January
**enfermo/enferma** (m/f) nurse
**enfrente de** opposite; **enfrente del hotel** opposite the hotel
**¡enhorabuena!** congratulations!
**ensalada** (f) salad
**entender** (verb) to understand; **no entiendo** I don't understand
**entonces** then, so
**entrada** (f) entrance, ticket (theatre etc); **entrada prohibida** no entry
**entrantes** (m pl) starters
**entre...** between...
**entrega** (f) delivery
**enviar por fax** (verb) to fax
**epiléptico** (adj) epileptic
**equipaje** (m) luggage; **el equipaje de mano** carry-on bag
**equipo de música** (m) music system
**equivocación** (f) mistake
**equivocado** (adj) wrong
**era** you were (formal): it/he/she was
**éramos** we were
**eran** they were
**eras** you were (informal)
**eres** you are (informal)
**es** you are (formal)
**es** it/he/she is
**escalera** (f) staircase;

**la escalera mecánica** escalator; **las escaleras** stairs
**escarcha** (f) frost
**escocés/escocesa** (m/f) Scottish
**Escocia** (f) Scotland
**escopeta** (f) gun (rifle)
**escuela** (f) school
**ese/esa** that; **ese autobús** that bus; **ese hombre** that man; **esa mujer** that woman; **¿qué es eso?** what's that?
**ese/esa** that, that one
**esmalte de uñas** (m) nail polish
**esos/esas** those, those ones; **esos hombres** those men; **esas mujeres** those women
**espalda** (f) back (body)
**España** (f) Spain
**español/española** (m/f) Spanish, Spaniard
**especialidad** (f) field of study
**espejo** (m) mirror
**esperar** (verb) to wait; **¡espere!** wait!
**espinacas** (f pl) spinach
**espuma de afeitar** (f) shaving cream
**espuma moldeadora** (f) mousse (hair)
**esquina** (f) corner (of street)
**esquís** (m pl) skis
**está** you are (formal)
**está** it/he/she is
**esta noche** tonight
**estaba** it/he/she was; you were (formal)
**estábamos** we were
**estaban** they were
**estabas** you were (informal)
**estaca** (f) tent peg
**estación** (f) station; **la estación de autobús** bus station; **la estación de esquí** ski resort; **la estación de metro** metro station
**estacionamiento prohibido** (m) no parking
**Estados Unidos** United States
**estamos** we are
**están** they are
**estanco** tobacconist
**estaquilla** (f) tent peg
**estás** you are (informal)
**estatua** (f) statue
**este** east; **el Este** the East
**este/esta** this, this one; **este hombre** this man; **esta mujer** this woman; **¿qué es esto?** what's this?; **este es el señor...** this is Mr....
**estómago** (m) stomach

**estos/estas** these, these ones; **estos hombres** these men; **estas mujeres** these women; **estos son míos** these are mine
**estoy** I am
**estrecho** (adj) narrow
**estrella** (f) star
**estudiante** (m/f) student
**estufa** (f) heater
**estúpido** (adj) stupid
**etiqueta** (f) label
**evidente** (adj) clear (obvious)
**excelente** (adj) excellent
**exceso de equipaje** (m) excess baggage
**excursión** (f) excursion, tour
**exposición** (f) exhibition
**externa** external
**extintor** (m) fire extinguisher
**extranjero/extranjera** (m/f) foreigner

# F

**fácil** (adj) easy
**factor de protección** (m) protection factor (SPF)
**factura** (f) invoice
**facturación** (f) check-in
**facturar** (verb) to check in
**falda** (f) skirt
**falta: no hace falta** there's no need
**familia** (f) family
**fan** (m) fan (enthusiast)
**fantástico** fantastic
**farmacia** (f) pharmacy
**faros** (m pl) headlights
**febrero** February
**¡felicidades!** happy birthday!
**feliz** (adj) happy
**feo** (adj) ugly
**feria** (f) fair (adj: just), trade fair
**ferretería** (f) hardware store
**ferrocarril** (m) railway
**ferry** (m) ferry
**fiebre** (f) temperature, fever; **la fiebre del heno** hay fever
**fiesta** (f) party (celebration)
**filete** (m) steak
**filtro** (m) filter
**fin** (m) end; **¡por fin!** at last!
**final** (m) end
**fino** dry (sherry)
**flash** (m) flash (camera)
**flauta** (f) flute
**flequillo** (m) bangs (hair)
**flexo** (m) angle-poise lamp
**flor** (f) flower
**folleto** (m) brochure, leaflet
**fonda** (f) inn
**fondo** (m) bottom
**fontanero/fontanera** (m/f) plumber
**foto** (grafía) (f) photograph

**fotocopiadora** (f) photocopier
**fotografiar** (verb) to photograph
**fotógrafo/fotógrafa** (m/f) photographer
**fotómetro** (m) light meter
**frambuesa** (f) raspberry
**francés** French
**Francia** France
**fregadero** (m) sink
**freír** (verb) to fry
**frenar** (verb) to brake
**freno** (m) brake; **el freno de emergencia** emergency brake; **el freno de mano** handbrake
**fresas** (f pl) strawberries
**fresco** (adj) cool
**frigorífico** (m) fridge
**frío** (adj) cold; **tengo frío** I'm cold
**frito** (adj) fried
**frontera** (f) border (between countries)
**fruta** (f) fruit
**frutería** (f) grocery
**fuego** (m) fire; **los fuegos artificiales** fireworks
**fuente** (f) fountain
**fuera** outside
**fuerte** (adj) strong
**fumar** (verb) to smoke
**funcionar** (verb) to work (function)
**fútbol** (m) soccer (game)

# G

**gabardina** (f) raincoat
**gafas** (f pl) glasses (spectacles); **las gafas de sol** sunglasses
**galería de arte** (f) art gallery
**Gales** Wales
**galés/galesa** Welsh
**galleta** (f) biscuit
**gambas** (f pl) shrimp
**ganga** (f) bargain
**garage** (m) garage (for parking)
**garantía** (f) guarantee
**garantizar** (verb) to guarantee
**garganta** (f) throat
**gas para el encendedor** (m) lighter fluid
**gasoil** (m) diesel
**gasolina** (f) gas
**gasolinera** (f) gas station
**gato** (m) cat
**gay** gay (homosexual)
**gel** (m) gel (hair); **el gel de ducha** shower gel
**gemelos** (m pl) binoculars, cuff links, twins (identical)
**general: en general** usually
**gente** (f) people
**gerente** (m/f) manager

**Gibraltar** Gibraltar
**gire** (a la izquierda/ derecha) turn (left/right)
**ginebra** (f) gin
**gobierno** (m) government
**Golfo de Vizcaya** (m) Bay of Biscay
**goma** (f) rubber band; rubber (material)
**goma de borrar** (f) eraser
**gordo** (adj) fat
**gorra** (f) cap (hat)
**gorro** (m) woollen hat
**gotas** (f pl) drops
**gotero** (m) intravenous drip
**grabar** (verb) to record
**gracias** thank you
**grado** bachelor's degree
**Gran Bretaña** Great Britain
**grande** (adj) big, large
**grandes almacenes** (m pl) department store
**granja** (f) farm
**granjero** (m) farmer
**grapadora** (f) stapler
**grasa** (f) fat (meat, etc.)
**gratis** (adj) free (no charge)
**grifo** (m) tap (water)
**gris** (adj) gray
**gritar** (verb) to shout
**grosellas negras** (f pl) black currants
**grueso** (adj) thick
**grupo** (m) party (group)
**guantes** (m pl) gloves
**guapo** (adj) attractive, beautiful, handsome (person)
**guerra** (f) war
**guía** (m/f) guide; **la guía telefónica** phone book; **la guía turística** guidebook
**guisantes** (m pl) peas
**guisar** (verb) to cook
**guitarra** (f) guitar
**gustar** (verb) to like: **me gusta...** I like...; **me gusta nadar** I like swimming

# H

**habitación** (f) room (usually in a hotel); **la habitación doble** double room; **la habitación individual** single room; **habitaciones libres** vacancies
**hablar** (verb) to talk; **¿habla...?** do you speak...?; **no hablo...** I don't speak...
**hacer** (verb) to do, make; **hacer autostop** to hitchhike; **hacer footing** to jog; **hacer punto** to knit; **hacer transbordo** to change (trains, etc.); **hace sol** (adj) it's sunny

**hacha** (m) *ax*
**hacia abajo** *down*
**hambre** *hungry;* **tengo hambre** *I'm hungry*
**hamburguesa** (f) *hamburger*
**hámster** (m) *hamster*
**harina** (f) *flour*
**hasta** *until*
**hay...** *there is/are...;* **¿hay...?** *is/are there...?*
**helado** (m) *ice cream*
**hepatitis** (f) *hepatitis*
**herida** (f) *injury*
**hermana** (f) *sister*
**hermano** (m) *brother*
**hervido** (adj) *boiled*
**hervidor de agua** (m) *kettle*
**hervir** (verb) *to boil* (water)
**hidroaleta** (f) *hydrofoil*
**hielo** (m) *ice*
**hierba** (f) *grass*
**hierro** (m) *iron* (material)
**hígado** (m) *liver*
**higo** (m) *fig*
**hija** (f) *daughter*
**hijastra** (f) *stepdaughter*
**hijastro** (m) *stepson*
**hijo** (m) *son*
**hincha** (m) *soccer fan*
**historia** (f) *history*
**hobby** (m) *hobby*
**hoguera** (f) *campfire*
**hoja** (f) *leaf, sheet* (of paper)
**hojalata** (f) *tin*
**hola** *hello*
**hombre** (m) *man*
**hombro** (m) *shoulder*
**homeopatía** (f) *homeopathy*
**honrado** (adj) *honest*
**hora** (f) *hour;* **¿qué hora es?** *what's the time?*
**horario** (m) *timetable;* **el horario de apertura** *opening times*
**horca** (f) *garden fork*
**horno** (m) *oven*
**horrible** (adj) *awful, horrible*
**hospital** (m) *hospital*
**hoy** *today*
**hueso** (m) *bone*
**huevo** (m) *egg*
**húmedo** (adj) *damp*
**humo** (m) *smoke*

# I

**idioma** (m) *language*
**iglesia** (f) *church*
**imperdible** (m) *safety pin*
**imposible** *impossible*
**impreso de solicitud** (m) *application form*
**impresora** (f) *printer*
**incendio** (m) *fire* (blaze)
**incluido** *included*

**indigestión** (f) *indigestion*
**infección** (f) *infection*
**información** (f) *information*
**informe** (m) *report*
**ingeniería** (f) *engineering*
**Inglaterra** (f) *England*
**inglés/inglesa** *English*
**inhalador** (m) *inhaler* (for asthma, etc.)
**inmediatamente** *immediately*
**insecto** (m) *insect*
**insolación** (f) *sunstroke*
**insomnio** (m) *insomnia*
**instrumento musical** (m) *musical instrument*
**intentar** (verb) *to try*
**interesante** (adj) *interesting*
**intermitente** (m) *indicator*
**internet** (m) *Internet*
**interpretar** (verb) *to interpret*
**intérprete** (m/f) *interpreter*
**interruptor** (m) *switch*
**intoxicación alimenticia** (f) *food poisoning*
**invitación** (f) *invitation*
**invitada** (f) *guest*
**inyección** (f) *injection*
**ir** (verb) *to go;* **ir a esquiar** *to go skiing;* **ir de compras** *to go shopping*
**Irlanda** (f) *Ireland;* **Irlanda del Norte** *Northern Ireland*
**irlandés/irlandesa** *Irish*
**isla** (f) *island*
**Italia** (f) *Italy*
**italiano/italiana** (m/f) *Italian*
**izquierdo** *left* (not right)

# J

**jabón** (m) *soap*
**jamón** (m) *ham*
**jarabe** (m) *syrup*
**jardín** (m) *garden*
**jarrita** (f) *mug*
**jarrón** (m) *vase*
**jaula** (f) *cage*
**jazz** (m) *jazz*
**jefe/jefa** (m/f) *manager*
**jengibre** (m) *ginger* (spice)
**jerez** (m) *sherry*
**jeringuilla** (f) *syringe*
**jersey** (m) *sweater*
**joven** (adj) *young*
**joyería** (f) *jeweler's*
**judías** (f pl) *beans*
**jueves** *Thursday*
**jugar** (verb) *to play*
**juguete** (m) *toy*
**julio** *July*
**junio** *June*
**junto a** *near;* **junto a la puerta** *near the door;* **junto a la ventana** *near the window*
**juntos** *together*

# K, L

**kebab** (m) *grilled meat* (pressed and cut in slices)
**kilo** (m) *kilo*
**kilómetro** (m) *kilometer*
**kiosko de periódicos** (m) *newsagent's*
**la** (f) *the*
**laca** (f) *hairspray*
**lado de** (f) *beside*
**ladrón/ladrona** (m/f) *thief*
**lago** (m) *lake*
**lámpara** (f) *lamp*
**lamparilla de noche** (f) *bedside lamp*
**lana** (f) *wool*
**langosta** (f) *lobster*
**lápiz** (m) *pencil*
**largo** (adj) *long*
**las** (f pl) *the*
**lata** (f) *can* (tin)
**lavabo** (m) *basin* (sink)
**lavandería automática** (f) *self-service laundry*
**lavavajillas** (m) *dishwasher*
**laxante** (m) *laxative*
**leche** (f) *milk;* **la leche limpiadora** *cleansing milk* (for skin); **la leche merengada** *milkshake with cinnamon*
**lechuga** (f) *lettuce*
**leer** (verb) *to read*
**lejía** (f) *bleach*
**lejos** *far, far away*
**lengua** (f) *tongue*
**lente** (f) (camera) *lens;* **las lentes de contacto** *contact lenses;* **las lentes de contacto semirígidas** *gas-permeable lenses*
**lento** (adj) *slow*
**letra** (f) *letter* (of alphabet)
**levantarse** (verb) *to get up* (rise)
**libra** (f) *pound* (sterling)
**libre** *free* (not engaged)
**libre de impuestos** *duty-free*
**libro** (m) *book;* **el libro de frases** *phrase book*
**licor** (m) *liqueur*
**ligero** (adj) *light* (not heavy)
**lima** (f) *lime* (fruit)
**lima de uñas** (f) *nailfile*
**límite de velocidad** (m) *speed limit*
**limón** (m) *lemon*
**limonada** (f) *lemonade*
**limpio** (adj) *clean;* **limpiar** (verb) *to clean*
**línea** (f) *line* (phone, etc.)
**linterna** (f) *torch*
**líquido lavavajillas** (m) *dishwashing liquid*
**lista** (f) *list*
**listo** (adj) *clever; ready*

**literatura** (f) *literature*
**litro** (m) *liter*
**llamar por teléfono** (verb) *to telephone*
**llave** (f) *key;* **la llave de las tuercas** *wheel brace;* **la llave inglesa** *wrench*
**llegar** (verb) *to arrive*
**lleno** (adj) *crowded, full;* **estoy lleno** *I'm full (up)*
**llorar** (verb) *to cry (weep)*
**lluvia** (f) *rain*
**lo/la** *it*
**lo antes posible** *as soon as possible*
**loción** (f) *lotion;* **la loción antimosquitos** *insect repellent lotion;* **la loción bronceadora** *suntan lotion*
**loco** *mad*
**lona impermeable** (f) *ground sheet*
**longitud** (f) *length*
**los** (m pl) *the*
**lo siento** *I'm sorry*
**luces de posición** (f pl) *side lights*
**lugar** (m) *place, sight;* **los lugares de interés de...** *the sights of...*
**luna** (f) *moon*
**lunes** *Monday*
**luz** (f) *light*

# M

**madastra** (f) *stepmother*
**madera** (f) *wood (material)*
**madre** (f) *mother*
**maduro** (adj) *ripe*
**malas hierbas** (f pl) *weeds*
**maleta** (f) *suitcase*
**maletero** (m) *trunk (car)*
**Mallorca** *Majorca*
**malo** (adj) *bad, poor (quality)*
**mama** (f) *mom*
**mañana** *tomorrow*
**mañana** (f) *morning;* **por la mañana** *in the morning*
**mandar** (verb) *to send*
**mandarina** (f) *tangerine*
**manga** (f) *sleeve*
**mano** (f) *hand*
**manta** (f) *blanket, rug*
**mantequilla** (f) *butter*
**manzana** (f) *apple*
**mapa** (m) *map;* **los mapas en línea** *online map*
**maquillaje** (m) *makeup*
**máquina cortacésped** (f) *lawn mower*
**máquina de escribir** (f) *typewriter*
**máquina de fotos** (f) *camera*
**mar** (m) *sea*
**marea** (f) *tide*

**mareado** *faint, dizzy*
**margarina** (f) *margarine*
**marido** (m) *husband*
**mariscos** (m pl) *seafood, shellfish*
**mármol** (m) *marble*
**marrón** *brown*
**Marruecos** *Morocco*
**martes** *Tuesday*
**martillo** (m) *hammer*
**marzo** *March*
**más** *more;* **más de...** *more than...;* **más tarde** *later;* **algo más** *something else;* **alguien más** *someone else*
**mascarilla** (f) *face mask*
**máster** *master's degree*
**mástil** (m) *tent pole*
**matrícula** (f) *number plate*
**mayo** *may*
**mecánico/mecánica** (m/f) *mechanic*
**media pensión** *half board*
**medianoche** (f) *midnight*
**medias** (f pl) *tights, stockings*
**medicina** (f) *medicine (subject)*
**médico/médica** (m/f) *doctor*
**medio** *half;* **media hora** *half an hour*
**mediodía** (m) *midday, noon*
**Mediterráneo: el Mediterráneo** *Mediterranean*
**medusa** (f) *jellyfish*
**mejillones** (m pl) *mussels*
**mejor** (m/f) *best/better*
**melocotón** (m) *peach*
**melón** (m) *melon*
**menos** *less*
**mensaje** (m) *message*
**mensajería de voz** (f) *voicemail*
**menú** (del día) (m) *set menu*
**menudo: a menudo** *often*
**mercado** (m) *market*
**merienda** *afternoon snack*
**mermelada** (f) *jam;* **la mermelada de naranja** *marmalade*
**mes** (m) *month*
**mesa** (f) *table;* **la mesa de escritorio** *desk*
**mesilla de noche** (f) *bedside table*
**metro** (m) *underground (railway)*
**mi** (s) *my;* **mi libro** *my book;* **mis llaves** *my keys*
**microondas** (m) *microwave*
**miel** (f) *honey*
**miércoles** *Wednesday*
**mil** *thousand*

**minusválido** (adj) *disabled*
**minuto** (m) *minute*
**mío** *mine;* **es mío** *it's mine*
**mirar** (verb) *to watch*
**misa** (f) *mass (church)*
**mismo** *same;* **el mismo vestido** *the same dress;* **la misma gente** *the same people;* **lo mismo otra vez, por favor** *same again, please*
**mochila** (f) *backpack*
**moda** (f) *fashion*
**módem** (m) *modem*
**mojado** (adj) *wet*
**moneda** (f) *coin*
**monedero** (m) *purse*
**monitor** (m) *monitor (computer)*
**montaña** (f) *mountain;* **montaña alta** *high mountain*
**monte** (m) *hill*
**monumento** (m) *monument*
**morado** *purple*
**moras** (f pl) *blackberries*
**mordedura** (f) *bite (dog)*
**morder** (verb) *to bite (dog)*
**morir** (verb) *to die*
**mosaico** (m) *mosaic*
**mosca** (f) *fly (insect)*
**mosquito** (m) *mosquito*
**mostaza** (f) *mustard*
**mostrador** (m) *countertop;* **el mostrador de facturación** *check-in desk*
**motocicleta** (f) *motorcycle*
**motor** (m) *engine (car)*
**motora** (f) *motorboat*
**mover** (verb) *to move (something);* **moverse** *move oneself;* **¡no se mueva!** *don't move!*
**móvil** (m) *cell phone*
**mucho** *much/many, a lot;* **mucho mejor** *much better;* **mucho más despacio** *much slower;* **no muchos** *not many*
**mudarse** (de casa) (verb) *to move (house)*
**muebles** (m pl) *furniture*
**muela** (f) *back tooth*
**muelle** (m) *dock; spring (mechanical)*
**muerto** (adj) *dead*
**mujer** (f) *woman, wife*
**muletas** (f pl) *crutches*
**muñeca** (f) *wrist*
**muro** (m) *wall (outside)*
**museo** (m) *museum*
**música** (f) *music;* **la música clásica** *classical music;* **la música folclórica** *folk music;* **la música** *pop music*
**músico** (m) *musician*
**muy** *very*

# N

**nací en...** *I was born in...*
**nada** *nothing;* **no queda nada** *there's nothing left;* **no sirve de nada** *it's no use*
**nadar** (verb) *to swim*
**nadie** *nobody*
**naranja** (f) *orange (fruit);* (adj) *orange*
**nariz** (f) *nose*
**nata** (f) *cream (dairy)*
**natación** (f) *swimming*
**náuseas** (adj) *sick;* **tengo náuseas** *I feel sick*
**navaja** (f) *penknife*
**Navidad** (f) *Christmas*
**necesario** (adj) *necessary*
**necesito...** *I need...*
**negar** (verb) *to deny*
**negativo** (m) *negative (photo)*
**negocio** (m) *business*
**negro** (adj) *black*
**neozelandés/ neozelandesa** *New Zealander*
**neumático** (m) *tire*
**ni...ni...** *neither...nor...*
**niebla** (f) *fog*
**nieta** (f) *granddaughter*
**nieto** (m) *grandson*
**nieve** (f) *snow*
**ninguno/ninguna: ninguno de ellos** *neither of them;* **en ninguna parte** *nowhere*
**niño/niña** *child (m/f);* **los niños** *children;* **el niño pequeño** *baby*
**no** *no (response), not;* **no hay de qué** *you're welcome;* **no importa** *it doesn't matter;* **no es/ está...** *(s) he's not...*
**noche** (f) *night*
**nombre** (m) *name;* **el nombre de pila** *first name*
**norte** (m) *north*
**nosotros/nosotras** *we, us;* **es para nosotros/ nosotras** *it's for us*
**noticias** (f pl) *news*
**novela** (f) *novel*
**noventa** *ninety*
**novia** (f) *girlfriend*
**noviembre** *November*
**novio** (m) *boyfriend*
**nudista** (m/f) *nudist*
**nuestro** *our;* **es nuestro** *it's ours*
**Nueva Zelanda** *New Zealand*
**nueve** *nine*
**nuevo** (adj) *new*
**nuez** (f) *nut (fruit)*
**número** (m) *number;* **los números** *figures*
**nunca** *never*

# O

**o** *or;* **o bien...o...** *either...or...*
**obra de teatro** (f) *play (theater)*
**obturador** (m) *shutter (camera)*
**Océano Atlántico** (m) *Atlantic Ocean*
**ochenta** *eighty*
**ocho** *eight*
**octubre** *October*
**oculista** (m/f) *optician*
**ocupado** (adj) *busy (engaged); occupied*
**oeste** (m) *west*
**oficina** (f) *office (place); branch (of company);* **la oficina de objetos perdidos** *lost property office;* **oficina de información turística** *tourist office;* **oficina del camping** *campsite office*
**oído** (m) *(inner) ear*
**¡oiga, por favor!** *excuse me! (to get attention); waiter/waitress!*
**oír** (verb) *to hear*
**ojo** (m) *eye*
**ola** (f) *wave*
**oler** (verb) *to smell*
**olivo** (m) *olive tree*
**olor** (m) *smell*
**oloroso** *sweet (sherry)*
**olvidar** (verb) *to forget*
**once** *eleven*
**ondulado** (adj) *wavy (hair)*
**operación** (f) *operation*
**operadora** (f) *operator (phone)*
**oporto** (m) *port (drink)*
**orden del día** (m) *agenda*
**ordenador** (m) *computer*
**oreja** (f) *ear*
**órgano** (m) *organ (music)*
**oro** (m) *gold*
**orquesta** (f) *orchestra*
**oscuro** *dark;* **azul oscuro** (adj) *dark blue*
**ostra** (f) *oyster*
**otra vez** *again*
**otro** *another; other;* **el otro** *the other one;* **en otro sitio** *somewhere else*

# P

**padastro** (m) *stepfather*
**padre** (m) *father;* **los padres** *parents*
**pagar** (verb) *to pay;* **pagar al contado** *to pay cash*
**página** (f) *page;* **página web** (f) *website*
**pago** (m) *payment;* **pago sin contacto** *contactless payment*

**país** (m) *country (state)*
**pájaro** (m) *bird*
**pala** (f) *spade*
**palabra** (f) *word*
**palacio** (m) *palace*
**palanca de velocidades** (f) *gear stick*
**pálido** (adj) *pale*
**pan** (m) *bread;* **pan con jamón** *bread with ham;* **pan con tomate** *bread with tomato*
**panadería** (f) *bakery*
**pañal** (m) *diaper;* **los pañales desechables** *disposable diapers*
**pandemia** *pandemic*
**paño de cocina** (m) *dish towel*
**pantalla** (f) *lampshade, screen*
**pantalón** (m) *pants;* **los pantalones cortos** *shorts*
**pantis** (m pl) *tights*
**pañuelo** (m) *headscarf;* **los pañuelos de papel** *tissues*
**papá** (m) *dad*
**papel** (m) *paper;* **el papel de envolver/regalo** *wrapping paper;* **el papel de escribir** *writing paper;* **el papel higiénico** *toilet paper;* **los papeles de filtro** *filter papers*
**paquete** (m) *package, packet*
**par** (m) *pair*
**para** *for;* **es para mí** *it's for me;* **para el viernes** *by Friday;* **¿para qué?** *what for?;* **para una semana** *for a week*
**parabrisas** (m) *windshield*
**parachoques** (m) *bumper*
**parada** (f) *stop (bus);* **la parada de taxis** *taxi stand*
**parafina** (f) *paraffin*
**paraguas** (m) *umbrella*
**parar** (verb) *to stop*
**pared** (f) *wall (inside)*
**pariente** (m) *relative*
**parque** (m) *park*
**parrilla** (f) *grill*
**parte de atrás** (f) *back (not front)*
**parterre** (m) *flowerbed*
**partido** (m) *match (sport); party (political)*
**pasajero** (m) *passenger*
**pasaporte** (m) *passport;* **el pasaporte de animales** *pet passport*
**pasas** (f pl) *raisins*
**paseo** (m) *walk, stroll;* **ir de paseo** (verb) *to go for a walk*
**pasillo** (m) *aisle, corridor*
**paso elevado** (m) *flyover*
**pasta** (f) *pasta*

**pasta dentífrica** (f) *toothpaste*
**pastel** (m) *cake* (small)
**pastelería** (f) *cake shop*
**pastilla** (f) *pill, tablet;* **las pastillas de menta** *peppermints;* **las pastillas para la garganta** *cough drops*
**patata** (f) *potato;* **las patatas fritas** *potato chips*
**patinar** (verb) *to skid*
**patines para hielo** (m pl) *ice skates*
**peatón** (m) *pedestrian*
**pecho** (m) *chest (part of body)*
**pedazo** (m) *piece*
**pedido** (m) *order*
**pegamento** (m) *adhesive, glue*
**peinar** (verb) *to comb*
**peine** (m) *comb*
**película** (f) *film, movie;* **la película en color** *color film*
**peligroso** (adj) *dangerous*
**pelo** (m) *hair*
**pelota** (f) *ball*
**peluquería** (f) *hairdresser;* **la peluquería de caballeros** (barbero) *barber*
**pendientes** (m pl) *earrings*
**pensar** (verb) *to think;* **lo pensaré** *I'll think about it*
**pensión completa** *full board*
**peor** *worse, worst*
**pepino** (m) *cucumber*
**pequeño** (adj) *little, small*
**pera** (f) *pear*
**percha** (f) *coat hanger*
**¡perdón!** *sorry!, excuse me!* (when sneezing, etc.)
**perejil** (m) *parsley*
**perezoso** (adj) *lazy*
**perfecto** (adj) *perfect*
**perfume** (m) *perfume*
**periódico** (m) *newspaper*
**perla** (f) *pearl*
**permanente** (f) *perm*
**permiso** (m) *license*
**pero** *but*
**perro** (m) *dog*
**persianas** (f pl) *blinds*
**persona de la limpieza** (f) *cleaning staff*
**pesado** (adj) *heavy*
**pesca** (f) *fishing*
**pescadería** (f) *fishmonger's*
**pescado** (m) *fish (food)*
**pescar: ir a pescar** (verb) *to go fishing*
**pez** (m) *fish (animal)*
**piano** (m) *piano*
**picadura** (f) *bite (by insect)*
**picaporte** (m) *handle (door)*
**picar** (verb) *to bite (insect)*
**picas** (f pl) *spades (cards)*
**pícnic** (m) *picnic*
**pie** (m) *foot*

**pierna** (f) *leg*
**pijama** (m) *pajamas*
**pila** (f) *battery (flashlight, etc.)*
**piloto** (m) *pilot*
**pimienta** (f) *pepper (spice)*
**pimiento** (m) *bell pepper (red, green)*
**pin** (m) *PIN*
**piña** (f) *pineapple*
**pinchazo** (m) *puncture*
**pinchitos/pinchos** (m) *grilled meat (on a skewer)*
**pino** (m) *pine (tree)*
**pintor/pintora** (m/f) *decorator*
**pintura** (f) *paint*
**pinza** (f) *peg;* **las pinzas** *tweezers*
**pipa** (f) *pipe (for smoking)*
**Pirineos: los Pirineos** *Pyrenees*
**piscina** (f) *swimming pool;* **la piscina municipal** *public swimming pool*
**piso** (m) *apartment; floor (storey)*
**pista** (f) *runway*
**pistola** (f) *gun (pistol)*
**pistón** (m) *piston*
**pizza** (f) *pizza*
**plancha** (f) *iron (for clothes);* **a la plancha** *grilled*
**planchar** (verb) *to iron*
**plano** (m) *town map, town plan, day's schedule;* (adj) *flat, level*
**planta** (f) *plant*
**planta baja** (f) *ground floor*
**plástico** (m) *plastic;* **el plástico para envolver** *plastic wrap*
**plata** (f) *silver (metal)*
**plátano** (m) *banana*
**plateado** *silver (color)*
**platillo** (m) *saucer*
**plato** (m) *plate;* **el plato principal** *main course;* **los platos preparados** *ready meals*
**playa** (f) *beach*
**plaza** (f) *square (in town);* **la plaza de toros** *bullring*
**pluma** (f) *pen;* **la pluma estilográfica** *fountain pen*
**pobre** (adj) *poor (not rich)*
**poco** *a little;* **poco común** (adj) *unusual;* **poco hecho/pasado** *rare (steak)*
**poder** (verb) *to be able*
**policía** (f) *police*
**policía** (m) *police officer*
**política** (f) *politics*
**pollo** (m) *chicken*
**polvo** (m) *powder;* **los polvos** *makeup powder;* **los polvos de talco** *talcum powder*
**pomada** (f) *ointment*

**poner** (verb) *to put;* **¿me pone...?** *can I have...?*
**poquito** *a little;* **solo un poquito** *just a little*
**por** *through, by, per;* **por avión** *by air mail;* **por la noche** *at night;* **por noche** *per night* **por todas** *for all*
**porcelana** (f) *china (wear)*
**por favor** *please*
**¿por qué?** *why?*
**porque** *because*
**portátil** (m) *laptop*
**portero** (m) *caretaker*
**Portugal** *Portugal*
**portugués** *Portuguese*
**posible** *possible*
**postal** (f) *postcard*
**póster** (m) *poster*
**postigo** (m) *shutter (window)*
**postre** (m) *dessert*
**precio** (m) *price;* **el precio de entrada** (m) *admission charge*
**precioso** *beautiful (object)*
**preferir** (verb) *to prefer*
**pregunta** (f) *question*
**presupuesto** (m) *budget, estimate, quotation*
**primavera** (f) *spring (season)*
**primer piso** (m) *first floor*
**primero** *first;* **de primera** *first class;* **primeros auxilios** *first aid*
**primo** (m) *cousin*
**prima** (f) *cousin*
**principiante** (m/f) *beginner*
**principio** (m) *start, beginning*
**prisa: tengo prisa** *I'm in a hurry*
**privado** (adj) *private*
**problema** (m) *problem*
**producto** (m) *product;* **los productos de belleza** *beauty products;* **los productos de limpieza** *household products;* **los productos lácteos** *dairy products*
**profesión** (f) *profession*
**profesor/profesora** (m/f) *teacher*
**profesor/profesora de universidad** (m/f) *lecturer (university)*
**profundo** (adj) *deep*
**programa** (m) *schedule*
**prohibido** *prohibited*
**prohibido estacionar** (m) *no parking*
**prometida** (f) *fiancée*
**prometido** (m) *fiancé*
**prometido/prometida** (m/f) *engaged (to be married)*
**propina** (f) *tip (money)*
**propuesta** (f) *business proposal*

**próximo** next
**prudente** (adj) careful
**prueba** (f) test
**público** public
**pueblo** (m) small town, village
**¿puede...?** can you...?
**puedo** I can; **no puedo** I can't
**puente** (m) bridge
**puerta** (f) door, gate; **la puerta de embarque** departure gate
**puerto** (m) harbor, port
**pulga** (f) flea
**pulpo** (m) octopus
**pulsera** (f) bracelet
**punta** (f) tip (end)
**puro** (m) cigar

# Q

**que** than
**¿qué?** what?
**quemadura** (f) burn
**quemadura de sol** (f) sunburn
**quemar** (verb) to burn
**querer** (verb) to want, love
**querido** (adj) dear (person)
**queso** (m) cheese
**¿qué tal?** how are you?
**¿quién?** who?
**quince** fifteen
**quirófano** (m) operating room
**quisquillas** (f pl) shrimps
**quizás** maybe, perhaps

# R

**rábano** (m) radish
**radiador** (m) radiator
**radio** (f) radio
**rápido** (adj) fast, quick
**raro** rare (uncommon)
**rastrillo** (m) rake
**rata** (f) rat
**ratón** (m) mouse
**raya** (f) part (in hair)
**rebajas** (f pl) sale (at reduced prices)
**rebeca** (f) cardigan
**recado** (m) message
**recepción** (f) reception
**recepcionista** (m/f) receptionist
**receta** (f) prescription
**recibo** (m) receipt
**recobrar algo** (verb) to get something back
**recogida** (f) collection (postal)
**récord** (m) record (sports, etc.)
**recuerdo** (m) souvenir
**redondo** (adj) round (circular)
**regalo** (m) gift; **el regalo de cumpleaños** birthday present
**regla** (f) ruler (for measuring)
**reír** (verb) to laugh
**rejilla de equipajes** (f) luggage rack

**relajarse** (verb) to relax
**religión** (f) religion
**relleno** (m) filling (in sandwich, cake)
**reloj** (m) clock, watch; **reloj de pared** (m) wall clock
**remar** (verb) to row
**remolque** (m) trailer
**remos** (m pl) oars
**resaca** (f) hangover
**reserva** (f) reservation
**reservar** (verb) to book
**resfriado** (m) cold (illness); **tengo un resfriado** I have a cold
**respirar** (verb) to breathe
**restaurante** (m) restaurant
**resto** (m) rest, remainder
**retrasado** (adj) delayed; **el autobús se ha retrasado** the bus is late
**reunión** (f) meeting
**revelar** (verb) to develop (film)
**revista** (f) magazine
**rico** (adj) rich
**rímel** (m) mascara
**rincón** (m) corner (of room)
**riñón** (m) kidney
**río** (m) river
**rizos** (m pl) curls
**robar** (verb) to steal; **lo han robado** it's been stolen
**robo** (m) robbery
**roca** (f) rock (stone)
**rock** (m) rock (music)
**rodilla** (f) knee
**rojo** red
**ron** (m) rum
**ropa** (f) clothes; **la ropa de cama** bed linen; **la ropa interior** underwear; **la ropa sucia** laundry (dirty)
**rosa** (adj) pink
**rosa** (f) rose
**roto** (adj) broken
**rotonda** (f) roundabout
**rotulador** (m) felt-tip pen
**rubí** (m) ruby (stone)
**rubio/rubia** (adj) blond(e)
**rueda** (f) wheel; **la rueda pinchada** flat tire
**rugby** (m) rugby
**ruidoso** (adj) noisy
**ruinas** (f pl) ruins
**rulos** (m pl) curlers

# S

**sábado** Saturday
**sábana** (f) sheet (bedding)
**saber** (verb) to know (fact); **no sé** I don't know
**sabor** (m) flavor
**sacacorchos** (m) corkscrew
**sacapuntas** (m) pencil sharpener
**sacar** (verb) to bring out

**saco de dormir** (m) sleeping bag
**sal** (f) salt
**sala de espera** (f) waiting room
**sala de pediatría** (f) children's ward
**salchicha** (f) sausage
**salida** (f) exit, departure; **las salidas** departures (airport etc); **la salida de emergencia** emergency exit
**salmón** (m) salmon
**salón** (m) lounge (in hotel)
**salsa** (f) sauce
**¡salud!** cheers! (toast)
**saludar con la mano** (verb) to wave
**sandalias** (f pl) sandals
**sangre** (f) blood
**sartén** (f) frying pan
**sauna** (f) sauna
**secador** (de pelo) (m) hairdryer
**seco** dry
**sed** (adj) thirsty; **tengo sed** I'm thirsty
**seda** (f) silk
**segundo** (m) second (noun; adj); **de segunda** second class
**seguro** (m) insurance; (adj) sure, safe (not dangerous)
**seis** six
**sello** (m) stamp
**selva** rainforest
**semáforo** (m) traffic lights
**semana** (f) week; **la semana pasada** last week; **la semana que viene** next week
**seminario** (m) seminar
**semiseco** medium-dry (wine)
**señal** (f) deposit
**sencillo** (adj) simple
**senderismo** (m) hiking
**señor** Mr., sir
**señora** Mrs., madam
**señorita** Miss
**sentido obligatorio** (m) one way
**separado** separated
**septiembre** September
**ser** (verb) to be
**serio** (adj) serious
**seropositivo** HIV-positive
**servicio** (m) service, department; **el servicio de habitaciones** room service; **el servicio de limpieza** housekeeping (at a hotel); **el servicio de radiología** x-ray department; **el servicio de urgencias** emergency department

**servicios** (m pl) *toilets* (in public establishment); **los servicios de caballeros** *men's toilets;* **los servicios de señoras** *women's toilets*
**servilleta** (f) *napkin*
**sesenta** *sixty*
**setas** (f pl) *mushrooms*
**setenta** *seventy*
**seto** (m) *hedge*
**si** *if, whether*
**sí** *yes*
**sida** (m) *AIDS*
**siempre** *always*
**siesta** (f) *nap*
**siete** *seven*
**significar: ¿qué significa esto?** *what does this mean?*
**siguiente** *next*
**silla** (f) *chair;* **la silla de bebé** *car seat (for a baby);* **la silla de paseo** *stroller;* **la silla de ruedas** *wheelchair*
**sillón** (m) *armchair*
**simpático** (adj) *friendly*
**sin** *without;* **sin plomo** *unleaded*
**sinagoga** (f) *synagogue*
**sitio** (m) *room, space;* **sitio web** *website*
**sobre** (m) *envelope*
**sobre todo** *especially*
**sobrina** (f) *niece*
**sobrino** (m) *nephew*
**soda** (f) *soda water*
**sofa** (m) *sofa*
**sofocante** *close, stuffy*
**sol** (m) *sun*
**solo** (adj) *alone;* **yo solo** *by myself*
**solo** *just, only*
**soltero/soltera** (m/f) (adj) *single (unmarried)*
**solución limpiadora** (f) *saline solution (for contact lenses)*
**sombrero** (m) *hat*
**sombrilla** (f) *sunshade*
**somnífero** (m) *sleeping pill*
**somos** *we are*
**son** *they are*
**sonreír** (verb) *to smile*
**sonrisa** (f) *smile*
**sopa** (f) *soup*
**sordo** (adj) *deaf*
**sostén** (m) *bra*
**sótano** (m) *basement*
**soy** *I am;* **soy de…** *I come from…*
**spray** (m) *inhaler (for asthma, etc.);* **el spray antipulgas** *flea spray*
**su** (s) *its/hers/his/your (formal);* **¿es suyo esto?** *is this yours?*

**subirse** (verb) *to get in, get on (of train, bus, etc.)*
**sucio** *dirty*
**sudadera** (f) *sweatshirt*
**Sudamérica** *South America*
**sudar** (verb) *to sweat*
**sudor** (m) *sweat*
**suelo** (m) *floor (ground);* **el suelo aislante** *ground sheet*
**sueño** (m) *sleep*
**suerte** (f) *luck;* **¡suerte!** *good luck!*
**supermercado** (m) *supermarket*
**suplemento** (m) *supplement*
**supositorio** (m) *suppository*
**sur** (m) *south*

# T

**tabaco** (m) *tobacco*
**taberna** (f) *bar*
**tabla de windsurfing** (f) *sailboard*
**tableta de chocolate** (f) *bar of chocolate*
**tacón** (m) *heel (shoe)*
**taller** (m) *garage (for repairs)*
**talón** (m) *heel (foot)*
**talonario de cheques** (m) *checkbook*
**también** *too (also)*
**tampones** (m pl) *tampons*
**tan** *so;* **tan bueno** *so good*
**tanto: no tanto** *not so much;* **tanto… como…** *both… and…*
**tapas** *small plates (food)*
**tapiz** (m) *tapestry*
**tapón** (m) *cap (bottle), plug (sink)*
**taquilla** (f) *box office, ticket office*
**tarde** (f) *evening;* (adj) *late; it's getting late* **se está haciendo** *tarde*
**tarifa** (f) *fare*
**tarjeta** (f) *card;* **la tarjeta de banco** *bank card;* **la tarjeta de crédito** *credit card;* **la tarjeta de débito** *debit card;* **la tarjeta de embarque** *boarding pass;* **la tarjeta de vista** *business card;* **la tarjeta telefónica** *phonecard;* **la tarjeta SIM** *SIM card*
**tarta** (f) *cake (large)*
**taxi** (m) *taxi*
**taza** (f) *cup*
**té** (m) *tea (usually black but can also refer to green, red, herbal, or fruit tea);* **té con leche** *tea with milk;* **té con limón** *tea with lemon;* **té negro** *black tea*

**techo** (m) *ceiling*
**teclado** (m) *keyboard*
**técnico/técnica** (m/f) *technician*
**tejado** (m) *roof*
**tejanos** (m pl) *jeans*
**tela** (f) *material (cloth)*
**teleférico** (m) *cable car*
**teléfono** (m) *telephone*
**televisión** (f) *television;* **la televisión por** *cable TV*
**temperatura** (f) *temperature*
**temprano** *early*
**tenedor** (m) *fork*
**tener** (verb) *to have;* **tengo** *I have;* **no tengo** *I don't have;* **¿tiene?** *do you have?;* **tengo que irme** *I have to go;* **tengo calor** *I feel hot;* **tengo que…** *must…*
**teñir** (verb) *to bleach (hair)*
**tenis** (m) *tennis*
**tenue** *faint (unclear)*
**tercero** *third*
**terminal** (f) *terminal*
**ternera** (f) *veal*
**terraza** (f) *terrace*
**testigo** (m/f) *witness*
**tía** (f) *aunt*
**tiempo** (m) *time, weather*
**tienda** (f) *shop;* **la tienda de alimentación** *grocer's;* **la tienda de discos** *record store*
**tienda (de campaña)** (f) *tent*
**¿tiene…?** *do you have…?*
**tierra** (f) *land, soil*
**tijeras** (f pl) *scissors*
**timbre** (m) *bell (door)*
**tinta** (f) *ink*
**tinto** *red (wine)*
**tintorería** (f) *dry cleaner*
**tío** (m) *uncle*
**tirantes** (m pl) *braces*
**tirar de** (verb) *to pull*
**tirita** (f) *plaster*
**toalla** (f) *towel*
**toallitas para bebé** (f pl) *baby wipes*
**tobillo** (m) *ankle*
**toca: me toca a mí** *it's my turn*
**tocadiscos** (m) *record player*
**tocar** (verb) *to feel (touch)*
**todavía** *yet;* **todavía no** *not yet*
**todo** *everything, all;* **eso es todo** *that's all*
**todos** *everyone*
**todos los días** *every day*
**tomar** (verb) *to take;* **tomar el sol** *to sunbathe*

**tomate** (m) *tomato*
**tónica** (f) *tonic*
**torero** (m) *bullfighter*
**tormenta** (f) *storm*
**tornillo** (m) *screw*
**toro** (m) *bull*
**torre** (f) *tower*
**tortilla** (f) *omelet* (egg); *tortilla* (flatbread)
**tos** (f) *cough*
**toser** (verb) *to cough*
**tostada** (f) *toast*; **tostada con mantequilla y mermelada** *toast with butter and jam*
**trabajar** (verb) *to work* (job)
**trabajo** (m) *job, work*
**tractor** (m) *tractor*
**tradición** (f) *tradition*
**traducir** (verb) *to translate*
**traductor/traductora** (m/f) *translator*
**traer** (verb) *to fetch*
**tráfico** (m) *traffic*
**traje** (m) *suit* (clothing)
**tranquilo** (adj) *quiet*
**trapo del polvo** (m) *duster*
**trasero** (m) *bottom* (part of body)
**tréboles** (m pl) *clubs* (cards)
**trece** *thirteen*
**treinta** *thirty*
**tren** (m) *train*
**tres** *three*
**triste** (adj) *sad*
**tú** *you* (informal)
**tu** (s) *your* (informal); **tu libro** *your book;* **tus zapatos** *your shoes;* **¿es tuyo esto?** *is this yours?*
**tubería** (f) *pipe* (for water)
**tubo de escape** (m) *exhaust* (car)
**tuerca** (f) *nut* (for bolt)
**túnel** (m) *tunnel*
**turismo** (m) *sightseeing*
**turista** (m/f) *tourist*

# U

**último** *last* (final)
**un/una** *a*
**uña** (f) *finger nail*
**único** *single* (only)
**universidad** (f) *university*
**uno** *one*
**urgente** (adj) *urgent*
**usar** (verb) *to use*
**uso** (m) *use, usage*
**usted** *you* (formal)
**utensilios de cocina** (m pl) *cooking utensils*
**útil** (adj) *useful*
**uvas** (f pl) *grapes*

# V

**vacaciones** (f pl) *vacation*
**vacío** (adj) *empty*
**vacuna** (f) *vaccination, vaccine*
**vacunar** (verb) *to vaccinate*
**vagón** (m) *carriage* (train); **el vagónrestaurante** *restaurant car*
**vainilla** (f) *vanilla*
**vale** *OK*
**valle** (m) *valley*
**válvula** (f) *valve*
**vapor** (m) *steam, steamer* (boat); **al vapor** (adj) *steamed*
**vaqueros** (m pl) *jeans*
**varios** *several*
**vaso** (m) *glass* (for drinking)
**váter** (m) *toilet* (item in bathroom)
**¡váyase!** *go away!*
**veces: a veces** *sometimes*
**vegetariano** (adj) *vegetarian*
**vehículo** (m) *vehicle*
**veinte** *twenty*
**vela** (f) *sailing; candle*
**velocidad** (f) *speed*
**venda** (f) *bandage*
**vender** (verb) *to sell*
**veneno** (m) *poison*
**venir** (verb) *to come;* **¡venga aquí!** *come here!*
**ventana** (f) *window*
**ventas** (f pl) *sales*
**ventilador** (m) *fan* (ventilator)
**ventisca** (f) *blizzard*
**ver** (verb) *to see;* **no veo** *I can't see*
**verdad** *true;* **es verdad** *it's true;* **¿verdad?** *isn't that so?*
**verde** *green*
**verdura** (f) *vegetables*
**verja** (f) *gate*
**vestido** (m) *dress*
**veterinario** (m) *vet*
**vez: de vez en cuando** *occasionally*
**viajar** (verb) *to travel;* **viajar en avión** *fly* (of person)
**viaje** (m) *journey;* **el viaje de novios** *honeymoon*
**vida** (f) *life*
**vídeo** (m) *video* (film); **el (aparato de) vídeo** *video recorder*
**videocámara** (f) *camcorder*
**videojuegos** (m pl) *computer/video games*
**viejo** (adj) *old*
**viento** (m) *wind*
**viernes** *Friday*
**vigilante nocturno** (m) *night porter*
**vinagre** (m) *vinegar*
**vinatero** (m) *wine merchant*

**vino** (m) *wine*
**violín** (m) *violin*
**visita** (f) *visit;* **las horas de visita** *visiting hours;* **la visita con guía** *guided tour*
**visitante** (m/f) *visitor*
**visitar** (verb) *to visit*
**visor de imagen** (m) *viewfinder*
**vista** (f) *view*
**vitaminas** (f pl) *vitamin pills*
**vivero** (m) *garden center*
**vodka** (m) *vodka*
**volar** (verb) *to fly* (plane, insect)
**volver** (verb) *to come/get back, return;* **nos volvemos mañana** *we get back tomorrow*
**vomitar** (verb) *to be sick* (vomit)
**voz** (f) *voice*
**vuelo** (m) *flight;* **el número de vuelo** *flight number*

# W, Y, Z

**whisky** (m) *whisky*
**y** *and*
**ya** *already*
**yo** *I*
**yogur** (m) *yogurt*
**zanahoria** (f) *carrot*
**zapatería** (f) *shoe store*
**zapatilla** (f) *washing machine*
**zapatillas** (f pl) *slippers*
**zapatos** (m pl) *shoes;* **los zapatos de deporte** *sneakers*
**zona peatonal** (f) *pedestrian zone*
**zoo** (m) *zoo*
**zumo** (m) *juice;* **el zumo de frutas** *fruit juice;* **el zumo de naranja** *orange juice;* **el zumo de tomate** *tomato juice*

# Acknowledgments

**FOURTH EDITION (2023)**
For this edition, the publisher would like to thank Aashline R. Avarachan for editorial assistance; Nobina Chakravorty, Gopika Gopakumar, and Mitravinda VK for design assistance; Mohammad Rizwan for technical assistance; Elsa Vicente, Eduardo Sepúlveda, and Cristina Gomez for the editorial review; Karen Constanti for assistance with artwork commissioning; Peter Bull Art Studio and Dan Crisp for illustrations; and Andiamo! Language Services Ltd. for foreign language proofreading.

**THIRD EDITION (2018)**
**Senior Editors** Angeles Gavira, Christine Stroyan
**Project Art Editor** Vanessa Marr
**DTP Designer** John Goldsmid
**Jacket Design Development Manager** Sophia MTT
**Jacket Designer** Juhi Sheth
**Pre-Producer** David Almond
**Senior Producer** Ana Vallarino
**Associate Publisher** Liz Wheeler
**Publishing Director** Jonathan Metcalf

**FIRST EDITION (2005)**
The publisher would like to thank the following for their help: Isa Palacios and Maria Serna for the organization of location photography in Spain; Restaurant Raymon at Mi Pueblo, Madrid; Magnet Showroom, Enfield, London; MyHotel, London; Peppermint Green Hairdressers, London; Coolhurst Tennis Club, London; Kathy Gammon; Juliette Meeus and Harry.

**Produced for Dorling Kindersley by** Schermuly Design Co.
**Language content for Dorling Kindersley by** g-and-w publishing
**Managed by** Jane Wightwick
**Editing and additional input** Cathy Gaulter-Carter, Teresa Cervera, Leila Gaafar
**Additional design assistance** Phil Gamble, Lee Riches, Fehmi Cömert, Sally Geeve
**Additional editorial assistance** Kajal Mistry, Paul Docherty, Lynn Bresler
**Picture research** Louise Thomas

## PICTURE CREDITS

The publisher would like to thank the following for their kind permission to reproduce their photographs.

Key: a-above; b-below/bottom; c-centre; f-far; l-left; r-right; t-top

**9 Getty Images:** Maskot (cla). **10 Getty Images / iStock:** E+ / Morsa Images (cr). **11 Getty Images / iStock:** pixdeluxe (tl). **12 Getty Images / iStock:** stocknroll (cr). **13 Dreamstime.com:** Monkey Business Images (br). **Getty Images / iStock:** E+ / kali9 (cla); monkeybusinessimages (cl); E+ / Orbon Alija (clb). **14 Dreamstime.com:** Nyul (crb/old woman). **Getty Images / iStock:** Prostock-Studio (crb). **15 Dreamstime.com:** Slobodan Mračina (c). **Dreamstime.com:** Arne9001 (cl). **Ingram Image Library:** cra, cb, cbr. **Getty Images / iStock:** agrobacter (clb). **17 Getty Images / iStock:** E+ / Morsa Images (b); pixdeluxe (ca). **18 Getty Images / iStock:** lutavia (cb). **18-19 Getty Images / iStock:** vasantytf (c). **19 Alamy Stock Photo:** nito (cb). **Shutterstock.com:** nelea33 (c). **21 Getty Images:** DigitalVision / 10'000 Hours (cla). **23 DK Images:** Dave King (cra). **24 Dreamstime.com:** Joe Sohm (bl). **Getty Images:** Stuart Snelling / EyeEm (cr). **25 Getty Images / iStock:** monkeybusinessimages (clb, bl); ShotShare (cla). **DK Images:** Andy Crawford (cra); Magnus Rew (cr). **Ingram Image Library:** cra. **26 Dreamstime.com:** Monkey Business Images (crb). **Getty Images / iStock:** kuppa_rock (tr); vasantytf (br). **28 Dreamstime.com:** Robert Kneschke (br); Laupri (cra). **Ingram Image Library:** bcr. **29 Alamy Stock Photo:** PhotoAlto / Michele Constantini (bl). **Shutterstock.com:** Africa Studio (clb); by-studio (cl). **DK Images:** Dave King (cr). **31 Getty Images / iStock:** E+ / AsiaVision (cl). **30-31 Alamy Stock Photo:** Comstock Images (clb); Think Stock (cla). **32 Getty Images / iStock:** E+ / kupicoo (cr). **33 Getty Images / iStock:** Moon Safari (tl, cla, cl, clb). **34 Dreamstime.com:** Roman Egorov (cl). **Getty Images:** fStop / Halfdark (cr). **Shutterstock.com:** Arad-dara (cb). **34-35 Dreamstime.com:** Jiri Hera (ca). **35 Dreamstime.com:** Oleg Dudko (cl). **Ingram Image Library:** cr. **36 Dreamstime.com:** Oleg Dudko (cra); Roman Egorov (ca). **36-37 Dreamstime.com:** Jiri Hera (tc).

**37 Getty Images:** Stuart Snelling / EyeEm (bl); fStop / Halfdark (cla). **38 Dreamstime.com:** Sean Pavone (cr). **39 Getty Images / iStock:** tommaso79 (tl). **40 DK Images:** Lee Riches (c). **Shutterstock.com:** Rodrigo Garrido (bl). **41 Dreamstime.com:** Valentin Lung Illes (tl). **Getty Images / iStock:** MarioGuti (cl). **42 Getty Images / iStock:** Tramino (cr). **43 Dreamstime.com:** Rndmst (cla). **Shutterstock.com:** Rodrigo Garrido (tl). **44-45 Shutterstock.com:** Nerthuz (c). **46 Dreamstime.com:** Btlife (ca). **Ingram Image Library:** c. **DK Images:** Lee Riches (cb). **Getty Images / iStock:** MarioGuti (tr). **Shutterstock.com:** Nerthuz (tc). **47 Dreamstime.com:** Sean Pavone (bl). **Getty Images / iStock:** Tramino (cl). **48 Dreamstime.com:** Edmac1717 (br); Rudolf Ernst (cb); Matthi (cb/Museum); Mmeeds (bc). **48-49 Dreamstime.com:** Amoklv (c). **49 Dreamstime.com:** A1977 (bl). **Getty Images / iStock:** ivotheeditors (tl). **50-51 Getty Images / iStock:** ewg3D (c). **50 Alamy Stock Photo:** Peter Titmuss (cb). **52 Getty Images / iStock:** krblokhin (cra). **53 Alamy Stock Photo:** Image Farm Inc. / James Dawson (cla/wheelchair); Matthew Ashmore / Stockimo (cla). **Getty Images / iStock:** Warchi (tl). **54 Alamy Stock Photo:** Moodboard Stock Photography (cla). **DK Images:** Andy Crawford (cb). **Alamy Stock Photo:** Jackson Smith (crb). **Getty Images / iStock:** E+ / martin-dm (crb). **55 Dreamstime.com:** Vinicius Tupinamba (cla). **Getty Images / iStock:** E+ / xavierarnau (tl). **56 Dreamstime.com:** A1977 (c); Rudolf Ernst (tc); Mmeeds (tr); Matthi (tc/Museum); Edmac1717 (ca); Amoklv (cr). **Getty Images / iStock:** ivotheeditors (ca/Cathedral). **56-57 Dreamstime.com:** Nerthuz (c). **58 Alamy Stock Photo:** Ingram Publishing (c). **DK Images:** cra. **Dreamstime.com:** David Brooks (crb). **Getty Images / iStock:** E+ / zeljkosantrac (crb/Family). **59 Dreamstime.com:** Denys Kovtun (tl). **Getty Images / iStock:** 0802290022 (clb). **60 Getty Images / iStock:** surachetsh (cb). **Shutterstock.com:** Sarymsakov Andrey (cr). **61 Alamy Stock Photo:** Cultura Creative RF / IS007 (cla). **Dreamstime.com:** Piotr Adamowicz (bl). **Getty Images / iStock:** yipengge (tl). **Alamy Stock Photo:** Robert Harding Picture Library (cla); Image Source (cl). **DK Images:** Steve Gorton (cl); Pia Tryde (cl). **Ingram Image Library:** c. **62-63 Dreamstime.com:** Jennifer Thompson (c). **64 Dreamstime.com:** Flydragonfly (crb). **65 Alamy Stock Photo:** Goodshoot (cla); Arcaid Images / Richard Bryant (clb/Bathroom). **Dreamstime.com:** Apiwan Borrikonratchata (cla/car); Vitalyedush (cla). **Alamy Stock Photo:** GKPhotography (bl). **Getty Images / iStock:** piovosempre (clb). **Shutterstock.com:** Sarymsakov Andrey (cl). **66 Alamy Stock Photo:** Arcaid Images / Richard Bryant (ca). **Dreamstime.com:** Jennifer Thompson (br). **67 Alamy Stock Photo:** Ingram Publishing (cr). **DK Images:** c. **Alamy Stock Photo:** Goodshoot (crb). **68 Alamy Stock Photo:** doughoughton (cr); CoverSpot (bl). **Lee Riches:** bl **Dreamstime.com:** Arne9001 (c). **Getty Images / iStock:** E+ / alvarez (cr); PK-Photos (cb). **Shutterstock.com:** Weho (cra). **69 Alamy Stock Photo:** ImagesEurope (clb). **Dreamstime.com:** Marcel De Grijs (cl); Nemesio Jim © nez Jim © nez (cla). **Getty Images / iStock:** nastya_ph (tl). **72 Getty Images / iStock:** doomu (bl). **73 Alamy Stock Photo:** imageBROKER / Harald Theissen (cla/wine). **Alamy Stock Photo:** imagebroker (cla); Image Source (cl); Comstock Images (tl). **Dreamstime.com:** Charlieaja (cla); Konstantin Iliev (clb). **Getty Images / iStock:** E+ / Drazen_ (cla). **74 Getty Images:** beyond fotomedia / Alessandro Ventura (r). **75 Ingram Image Library:** c. **Getty Images / iStock:** leolintang (br). **76 Dreamstime.com:** Arne9001 (fbr); Marcel De Grijs (crb); Efmradio (cb). **Getty Images / iStock:** PK-Photos (bc). **Shutterstock.com:** Weho (br). **78 Alamy Stock Photo:** Luca DiCecco (br). **79 Getty Images / iStock:** E+ / shapecharge (tl, cla, cl, clb). **Shutterstock.com:** zhu difeng (bl). **80 Dreamstime.com:** Robert Kneschke (cra). **82 Ingram Image Library:** c. **Alamy Stock Photo:** JSP Studios / Momentum Creative (cr). **Getty Images / iStock:** Bim (crb). **Shutterstock.com:** Gorodenkoff (cra). **83 Alamy Stock Photo:** wildphotos.com (cla). **84-85 Shutterstock.com:** Pressmaster (c). **84 Shutterstock.com:** Ground Picture (bl). **85 Getty Images / iStock:** PeopleImages (tc). **Shutterstock.com:** Drazen Zigic (c). **Ingram Image Library:** cr. **86 Alamy Stock Photo:** Luca DiCecco (br). **88 DK Images:** cr. **Ingram Image Library:** clb. **89 Alamy Stock Photo:** Brand X Pictures (tl). **Getty Images / iStock:** Damir Khabirov (tl). **DK Images:** Stephen Oliver (cl). **92 Getty Images / iStock:** E+ / FatCamera (cr). **91 Dreamstime.com:** Sebnem Ragiboglu (tl). **93 Dreamstime.com:** Roman Egorov (cb); Prostockstudio (tl). **94 Getty Images / iStock:** E+ / Morsa Images (cra); E+ / Tempura (br). **95 DK Images:** Stephen Oliver (cla). **Dreamstime.com:** Shawn Hempel (clb). **Getty Images / iStock:** seb_ra (clb/Doctor). **96 DK Images:** cr. **Ingram Image Library:** clb. **97 Dreamstime.com:** Prostockstudio (bc). **Getty Images:** beyond fotomedia / Alessandro Ventura (tl). **98-99 Alamy Stock Photo:** Andrew Linscott (c). **98 Dreamstime.com:** Rawf88 (bl). **99 Alamy Stock Photo:** Itsik Marom (tc). **Dreamstime.com:** Laupri (ca). **Getty Images / iStock:** E+ / CreativaStudio (c). **Shutterstock.com:** Gajus (tl). **100 Dreamstime.com:** Draftmode (cb). **Getty Images / iStock:** sihuo0860371 (cr). **102 Getty Images / iStock:** cjp (cr). **102-103 Getty Images / iStock:** DigiStu (b). **103 Dreamstime.com:** Welcomia (cla). **Getty Images / iStock:** Imagesines (tl). **104 DK Images:** Paul Bricknell cl (6); Jane Burton (bcl); Geoff Dann cl (2); Max Gibbs cl (4); Frank Greenaway cl (3); Dave King cl (1), TracyMorgan c (5). **105 DK Images:** Dave King (cla) **106 Dreamstime.com:** Draftmode (bc). **Getty Images / iStock:** sihuo0860371 (cr). **107 Alamy Stock Photo:** Itsik Marom (cl). **Getty Images / iStock:** DigiStu (bl). **108 Dreamstime.com:** Akhilesh Sharma (cr/Envelope). **Shutterstock.com:** PaulSat (cr). **109 Getty Images / iStock:** mediaphotos (cla). **110 Getty Images / iStock:** Biserka Stojanovic (cr). **111 Dreamstime.com:** Welcomia (clb). **112 Getty Images / iStock:** E+ / freemixer (cr). **Dreamstime.com:** E+ / BraunS (bl). **113 Getty Images / iStock:** RossHelen (br). **Shutterstock.com:** Evgeny Atamanenko (clb). **114 Dreamstime.com:** Amsis1 (br); Brett Critchley (crb). **Getty Images / iStock:** Ridofranz (cr). **115 Dreamstime.com:** Ulianna19970 (cla). **Getty Images / iStock:** Tatsiana Volkava (cl). **Shutterstock.com:** Gerardo onandia (br). **116 Dreamstime.com:** Laupri (ca); Welcomia (cra). **Getty Images / iStock:** mediaphotos (br). **Shutterstock.com:** PaulSat (br). **118-119 Alamy Stock Photo:** mauritius images GmbH / Rene Mattes (c). **119 Dreamstime.com:** Prostockstudio (c). **120 Dreamstime.com:** Sergeyoch (bc/Ball); Wavebreakmedia Ltd (cr); Skypixel (cb); Volkop (bc). **121 Getty Images / iStock:** E+ / AscentXmedia (tl). **122-123 Alamy Stock Photo:** Tony Tallec (c). **123 Getty Images / iStock:** nastya_ph (tl). **124 Dreamstime.com:** Sergeyoch (crb/Ball); Skypixel (crb); Volkop (crb/racket); Wavebreakmedia Ltd (bc)

All other images © Dorling Kindersley